The All-American Dollar

Also by the Author

Casey: The Life and Legend of Charles Dillon Stengel
The Days of Mr. McGraw
Amazing: The Miracle of the Mets

The All-American Dollar

THE BIG BUSINESS OF SPORTS

Joseph Durso

Illustrated with Photographs

HOUGHTON MIFFLIN COMPANY BOSTON
1971

First Printing **w**

To my son Christopher

Foreword

This is not a survey of sports, nor an encyclopedia. It is a report on the major professional sports in the nineteen sixties and the things that changed them for the seventies and beyond — *revolutionized* them, in fact. And the chief thing was money.

It is true that money revolutionized a lot of things in the sixties and early seventies. Presidential campaigns were focused on it. The cost of living in the United States increased about 3 per cent every year, and 12 per cent between presidential elections. Inflation built some careers and destroyed others. The dollar was assaulted, the pound devalued. Interest rates gyrated. Welfare costs soared in the midst of prosperity. Workers rioted in Poland and other countries. Teachers and policemen went on strike along with everybody else, and so did football players and umpires. The price of a subway ride in New York rose to thirty cents. The price of a college education rose to $20,000. The price of a stadium rose to $50,000,000.

So this report is made with the realization that money changed many things in the world besides the price of a box seat. But it also is made with the realization that people in the twentieth century increasingly craved leisure, increasingly earned the time and money for it, and increasingly built their way of life around it.

It was a social revolution a great deal like that after World War I, with many of the same elements: public hunger for ease and even fantasy following the rigidity of the war years, inflation in the economy, new heroes, new values, new communications, new styles of living. That time, it grew through the Roaring Twenties and the message was spread by radio and the automobile. This time, in the years after World War II, the changes were spread over the decades of the fifties and sixties, and the chief carriers were television and the jet airplane.

The revolution of the twenties put professional sports in business; the revolution of the sixties put them in big business. And this report reflects how sports have acquired the opportunities — and the headaches — of big business.

Teams sprouted like supermarkets, causing leagues to divide themselves into "conferences" and conferences into "divisions." The National Hockey League, for example, started the sixties with half a dozen teams and the seventies with fourteen. This was the alignment, with the come-lately cities marked by asterisks:

East	*West*
Boston	California *
Buffalo *	Chicago
Detroit	Los Angeles *
Montreal	Minnesota *
New York	Philadelphia *
Toronto	Pittsburgh *
Vancouver*	St. Louis *

Never mind that Vancouver now was mapped into the East and Philadelphia into the West. The central thing was that if the customer could absorb that topsy-turvy geography, he was ready to tackle the more complex alignment in the National Basketball Association, which grew to this:

East		West	
Atlantic	*Central*	*Midwest*	*Pacific*
Boston	Atlanta*	Chicago	Los Angeles
Buffalo*	Baltimore	Detroit	Portland*
New York	Cincinnati	Milwaukee*	San Diego*
Philadelphia	Cleveland*	Phoenix	San Francisco
			Seattle*

Then, just when he was beginning to grasp this situation, the American Basketball Association sprang from the soil like dragons' teeth with eleven new teams arrayed like this: Carolina, the Floridians, Kentucky, New York, Pittsburgh, and Virginia in the East; Denver, Memphis, Indiana, Texas, and Utah in the West. All new, all symbolizing the trend toward "regional" franchises instead of the old-fashioned "hometown" franchises.

In baseball, meanwhile, the long-standing big leagues began to move like nomads in the sixties, pressing into the Far West, the Southwest, and the Northwest, on into Canada, and then splitting in 1969 into divisions within leagues while the more visionary people in the board rooms began to clamor for even more splitting in the seventies. For the time being, at least, they broke down like this:

National League		American League	
East	*West*	*East*	*West*
Chicago	Atlanta*	Baltimore	California*
Montreal*	Cincinnati	Boston	Chicago
New York	Houston*	Cleveland	Kansas City
Philadelphia	Los Angeles	Detroit	Milwaukee*
Pittsburgh	San Diego*	New York	Minnesota*
St. Louis	San Francisco	Washington	Oakland*

Now the public was ready for the advanced course in social

geography, and it was provided by the merger of the National
Football League and the American Football League into this
kaleidoscopic network of clubs with nicknames like the Saints,
Dolphins, Bills, Oilers, and Broncos:

National Conference

Eastern	Central	Western
Dallas *	Chicago	Atlanta *
New York	Detroit	Los Angeles
Philadelphia	Green Bay	New Orleans *
St. Louis	Minnesota *	San Francisco
Washington		

American Conference

Eastern	Central	Western
Baltimore	Cincinnati *	Denver *
Boston *	Cleveland	Kansas City *
Buffalo *	Houston *	Oakland *
Miami *	Pittsburgh	San Diego *
New York		

To keep people from growing too provincial, the baseball
hierarchy began to visit Japan and Japanese teams began to visit
the United States, foreshadowing the time when the major
leagues might expand to include the Far East, Mexico, and
maybe Latin America. And Walter Kennedy, the commissioner
of basketball, began to predict that his sport in the seventies
would expand to Italy, Spain, and Greece.

But before the blessings of the American sports revolution
could be exported wholesale, some saner heads — or perhaps
stodgier heads — were pointing out that Edward Heath had
spent only $2590 to retain his seat in Parliament and become
Prime Minister in 1970 while Nelson Rockefeller was spending
$6,000,000 to retain his seat as governor of New York. Not only

that, but Rockefeller's Department of Environmental Conservation later warned that the trout season would be leaner because the shortage of money had prevented the state from stocking its streams.

Then, one day in 1971, Madison Square Garden was forced to file certificates of deposit totaling $348,246.50 in the Chemical Bank of New York on behalf of Joe Frazier and the same amount on behalf of Muhammad Ali. The state was assessing each fighter that much from his purse of $2,500,000, earned (and otherwise taxed at several levels) after fifteen rounds of fighting that also earned Frazier the title of "undisputed heavyweight champion of the world." They disputed the assessment, though, and Harry Markson of the Garden boxing command mourned: "It effectively puts us out of business."

On the same day, Representative Morris K. Udall of Arizona, a onetime professional basketball player, filed a bill to limit the televising of sports. It was a bill, he told the House of Representatives, that "will undoubtedly arouse outrage in the breasts of professional sports teams" but that "will save some marriages, perhaps give fathers and sons a chance to know each other."

His bill intended to confine the TV reports of baseball between the opening week of April and the second Sunday of September; football between September 1 and the second Sunday in January; and basketball between December 1 and the second Sunday in April.

"Virtually every professional sport is now controlled, coached, and managed by television," he said, "and franchises are marketed around the country like so many hamburger stands. Who won the last Super Bowl? The World Series? How many teams are there in the NFC? In the AFC? The NBA? Major league baseball? What teams were the champions of each? Who were the combatants in this year's Rose Bowl?"

His purpose, Mr. Udall suggested, was to return to "the marking of time by the ebb and flow of the athletic equinox" —

something that had supplied stability to his life as a boy in Arizona.

But stability was not one of the products of inflation, in economics or sports, and a generation of inflated growth had produced a wealth of trouble in addition to just plain wealth:

— The 1964 Olympic Games were embroiled by charges that equipment makers had made payoffs to athletes.

— The 1968 Olympics were embroiled by protests from black athletes, who first threatened to boycott the games and who then gave the Black Power salute during the playing of "The Star-Spangled Banner" in Mexico City.

— The 1968 Kentucky Derby was plunged into a historic dispute, and long litigation, after illegal medication reportedly was found in the winner, Dancer's Image.

— A power struggle was waged for control of amateur sports by the Amateur Athletic Union and the National Collegiate Athletic Association.

— A boycott by horsemen closed down the Aqueduct racetrack in New York, and a boycott of several tracks was threatened by jockeys when exercise girls began to win their crusade to be licensed as regular riders.

— Baseball umpires won the right to unionize under the National Labor Relations Board and later went on strike during the 1970 play-offs.

— Joe Namath quit football during a battle with Commissioner Pete Rozelle over the quarterback's ownership of a Manhattan bar frequented by "undesirables," but then relented, sold the bar, and returned to the wars.

— The touring professional golfers seceded from the PGA in a fight over prize money, then returned under their own commissioner.

— Wally Butts and Bear Bryant, two prestigious football coaches who were accused of rigging college games, sued for slander, and won the suit.

— Turbine engines were banned at Indianapolis.

— Ara Parseghian ordered his Notre Dame football team to run out the clock for a 10–10 tie with Michigan State in their 1966 "game of the decade," rather than risk an interception — a decision that prompted some alumni to groan, "He tied one for The Gipper."

—The closed-circuit TV of the Ali-Frazier "fight of the century" packed 369 halls and auditoriums with people who paid up to twenty-five dollars a seat — which was five dollars more than people paid to sit in the upper balcony of Madison Square Garden, where the fight was held. In Pittsburgh, a lumpy screen was set up on the infield of Three Rivers Stadium and the temperature was seventeen degrees, but 5000 fans coughed up fifteen dollars anyway. In Harlem, 11,000 tickets were sold in the 369th Regiment Armory. But in Kansas and Iowa, a promoter who had paid $200,000 in advance for his "territory" complained later that he had lost $75,000 because "the boys in New York were too smart." And in Chicago, when the television picture failed, the crowd of 6900 responded by throwing chairs and bottles from the balcony and hurled ticket counters through windows.

Nor was stability restored when a national recession began to dent the inflation late in the sixties. Half the baseball teams in the American League lost attendance in 1970, led by the Boston Red Sox, who lost 238,000 customers in one year and 445,000 in two. Half the teams in the National League slid too, and they were led by the Atlanta Braves, who lost 380,000 fans as the most migrating franchise in the majors. And while twenty-three cities were added to baseball, football, hockey, and basketball between 1966 and 1969, the price for each franchise began to slip back — and five of the eleven clubs in the American Basketball Association changed locations in one year.

Even the man in the street began to feel the pinch of the dollar. The tax assessment on a country club near Cincinnati leaped in one year from $58,000 to $304,000. Private clubs remained almost stationary at about 4500 during the forty years after 1931, while daily-fee courses jumped from 700 to 4248. And some clubs demanded an initiation fee of $6000 a member followed by a bond that cost $6000 more.

Yet in 1971, lady golfers stopped being the poor cousins of the links with a record-setting purse of $60,000 for one tournament, Rod Laver won thirteen straight tennis matches and $130,000 in a three-month spree, and Carl Yastrzemski signed a three-year contract with the Red Sox that guaranteed him $500,000. So it was still a good question whether the bubble was bursting or just growing distended under heavy pressure.

This report on the situation grew from an article in the *New York Times* suggested by James Reston, who once wrote:

"Sport in America plays a part in our national life that is probably more important than even the social scientists believe. Sports are now more popular than politics in America, increasingly so since the spread of television. The great corporations are now much more interested in paying millions for sports broadcasts than they are for all political events except for the nominations and inaugurations of Presidents, because the general public is watching and listening."

The other people who contributed to this report are too numerous to mention fairly. But they include James Roach, the sports editor of the *Times;* old performers like Ken Strong and new ones like Tom Seaver; commissioners like Pete Rozelle and Bowie Kuhn, and especially Joe Dey; ringmasters like Michael Burke, Harry Dalton, Alvin Cooperman, Bob Wolff, George M. Weiss, James K. Thomson, Lee MacPhail, Bill Veeck, Robert O. Fishel, and Harold Weissman; and my colleagues at the *Times,* Steve Cady, Dave Anderson, William N. Wallace, Leonard Koppett, John Radosta, Gerald Eskenazi, and Sam Goldaper.

Then there was my editor and muse, Jacques de Spoelberch

of Houghton Mifflin, a Princeton man and onetime catcher who went straight — into the literary life — instead of turning professional and pursuing the All-American dollar.

Joseph Durso

Contents

Illustrations

(The photographs in this book, except where noted, are by United Press International.)

Everybody is out for the Big Buck,
and the television contracts are king.
— *James Reston*

1

$200,000 a Minute

AUGUST A. BUSCH JR. owns nine breweries, three powerboats, two wildlife preserves, a bunch of elephants and camels — and one baseball team, the St. Louis Cardinals.

He inherited two things from his rich family: the Anheuser-Busch brewing company and an overworked sense of civic pride. His grandfather, a public lion at the turn of the century, once sent a small fortune in cash to the victims of the San Francisco earthquake. In his own time, Gussie Busch served as head of the United Fund charity campaign, the St. Louis University Fund campaign, and a development company called Civic Progress, which was bent on rebuilding much of the Mississippi riverfront.

But he reached the peak of zeal in 1953, when the city's baseball team was floundering and threatening to leave town. So Busch shelled out three and three-quarter million dollars and bought control "to save the Cardinals for St. Louis."

Now it was fifteen years, two National League pennants, and one world championship later, and Busch sat in his office on the third floor of the main brewery, a red brick fortress embedded on the west bank of the Mississippi like some great relic. The gleaming Gateway Arch rose 630 feet into the air over his shoulder, a monster croquet wicket symbolizing the city's title of "Gateway to the West."

The thing was that Busch owned something else besides all

those beer vats and elephants: the only million-dollar payroll in professional baseball. He owned Bob Gibson at $125,000 a year, Curt Flood at $90,000, Lou Brock at $90,000, Tim McCarver at $70,000, Mike Shannon at $60,000, Orlando Cepeda at $85,000, Julian Javier at $57,000, and Dal Maxvill, a man whose lifetime batting average was .232, at $53,000.

The office had mailed out registered letters containing these contracts six weeks earlier and, even at the bid-price, Busch owned the most expensive payroll in a chancy business.

But that's not what was troubling him on this day as he sat drumming his fingers on the broad, clean desk in the brown fortress. What was bothering Gussie Busch that day was that somehow none of the highest-priced contracts in baseball history had been mailed back to St. Louis — signed. Somewhere out there, the natives were getting restless.

• • •

Tom Tresh flew from Detroit to New York that day, took a taxicab from Kennedy Airport to midtown Manhattan, and stepped out at the Roosevelt Hotel at Madison Avenue and Forty-fifth Street. He took the elevator to the eighteenth floor, which was swarming with baseball players.

Roberto Clemente came from Puerto Rico, Tommy Davis from California, and the 123 others from places in between. They filed into a board room, sat down in long rows of chairs, and listened closely while an economist named Marvin Miller addressed them on the subject of "deferred income" and "benefits plans."

Tresh, who studied and taught at Western Michigan University, sat near Steve Hamilton, who taught school at Eastern Kentucky State, and Fritz Peterson, who taught school at Eastern Illinois University. He had joined the New York Yankees eight years earlier, when they were winning, and now he was one of the old warhorses, when they were losing. He was a onetime left fielder converted to shortstop, and he was thirty years old.

Tresh tried to "psych" himself by reading books on psycho-cybernetics. Mind over matter, self-inspiration, play the ground ball and don't let the ground ball play you. He was, observed Professor Sidney Hook, the philosopher, like a Mohammedan on the eve of battle.

But now it was the eve of the 1969 baseball season, and Tresh sat wondering whether *anybody* would be counting the bounces on ground balls. The 125 players in the room represented the 475 others in the major leagues, and they were trying to decide whether to go on strike, like steelworkers. They averaged about twenty-five years of age, and the critical issue was a pension they might collect a quarter of a century later.

"My father Mike was eligible for a pension at fifty after he'd quit catching," Tresh recalled. "But when he was forty-nine, he found out that he had cancer. So he had the terrible choice of letting his pension start the next year and collecting two hundred fifty dollars a month for life — however long that was — or of not starting his pension and preserving his life-insurance protection.

"He wanted the pension, too. He loved to go off on the frozen lakes in Michigan and spend his time fishing, and he could've used the money for some pleasure at that stage of his life. But that would have meant leaving my mother without the protection of his insurance.

"He decided to skip the pension. He sacrificed the monthly check that he could have used to make life easier, and he died two years later. He left my mother with twenty thousand dollars insurance instead."

Tresh was roused from his reverie by Miller's voice at the microphone. He was explaining the value of a pension as a form of deferred income and a hedge against inflation, and Mike Tresh's son sat straight and listened closely.

•   •   •

Nine blocks away, in a tailored suite of offices rich with polished wood, a man named Pete Rozelle paced the carpet. The address was 410 Park Avenue and the sign on the outer door read starkly: Professional Football.

Unlike Tom Tresh, Rozelle wasn't worrying about the urgency — or even the desirability — of a pension. Six months earlier, the football players had gone through all the stages of economic warfare on that issue — negotiation, impasse, ultimatum, boycott, strike, renegotiation, and finally settlement.

Now the 640 players in the National Football League were guaranteed $1600 a month when they reached sixty-five, a tidy increase of 100 per cent in that particular "deferred payment." And the 400 men of the American Football League could count on $1132 a month besides their Social Security. In both leagues, every athlete and every member of his family had $50,000 worth of medical insurance.

Nor was Rozelle troubled by business. The NFL was already 90 per cent sold out for its games and was certain that 54,000 persons would pay five dollars or six dollars or more every time two teams played. The AFL was averaging 40,000 for each show, and the television money was worth $27,000,000 a season for both. No, business was great; maybe a little too great.

Rozelle was troubled by a trip he was about to take to Palm Springs, the lush oasis in the California desert. He said, a little bravely, several times: "We'll stay there all week if we have to, until we get this thing straightened out." He didn't know it at the time, but two months later the owners in one of the two leagues would sit around a table for thirty-six hours trying to unsnarl the things that were on Rozelle's mind that day. One of them, Art Modell of Cleveland, would even be in a hospital with an ulcer and would horrify his doctors by taking part in the sessions by long-distance telephone.

Pete Rozelle's problem, in a nutshell, was how to realign the twenty-six teams into two equal leagues covered by two or maybe even three television networks. He wasn't worried about sitting in Palm Springs all week. He was really afraid they might have to stay there all *spring* before the money men straightened that one out.

His misgivings were not soothed when somebody announced later that the problem of stacking thirteen teams into one league alone had been fed into an exceptionally bright computer. The machine was asked to balance things like stadium capacity, geography, weather, natural rivalries, and strength of competition. The computer reported that Rozelle had 90,090 possible variations to consider.

· · ·

O. J. Simpson checked his signals, as he had done while carrying footballs during thirty games as the most celebrated running back in the history of the University of Southern California. One of the twenty-six teams furrowing the brow of Pete Rozelle had just drafted Simpson, and he was bound not to negotiate with anybody else. His senior classmates at Southern Cal who were engineers or lawyers could shop around, but O.J. had been "claimed."

Like any of the 792 baseball and football amateurs who had just been drafted during two weeks of the biggest grab bag of American talent, he might simply show up with lawyer and briefcase and challenge the entire system. He might even shatter the entire system. That way, he would go down in history as a legal footnote. If he did not sue, though, and eventually signed a contract, Simpson knew that he might wind up a millionaire.

What troubled him this day was not so much the prospect of becoming a millionaire, but the tortuous choice of routes open to him in reaching that goal. He had been claimed by the Buffalo Bills, a team that played 3000 miles from Simpson's home in a city that was sometimes snowbound, a team that had fashioned the worst record in professional football the season before by winning only one of fourteen games.

The thing on Simpson's mind was also on Ralph Wilson's

mind. Wilson, as the owner of the Buffalo team, had cast the vote that made Simpson the nation's number one draft choice — cast the vote, that is, that automatically made Simpson the nation's most expensive football player.

Wilson had just endured a season during which he had lost half a dozen quarterbacks and one head coach, and it was not far-fetched that he also might lose one city and one top draft choice. He knew that Erie County had approved $50,000,000 in bonds to build a stadium for a baseball team — which wound up in Montreal. And now he knew that O. J. Simpson was unhappy, unwilling, or unconvinced that his future lay along the cold shore of Lake Erie.

Chuck Barnes, a talent specialist for Sports Headliners, worsened Wilson's afternoon by making a potent pitch: $650,000 for five years of O.J.'s services running with footballs. That would include an annual salary of $100,000 and a bonus of $150,000. The gap looked like nearby Niagara Falls to Wilson. He had offered $50,000 a year. They were $400,000 apart.

Somebody remembered that bonus money had been even higher a few seasons earlier, before the two football leagues had quit bidding each other up, and told Simpson: "You were born five years too late."

O.J., realizing that he could not be "traded" by Buffalo to a rich National League club until the following season, smiled ruefully and said: "Or one year too soon."

Then he tried to relax Wilson by some badinage. He had had a dream after his senior season, O.J. said. "It was a nightmare. I was drafted by the Buffalo Bills."

Wilson, remembering those half-dozen injured quarterbacks and the size of the check Simpson was demanding, replied: "I had a nightmare, too. I dreamed that you were a flop."

• • •

Charles Engelhard sat in front of the fireplace in a cottage at Blewbury, high on the Berkshire Downs, sipping tea with Mrs.

Johnson Houghton. A terrier, a cat, and a duck wandered around the floor, but Engelhard and Mrs. Houghton were intent on horses — thoroughbred horses, to be exact, like the beauties in the stalls outside.

The horses were part of the $8,000,000 worth of animals kept in training by Charles Engelhard, and they were part of the $15,000,000 in horseflesh that he fed, trained, and raced from the United States to Europe to South Africa. They were, he insisted, "a hobby, a relaxation."

But Charles Engelhard also owned three airplanes; an estate in Far Hills, New Jersey; homes in Maine and Florida; apartments in New York, London and Rome; an art collection rich with Degas, Renoir, Monet, Corot, Cézanne, and Winslow Homer; a kennel of prize golden retrievers; a quarter-of-a-billion-dollar financial empire, and forty-seven broodmares, plus investments in syndicates that controlled the great racers Buckpasser, Damascus, Tom Rolfe, and Dr. Fager. And to him, racing was "a hobby and a relaxation" with a rather urgent goal.

The immediate goal that day, as he sipped tea and munched on scones with Mrs. Houghton in the English cottage, was the Epsom Derby. If only his promising colt Ribofilio could somehow survive the course and carry home the green and gold silks ahead of the field, then it might have all been worthwhile. He sat there that afternoon, the adviser to presidents and kings and prime ministers, and considered what was at stake as the sun slanted down across the hedgerows.

"You hope," he said, bringing life's opportunities and challenges into focus, "that you will get one horse now and then that will pull you out, that will make up for the deficit."

• • •

Clarence Bigelow of Dickeyville, Wisconsin, parked his car alongside the bus depot in Chicago and steered his twelve-year-old son Charles toward the ticket window. He fished a twenty-dollar bill from his wallet, slid it beneath the grillwork on the window, and said: "Two in the mezzanine for the Black Hawks and Detroit on the twenty-sixth."

The man in the window of the bus depot took the twenty, punched a coded sentence of information onto a tape machine, and waited expectantly. People all over the depot were swarming toward ticket windows for seats on the 6:12 to Milwaukee and the 6:32 to South Bend; Clarence Bigelow of Dickeyville, Wisconsin, was waiting for two in the mezzanine for the Black Hawks.

The coded request from the man in the window was flashed to a computer in New York, was registered there, was sorted out, was fed into a seating diagram of the Stadium back in Chicago, and was returned to the bus depot with the notation that such-and-such seats were available for the twenty-sixth. Mr. Bigelow could have driven downtown to the box office at the Stadium itself, but that was all of four miles off in heavy traffic and, besides, his son Charles wanted to put the computer to work.

People were buying tickets the same way that day in "computer windows" of department stores, supermarkets, banks, and airline offices around the country. Their requests were fed to the electronic marvels in either Los Angeles or New York, which in turn figured out which seats were available and then, if the customers were willing, even printed the actual tickets that were slid back through the windows of department stores, supermarkets, banks, and airline offices.

"Pretty neat," murmured Charles, gleaming.

"Sorry, sir," the man in the bus depot window said to Charles's father, holding back the $6.40 in change that Mr. Bigelow had coming to him. "The computer is jammed right now with requests for tickets. Can you wait fifteen minutes or so and we'll give it another try?"

• • •

Dennis Dale McLain sat in a contour chair in the living room of his house at 407 Princess Drive, Lakeland, Florida. It was a corner house in a solid residential resort development, with green wall-to-wall carpeting, flower-print wallpaper, modern furniture, and a purple Dodge convertible parked under a palm tree in the driveway. McLain was twenty-five years old, had pitched thirty-one victories for the Detroit Tigers in 1968, and reportedly had an income of $200,000 a year. The house was one of the few things left that he owned free of debt.

"I'm smart to a point," he said without spirit, like any $200,-000-a-year young man whose world has just come apart at the seams. "I know how to pitch. But I've made many bad business deals. All my problems stem from my business obligations. I act a lot of times before I think. I'm stupid that way."

Some of the things that McLain did before thinking included playing the organ in nightclubs, piloting a twin-jet airplane, investing in a paint factory, and moonlighting as a bookmaker. The first three got him cheers, thrills, and debts; the last got him suspended from baseball.

"Yes, I think I spread myself too thin," he said. "Put all my eggs in one basket. I like nightclub work, but the paint company dragged me down. We make plastic paint coatings. Great products, but we ran out of money. You can't sell paint in November and December."

Once, McLain had been so successful pitching for Detroit that his teammates rigged a cardboard sign in the locker room for the guidance of the newspapermen and broadcasters who besieged him. It read: "This way to McLain's locker."

Another time, he was selected to pitch an exhibition game with the experimental jackrabbit baseball, the I-X. He was asked if he saw any significance in that, in view of the fact that he had led the American League in throwing home-run balls two of the last three years — with the regular baseball. And he laughed and said: *"Three* of the last three years."

Another time, he was late for the All-Star Game in Washington because he had flown home to Detroit overnight to have his teeth capped. He arrived back in the stadium just in time to see his replacement, Mel Stottlemyre of the New York Yankees, throw two home-run pitches. Stottlemyre was understandably vexed. But not nearly so vexed as Mickey Lolich, a teammate of McLain's, who later was left stranded at the airport by the flying pitcher.

At a public dinner that winter, McLain acknowledged his thoughtlessness by grinning and saying: "I hear Lolich is taking flying lessons and is going to leave *me* at the All-Star Game this year."

At Christmastime, just before his appearance before a federal grand jury on bookmaking activities, he strolled through his paint factory and office, shaking hands with the staff. He said he was sorry there was no Christmas bonus, and even sorrier there were no regular paychecks. Two days later, a bank reported the factory had $144.93 in its account.

"How much did we lose?" McLain asked, as he sat in his Florida living room, reflecting on his success in business. "It's still being computed. People think you don't need help. There just isn't that cabin in the sky where you've got fifty big ones put away."

His four-year-old daughter Kris edged through sliding doors into the room, wearing a red dress and trailing a small black stuffed poodle named Snoopy. "I want to give you a kiss," she whispered.

McLain said okay, and she climbed up onto his lap and kissed him. Then McLain said, "Go watch TV now, and take Snoopy with you."

Kris left, and the boy wonder of baseball shook his head and said: "I'm twenty-five going on twenty-six. I guess my character is being built."

•   •   •

Louis J. Castellano was a forty-two-year-old lawyer in Hempstead, Long Island, and the manager of the local Little League baseball team and he had a problem: namely, his star pitcher's mother. There was no real money involved, but Castellano knew that once you let a baseball player's mother veto your opening-day lineup, there was no telling how far-reaching the mess would become.

The problem was that his star pitcher's mother had checked the star pitcher's report card and had decided that he should spend opening day cracking the books instead of pitching for Louis J. Castellano's team.

Without their ten o'clock scholar, the Hempstead Orioles promptly lost the opening game. So, like many other managers, Louis J. Castellano blew his top. Like many other pitchers' mothers, his star pitcher's mother in turn blew her top, and she did it so vigorously before the president of the Little League that Louis J. Castellano immediately was fired. That's when Castellano the ex-manager turned himself back into Castellano the lawyer.

He presented himself before the New York State Supreme Court as a plaintiff and opened suit to have himself reinstated. He had been bounced, he argued *ex lege* and *de facto,* without due cause. The judge, though, ruled against him. The star pitcher's mother, the court decreed, was within her constitutional — to say nothing of her parental — rights in benching her twelve-year-old son, opening game or no opening game.

Louis J. Castellano sat behind his desk, behind his shingle, alongside his case of lawbooks. He looked fretfully out the window and pondered man's inhumanity to man. That was a tough combination to beat: a Little League mother and a Supreme Court judge who was probably a Little League grandfather. Castellano drummed his fingers on the desk, weighing the overriding issues. He could, he reasoned, recapturing the overriding spirit of the day, appeal his case to a *higher* court . . .

•   •   •

It was the best of times, it was the worst of times. It was a time of booming population, inflation and television, of $24,000,000,000 space programs, $50,000,000 stadiums, and $200,000-a-minute commercials during the Super Bowl football game.

It was a time when the public had the leisure and the cash to spend on sports, and to reward its heroes like capitalists. A time when Braulio Baeza made a quarter of a million dollars a year riding horses, when a college senior named Lew Alcindor antici- pated $1,000,000 for playing professional basketball — and when Joe Willie Namath made a fortune playing football and walked on a white llama rug in the splendor of his East Side pad.

It was the nineteen sixties, and money was giving professional sports its biggest opportunities and biggest headaches since World War II. And it was a time when the nineteen seventies dawned with question marks as big as the dollar signs.

During one week of 1969 alone, as the decade of astronomical performances and astronomical price tags came to a close, the sports world was confronted by this extraordinary tide of the economic, legal, and political crises of big business:

— In baseball, the 600 players in the two major leagues stood on the brink of their first general strike. The issue was pensions and $50,000,000 in television money. The new commissioner of baseball, the fifth in half a century but the second in less than four years, was a Wall Street lawyer who had been negotiating for the twenty-four club owners and who realized that an even more fundamental struggle was developing over the "reserve clause" in players' contracts.

— In football, the twenty-six teams in the two major leagues were preparing for the critical realignment hassle that was al- ready furrowing the brow of the Commissioner of Football, Pete Rozelle.

— In golf, a "revolt" by the 200 touring professionals had just led to a restructured high command, three factions, and one new high commissioner. His job was to oversee $7,000,000 in tournament prizes.

— In basketball, the twenty-five teams in the two warring leagues were headed for rival play-offs and rival stampedes for Alcindor, whose final college game touched off a gold rush. One league was afraid that it might not survive if it didn't sign him.

Even governments were feeling the bind of the dollar signs. The mayor of Montreal threatened to resign because "austerity" was undermining cultural projects like the exposition, Man and His World. Montreal's problem was steepened by a "blessing" that other cities had fought for and lost — a new baseball franchise.

The basic problem was not just that people in sports were suddenly learning the economic facts of life. Nor that the dollar of 1969 bought only eighty cents' worth of the things of 1959 and fifty cents' worth of the things of 1949. Nor was it the fact that more corporations were buying sports teams because inflation and the tax scales were making it difficult for anybody else to buy them. Nor that the number one corporate taxpayer in the state of New York was the New York Racing Association. Nor that football and baseball had just drafted 792 amateur athletes under a procedure that any one of the amateurs might decide to challenge in court.

Nor was it that all those factors were being influenced by the great god television, which broadcasts sports with all their wonders and woes for the largest audiences in history. Nor that a 400-yard race for quarter horses at Ruidoso Downs in New Mexico was worth $602,000 in prizes without television.

It was, and is, all of these things, the accountants of sports agreed — record gate receipts, spiraling costs, stiff taxes, expensive talent, athletes who doubled as stockbrokers, and a generation of inflated money.

For the public, it meant lavish entertainment like the Super

Bowl and prolonged play-offs in all the major sports. But it also meant a proliferation of leagues, higher prices, and a kaleidoscopic switching of franchises. Boston was abandoned for Milwaukee, then Milwaukee was abandoned for Atlanta.

For the athletes, it meant greater rewards, wilder competition for jobs, and more desperate stakes for those who became injured, outplayed, or merely ill-advised.

For their employers, it meant unlimited opportunities for staging extravaganzas and making money — but it also meant steeper urgency because the paying public had a wider choice than ever before. And so it became a scramble for new talent, new markets, new sources of cash, and a whole new class of entertainment specialists and money men to mastermind the whole show.

"Now that sports are becoming bigger business," said Marvin Miller, the labor economist who advises the baseball players, "they are adopting the problems of big business. Any affluent society makes people more security-conscious, and it's happening in sports."

"I find myself using words like 'diversification,'" said Alvin Cooperman, the new impresario of Madison Square Garden. "I've been in the business for thirty years — the entertainment business. What we're doing now is looking for new ways of generating revenue."

"In nineteen thirty," recalled John Quinn, the general manager of the Philadelphia Phillies, "a baseball team could break even with four hundred thousand spectators a year. Now it takes close to a million."

"I'm twenty-nine years old and have two children," said Jack Fisher, then a pitcher for the Cincinnati Reds who attended the mass meeting of 125 players along with Tom Tresh. "A pension becomes a big consideration when you have a family and a short career. It's a deferred payment."

"Deferred payment" is only one of the economic terms of the

new vocabulary of sports, and the athletes toss it off as expertly as "hit and run." Casey Stengel rode a bus from Alabama to Brooklyn in 1912 to join the big leagues. Today they fly in with college degrees, diversified portfolios, agents and advisers like Mark H. McCormack, and lawyers like Namath's counselor, Mike Bite.

One of the most dramatic signs of the restless times was probably the threat of a baseball strike. Players had held out for more money in the past. Sandy Koufax and Don Drysdale even held out in 1966 as a package. But all 600 players had never held out before 1969, especially over pensions.

This was the economic issue: The players' pension fund got 60 per cent of the TV money from the World Series and 95 per cent from the All-Star Game. The money came from a $50,000,-000, three-year contract between baseball and the National Broadcasting Company. The share for pensions totaled $1,400,-000 a year — before the athletes banded together and decided not to return those contracts to owners like Gussie Busch.

For a player, the pension meant that he could collect if he spent five seasons in a major league uniform. If he elected to start collecting at the minimum age of fifty, his pension was worth $250 a month. If he played ten years and collected at fifty, it was worth $500 a month. If he somehow played twenty years and waited until sixty-five to start collecting, it was worth $1487 a month.

Since the World Series of 1968, a couple of dozen meetings had been held on the future format for the pension plan. The owners agreed to raise the ante by $1,000,000 a year, but with no reference to television as the source. The players, though, insisted on hitching the formula to the rising star of TV revenue.

"If they thought TV revenue would fall," Miller said at the height of the impasse, "the owners would be stuffing this formula down our throats. Ten years ago, TV income for baseball was three and a quarter million a year. This year it's sixteen and a half. We don't know what it will be ten years from now."

Miller symbolizes the new era in economics on the playing fields. He has degrees from Miami University of Ohio and New York University. He served as chief economist for the United Steelworkers of America. He was hired as the players' adviser in July, 1966, and now conducts their affairs from a Park Avenue office in Manhattan with a sign on the door reading: Major League Baseball Players Association.

"This all started," he said, "during the wage stabilization days of World War Two. Salaries were held down because a raise might force up prices. It was inflationary. So fringe benefits were used as safety valves. A guy couldn't go out and buy a five-hundred-dollar used car with a health plan.

"Now an individual gets more by taking it as a deferred payment. If he takes twenty-five dollars in pay, he can't buy twenty-five dollars of insurance with it, considering the tax structure. But if his employer puts the twenty-five dollars into insurance, the worker gets twenty-five dollars worth of insurance."

The baseball owners replied that their sources of revenue were drying up too. The biggest attraction in baseball since Babe Ruth is the giveaway promotion, Bat Day. The Baltimore Orioles in 1968 operated at a loss of $186,460; then they sold six players to the new teams at Seattle and Kansas City and turned a profit of $737,765.

For the new cities, though, the cost of getting franchises spiraled to a record of $10,000,000. That's three times as much as the New York Mets paid in 1961, and it doesn't include a stadium that may cost $30,000,000 more.

Even the novelty of the first domed stadium can wear thin. In 1965, the Houston Astros drew 2,151,470 customers into the Astrodome. By 1968, the total had dropped to 1,312,887. The owner of the team promptly "diversified." He bought control of the Ringling Brothers–Barnum & Bailey Circus.

Baseball's troubles even attracted the attention of the *Wall Street Journal,* which knows a business conglomerate when it sees one. In an editorial on the new economics of baseball — one day after the deadlocked owners had named Bowie Kuhn "commissioner pro tem" — it said:

"The official view, then, appears to be that those who run the business of baseball should do pretty much as they please, with no effective regulation — by themselves or anyone else. And their employees ought to be thankful that the bosses let them work.

"That, of course, is largely the way many businessmen operated half a century or so ago. But somehow we can't help thinking that baseball's ills require remedies more rational than merely turning back the clock."

The pension problem, though, was past history to pro football. The summer before, many of the players in the National Football League stayed away from their training camps while their agents argued with the owners about pensions, medical coverage, and nineteen other issues. In the newer American Football League, the argument was shorter and the settlement smaller. But in both leagues — now conferences of a merged league — the handwriting was on the wall for the nineteen seventies.

The upheaval was marked by soaring populations, new stadiums, and television. The NFL entered its first deal with a single network in 1962 and got $4,650,000 from the Columbia Broadcasting System. By the time the leagues merged in 1969, the price had zoomed to $18,800,000 for a season. The American League, meanwhile, was running out a five-year deal with the National Broadcasting Company and it was worth $42,000,-000. And now there are twenty-six teams, three networks, and millions more in the till.

But for Rozelle and his athletes, the economic facts also included these: NFL teams were already playing in stadiums that were 90 per cent sold out, prices could not be raised freely, and the networks were beginning to suggest that there even was a limit on the TV gold.

"Football and baseball are like loss leaders in department stores," a network man said. "The networks don't get big profits from them. They get two things: prestige and a better grip on holding their affiliated stations."

Still, the rush for television money went on. Letters were delivered to the three networks advising them that sealed bids would be entertained for exclusive rights to a table tennis tournament. And a man in the Midwest notified a network that he had developed a new game, "broom ball," which was "sweeping" his neighborhood. He offered the match to national TV for $25,000. National TV, despite his talent with a pun, declined.

A television crew in Mexico was covering an auto race and decided to film a ten-minute segment of high diving from the cliffs of Acapulco. "Sure," replied the Mexican spokesman for the divers, "we would be happy to dive for one hundred thousand dollars."

The producer demurred and started to leave. But the Mexican impresario said quickly: "Would six divers at ten dollars each be too much, señor?"

So the astronomy of sports financing in the sixties and seventies may be rough on high divers, to say nothing of baseball's minor leagues and medium-sized cities with ambition. But it is spread across the board for big-league performers.

In thoroughbred racing, Eddie Neloy trained horses that won $1,233,101 in one year. Baeza rode horses that won $2,835,108 in one year. Angel Cordero Jr. rode 345 winners and his mounts won $2,638,680. At 10 per cent of the purses, both jockeys collected a quarter of a million dollars.

On Labor Day alone at the end of the decade, the Lindheimer Stakes at Arlington Park outside of Chicago fetched $13,850 in prizes; the Aqueduct Stakes in New York had a purse of

$108,200; and ten quarter horses in New Mexico sprinted in the $602,000 fantasia at Ruidoso Downs. The same day, Rockingham Park in New Hampshire treated the betting public to fourteen races spread across the morning and afternoon, and Shenandoah Downs in West Virginia staged nineteen races in the afternoon and evening.

There were close to 6000 racing dates on the continent in one year, most of them in the United States, and 48,000,000 customers bet more than $4,000,000,000. And where do they go from here?

Some tracks already hold ten races a day regularly, some run in the snow, and, said one horseman surveying the horse traffic, "there's no place else to go but Sunday."

One place that some horses go is the breeding farm, and syndication prices soared along with everything else. When Buckpasser retired from racing in 1967 and was syndicated as a stallion, his capital worth was valued at $4,800,000. When the great Dr. Fager left the track a year later for the life of a sire, his evaluation was $3,200,000. And shortly after, Vaguely Noble was syndicated at $5,000,000.

The harness tracks pay off in greenbacks too. Neither rain nor sleet nor gloom of night stayed the trotters from their swift rounds as 24,000,000 spectators bet more than $1,600,000,000 in one year on horses competing for $65,000,000 in purses.

Nevele Pride won twenty-three of twenty-six races in 1968 and earned $427,000. Cardigan Bay retired at the age of twelve after having become the first millionaire in a harness. Romunda Hanover, a yearling, was sold at auction for $115,000, and horses driven by Billy Haughton won $1,600,000 in one year.

In golf, economic pressures caused the touring pros to secede from the Professional Golfers' Association. Then they returned under a separate flag and under the first commissioner of the pros, Joseph C. Dey Jr.

"The growth is fantastic," Dey said. "About three hundred

golf courses are opened in the United States every year. There are nine thousand now and ten million players of all kinds. The courses doubled in the last generation and will probably double in the next.

"In eighteen ninety-five, the total purse for the first United States Open was three hundred thirty-five dollars. Now it's around two hundred thousand dollars. That year there were fifty-six entrants in the first three championships; now there are more than twelve thousand in the nine championships run by the United States Golf Association."

Somebody figured out that Arnold Palmer had taken 100,-000 shots as a touring pro — and had been rewarded to the tune of $11.65 a stroke. A decade ago he was the leading winner at $42,607; now Lee Trevino has gone past $209,000 in half a year.

But you could probably make more money working for Palmer than playing against him. He has a business empire managed by Mark McCormack, who also counts the money for Gary Player and other athletes. And Arnie alone has a *payroll* of $1,000,000 for his own employees.

In tennis, long the domain of the "kept" amateur, professionals started competing in the major tournaments as the last pretenses of amateurism left with the sixties. When the first United States Open was held at Forest Hills in September, 1968, $100,-000 in prizes was distributed. The tournament ironically was won by an amateur, Arthur Ashe, who could not accept the money.

In keeping with the temper of the times, though, he later received an anonymous gift of 100 shares of General Motors stock. It was then worth $8900.

The National Basketball Association in one year added Phoenix and Milwaukee and grew to fourteen teams, then added Cleveland, Buffalo, and Portland and grew to seventeen. Its attendance grew past three and a half million, and its payrolls grew too. Wilt Chamberlain went from Philadelphia to

Los Angeles and commanded a many-splendored package that guaranteed him $250,000 a year. Then along came Alcindor, and Milwaukee lunged at the chance to draft him and to guarantee him more money than it figured to net as a corporation.

In hockey, the National League expanded overnight from six teams to twelve, went on national television, and then expanded to fourteen teams. The new franchises cost $2,000,000 apiece at first, then quickly went to $6,000,000 in 1970. Within the last four years, every club has raised admission prices 15 per cent, but the public still swarms into the arenas and Clarence Bigelow of Dickeyville, Wisconsin, still waits in line trying to pry loose a pair of tickets.

The established teams play to 90 per cent of capacity and more; Montreal and Toronto to 100 per cent. Detroit once played to 110 per cent of its seating capacity. And the Maple Leafs have a waiting list of 10,000 for an arena in Toronto that seats 16,000.

But the costs keep rising too. A quarter-century ago, Eddie Shore of Boston earned $12,000 and was "stopped" by a pay ceiling imposed by the owners. He pressed for fringe benefits and got his rent paid. Now Bobby Hull makes $100,000 and Bobby Orr of Boston, a bruised and fresh-faced boy veteran, started dropping hints about $100,000 before he reached twenty-one.

When does the bubble burst? Will the inflation of the nineteen sixties lead to deflation in the nineteen seventies? Are the new athlete-capitalists on a collision course with their employers? Or is everybody on a collision course with antitrust laws and a decade of legal tangles?

Al Cooperman, who took over the productions for the new Madison Square Garden late in 1968, sits in a spacious office on the eighteenth floor over Pennsylvania Station in New York and contemplates the boom. He once booked plays for the Shubert theaters and supervised special programs for NBC, and presides over the Garden as a specialist in the business of entertainment.

He knows that the payrolls for the Knickerbockers in basketball and the Rangers in hockey have quadrupled in ten years.
But he knows there are cash customers out there, and he is opti-
mistic.

"We have two hundred eighty or three hundred events a
year," he said, "and we're looking for other ways of generating
revenue. The Felt Forum seats five thousand and the main
arena can go to twenty thousand, and we have forty-eight bowling lanes. But whether you make suits, cars, or furniture, there's
a whole new generation that was born into a visual environ-
ment. It's more competitive, but the horizon is wider and
brighter."

In the old days, dances were held before basketball games to
bring in the customers. The Knicks now go to 19,000 without
music. The Garden even put on a rock concert by the Doors as a
kind of experiment: one performance promoted by two newspaper ads. The Doors packed in 19,000 of the new generation of
customers and the Garden grossed $105,000.

But the search for new sources of revenue goes on and, while
it does, professional sports get deeper into the hazards of big
business. For one thing, they are now competing for that capricious "recreation dollar" with skiing, surfing, sailing, camping,
boating, flying, and all the other pastimes of a generation that
will pay to relax.

For another thing, they face the legal challenges of all businesses. Baseball, for one, has operated since 1922 under a special
exemption from the antitrust laws, but the "umbrella" keeps
coming under new pressure.

"Baseball has a pretty good lobby," Miller said. "The railroads and airlines get privileges, too, but they also get regulations. Some congressmen still think baseball is apple pie, but it's
a profitable business and bears examination.

"It gets help from the capital-gains tax, the depreciation of
contracts, and the writing-off of losses. Also, the free-agent draft

lets you take an athlete and force him to deal only with a perfect stranger. The reserve clause is in the same category. It's a euphemism to say you own a contract. You own an athlete.

"It would be far better to plan now than to have somebody come along and trigger a lawsuit that would challenge the whole structure."

"The business of baseball and football," observed Michael Burke, who runs the New York Yankees for CBS, "has grown so complex that you need people running these enterprises with a breadth of background and a breadth of vision.

"In a simpler time you might have an old entrepreneur who had been a catcher, coach, manager, general manager, and then owner. Now it's definitely more competitive for all leisure-time sports. You must have people with the background and vision to run your show. If not, you jeopardize it all."

. . .

Glendale, California, has the only set of bank doors engraved with the full figure of a man in a baseball suit. The doors belong to the Valley National Bank and the figure belongs to Charles Dillon Stengel. He was born when Victoria was Queen and Benjamin Harrison was President, and he began playing in the big leagues in 1912 when William Howard Taft first started slipping out of the White House on an April afternoon to throw out the first ball.

Long before television, long before Bat Day, long before "deferred payments" for athletes, Stengel had developed an intimate understanding of the impact of money on society. He was paid twenty-five cents for pumping the organ in St. Mark's Episcopal Chuch in Kansas City; $1 a day for pitching with the Kansas City Red Sox; $135 a month for playing the outfield at Kankakee, Illinois; and $100,000 a year for managing the New York Mets.

He had been a player, coach, or manager on seventeen professional baseball teams. He had been traded four times as a left-handed outfielder in the major leagues. He had been dropped or relieved three times as a manager in the big leagues. He had even been paid twice for *not* managing.

Along the way, he had watched the United States grow from the horse-drawn surrey to the lunar module, and he had seen it endure two world wars and a catastrophic depression. He had made, and lost, a fortune in oil and real estate, and now he was the vice president of the bank with the baseball figure carved into its double front doors.

He knew the value of a dollar, the lure of a dollar, and the danger of a dollar. And, in his own indescribable idiom, he surveyed the nineteen sixties and the nineteen seventies from the shrewdness of his start in the eighteen nineties.

"I got paid $2100 a year when I joined the big league," Casey Stengel said, reducing things to their simplest terms. "And they get more money now."

2

Behind Hagemeister's Brewery

IN THE DAYS BEFORE TELEVISION COMMERCIALS during professional football games cost $200,000 a minute — in the days before television commercials *or* professional football, for that matter — life in the United States was hinged on one central fact: The war to make the world safe for democracy was over.

It didn't particularly matter that the world was *not* especially safe for democracy. The main thing was that the war — the World War — was over, and not even the Bolsheviks could frighten people away from the era of wonderful nonsense that was about to unfold. It was 1919, the 77th Division paraded from Washington Square to 110th Street in a roaring return home, mail was being flown by air, and a brigadier general named Douglas MacArthur was appointed commandant at West Point.

It was a gathering time of suffragettes, heavyweight contenders, heroes like Jack Dempsey, heroines like Suzanne Lenglen, horses like Man o' War, hoofers like Jackie Coogan in *Peck's Bad Boy* at the Brooklyn Strand, and high-speed motorcars like the Amesbury Berlin, one of which was advertised in the *New York Times* "with Westinghouse shock absorbers, bumper, two spare shoes and other extras; just overhauled, painted and re-upholstered," and which could be viewed "on inspection by appointment."

True, the "reparations problem" was causing daily consternation among the international graybeards like Lloyd George, the King's Prime Minister, and the Allied armies were threatening to march again within six days in case the Germans failed to pay up. The armies did most of their marching on Fifth Avenue, though, and the Germans still failed to pay up. And, when the great tide of Prohibition flowed over the land, the war-weary American public did some marching of its own — to the new speakeasies and to the even newer "rum courts," both of which did a landslide business as the country tumbled into the Roaring Twenties.

For reassurance during all such tribulations, people had only to turn toward their idols and follow them down the postwar primrose path. Ethel and John Barrymore at the Empire Theatre. Tex Rickard at Madison Square Garden. John McGraw at the Polo Grounds. John McGraw in the grill room of the Lambs Club. Thomas A. Edison in his laboratory at Menlo Park, New Jersey. Babe Ruth packing his gear in Boston and heading for New York, where the Yankees soon would construct a stadium contoured for his "thing" with a baseball bat. John D. Rockefeller contributing $1,000,000 to "the starving children of Central Europe" and occasionally contributing shiny new nickels and dimes in hotel lobbies to starving ballplayers like Casey Stengel.

Even in matters of public morals, the straight and narrow path was being bent. The only cities that permitted Sunday baseball were Chicago, Cincinnati, and St. Louis, but Cleveland and Detroit were leaping into line and so was New York, under a bill sponsored in the Legislature by State Senator James J. Walker. The last holdouts, Philadelphia and Pittsburgh, did not capitulate until ten years later, though in Pittsburgh the owner of the team, Barney Dreyfuss, had often pointed out that Sunday baseball was risky because it was likely to kill the Saturday gate.

In Green Bay, Wisconsin, the rush toward social action focused on two men: a businessman named Frank Peck and a twenty-one-year-old dropout from the University of Notre Dame named Earle Louis Lambeau. It was a marriage of true minds. Peck owned the Indian Packing Company and had $500 to spend. Lambeau, who had been the captain of the football team at Green Bay's East High School in 1916 and 1917 and the fullback at Notre Dame in 1918, had a job at the packing company and plenty of free time.

When Frank Peck turned over his $500 for sweaters and stockings to "equip" an athletic team, Curly Lambeau called the boys together and put Green Bay — and professional football — on the map. The date was August 11, 1919.

"We played for the love of the game," recalled Lambeau, who was making $250 a month at the time in Frank Peck's packing house. "We agreed to split any money we got and each man was to pay his own doctor bills."

The players all came from Green Bay except one, Sam Powers of nearby Marinette, and they were rough. They swept through ten games against town teams in Wisconsin and the upper peninsula of Michigan, scoring 565 points behind the coaching, running, and passing of Lambeau; their opponents scored six. There were twenty-one pioneers in all who wore the sweaters and stockings of the Indian Packing Company, and when they played in the grassy park behind Hagemeister's Brewery in Green Bay, a newspaperman and booster named George W. Calhoun would filter among the standing crowd and pass the hat.

At the end of the season, each of the regulars pocketed $16.75.

One year later, though, things began looking up. Lambeau's father, who was a carpenter, built a wooden grandstand with 3000 seats and encircled the lot with a fence. This time, it cost fifty cents to get inside the fence to watch the "Packers" massing in front of Lambeau, who now was a full-time impresario as well as a part-time halfback.

In both respects, he was probably better set than George Stanley Halas, who was patching together a similar football team for a similar company across the state line in Decatur, Illinois: Staley's Bears. They were named for A. E. Staley, whose company produced cornstarch but whose abiding passion was sports.

This was a marriage of true minds, too. Halas had been born February 2, 1895, the son of a Czechoslovakian tailor in the working-class neighborhoods of southwest Chicago. He was a skinny, quick-witted sort who graduated in 1918 from the University of Illinois with a degree in ceramic engineering but with a runaway desire to become a working athlete. It wasn't a bad idea except for the economic fact that the only working, and eating, athletes in business at the time seemed to be chiefly baseball players. And in 1917, when Halas was interrupting his campus career to join the Navy, a flop-eared outfielder named Casey Stengel was taking a $2600 cut in pay from the Brooklyn Dodgers — a couple of months after he had banked a World Series check for $2834.

But Halas went up to the Great Lakes Naval Training Station anyway, became an ensign, made the football team as a 6-foot-170-pound end, and was named to the second team All-America. When the war ended, he tried to make it as a railroad engineer for a while, then turned up in the New York Yankees' training camp in the spring of 1919 as an outfielder. He went to bat against Rube Marquard of the Dodgers one afternoon, hit a triple off the center-field fence, and injured his right hip sliding into third base.

After that he played in only nineteen games with the Yankees, batted .091, retired with the damaged hip, and, he observed later, was "replaced" in right field by Babe Ruth.

That was when Halas consented to a marriage of minds with the Staley Starch Company, and in 1920 Staley's Bears were born. They played fourteen games, won eleven of them, lost one, were tied twice, scored 169 points, gave up only one touchdown, switched their football operations the next year to Chicago — and lost $71.63.

By then, Halas was putting in eighteen hours a day, and none of it was producing cornstarch. He played end for the Bears, coached the club, handled the administrative details, collected tickets, wrote publicity releases, and booked the games. On the side, he sold automobiles to earn money while his partner, Dutch Sternaman, pumped gasoline in a filling station.

What they needed, though, was some kind of organization or league to rescue them from the sandlots plus some "names" to rescue them from the poorhouse. They got the organization after a caucus in Canton, Ohio. A bunch of other refugees from the poorhouse stood around on the running boards in Ralph Hay's automobile agency and formed the American Professional Football Association. The membership fee was $100, and the teams that anted up were the Canton Bulldogs, the Cleveland Indians, the Dayton Triangles, the Akron Professionals, the Massilon Tigers, the Rochester Kodaks, the Rock Island Independents, the Chicago Cardinals, the Decatur Staley's, and a pair of town teams from Hammond and Muncie, Indiana.

The first president of the troupe was Jim Thorpe, the grandson of a Sac warrior, who had gone to school on the Carlisle Indian Reservation in Western Pennsylvania and who had done after-school chores for a young teacher named Marianne Moore. He earned her lasting thanks as "a good boy" for that, but he earned greater distinction as the bulldozing hellcat of the Carlisle football team from 1908 to 1910. By the time George Halas and his cronies were organizing the first pro football league ten years later, Thorpe had dominated the 1912 Olympic Games, played shortstop for the New York Giants, played football for the Canton Bulldogs, and lost his Olympic medals because of "professionalism."

Thorpe's career as a player in the new league lasted longer than his career as president. After one hand-to-mouth season, the association was reorganized in 1921 under Joe F. Carr, a promoter from Columbus, Ohio, who kept it afloat until his death in 1939. Two other things happened to the association that

year: the Green Bay Packers (now owned by the Acme Packing
Company) were admitted and the clubs decided to change their
name to the National Football League. They also decided to
reduce the franchise fee from $100 to $50.

That is, they now had the organization but still lacked some
grip on the public's imagination. They were like the mule
driver who rapped his most stubborn critter over the snout with
a plank — to get his attention so that he then could get down to
some serious training. Except that professional football in those
primeval days could not even get the public to stand still long
enough to command its attention.

"Truly," editorialized the *New York Times* in 1922, zeroing
in on the situation, "baseball is the national game. From east
and west, from north and south, the fans are gathering to see two
New York teams battle in the blue-ribbon event of the diamond,
the World Series."

The *Times* was commenting on a specific phenomenon, a
World Series between the New York Giants and New York Yankees — that is to say, between John McGraw and Babe Ruth.
But its focus was true enough in a general way. Baseball truly
was the national game, and football was considered a sport that
reached its peak on Saturday afternoons when the college elev-
ens met before huge crowds with bands playing and cheerleaders
tossing megaphones onto the grass before doing backflips.

But even college football had trouble commanding anybody's
attention until after the World Series had ended in October and
baseball finally yielded its place on the national sporting scene
for a few months. A World Series, especially one between the
Giants and the Yankees, would be approached with all the tumult and clamor of a political convention, and it probably attracted more politicians than many political conventions.

"J. P. Morgan is a boxholder," the press reported on the eve
of the 1922 Series, "as are also Harry F. Sinclair, Harry Payne
Whitney, Finley J. Shepard and Charles H. Sabin." In a box

near the dugout, Mary Roberts Rinehart entertained a group of friends while George M. Cohan, Louis Mann, and Jack Dempsey took bows. And when General John J. Pershing made an unexpected appearance, the crowd rose and cheered mightily, as it did for Al Smith and the old brown derby.

"Hear the crowd roar at the World Series games with Radiola," the public was exhorted in great advertisements that announced the arrival of radio onto this busy scene. "Grantland Rice, famous sports editor of the *New York Tribune,* will describe every game personally, play by play, direct from the Polo Grounds. His story, word by word, as each exciting play is made by the Yankees or Giants will be *broadcasted* from famous Radio Corporation–Westinghouse Station WJZ. There's an R.C.A. set for every home and every purse. As low as twenty-five dollars."

The broadcasting of a World Series marked the zenith of experiments that had been conducted for ten years: transmitting sports events from arena to studio. But the experiments had been pretty much of a university laboratory affair, as when pioneers at the University of Minnesota attempted to radio football games by using a spark transmitter and telegraph signals. And even as late as 1922, Texas A. & M. was experimenting in a play-by-play account of its Thanksgiving Day game against Texas.

But football's piece of the action was restricted to the college game. Not so with prize fighting, though, or with any of the other events picked for coverage by the new-fangled medium. From Pittsburgh, station KDKA carried a description of the Johnny Ray–Johnny Dundee fight in April of 1921 and, three months later, station WJY carried the heavyweight championship match between Jack Dempsey and Georges Carpentier from Jersey City. The next year — the year the National Football League was trying to get off the ground — WJZ in New York began carrying *baseball* scores every fifteen minutes every afternoon and WGN regaled Chicago for seven hours with a nonstop description of the Indianapolis Speedway Classic as the racing cars whipped past the microphone at close to 100 miles an hour. And by 1925, all home baseball games — not just the scores — were being carried by WMAQ, Chicago, and KHJ, Los Angeles, which wasn't even in the major leagues.

By then, the baritone voice behind the microphone customarily belonged to a concert singer from the Northwest named Graham McNamee, who always opened his broadcasts with "Good afternoon, ladies and gentlemen of the radio audience" and ended them with "Good night, all," and who once received 50,000 letters after a World Series — from *baseball* fans.

But there were the pro football players, while all this was going on, forming their leagues and their flying wedges on clawed-up little fields behind Hagemeister's Brewery and in other obscure sandlots from Rock Island to Muncie. They were still there looking for the "names" who would capture the public's fancy the way McGraw and Ruth and Cobb and Mathewson and Dempsey and Tilden did. Bob Zuppke, who was George Halas's coach at Illinois, had been right when he told the graduating Halas and his teammates: "Why is it that when you fellows begin to know something about football, you leave me and stop playing? Football is the only sport in which a man's career ends when it should be beginning."

He was so right, agreed Halas as he collected tickets and sold automobiles; he was right, agreed Dutch Sternaman, as he pumped gas between those weekend slugfests that passed for football games in the new professional league. He was right, agreed Jim Thorpe, as he escorted Halas into the record book one November afternoon in 1923 by catching him from behind and slamming him into the end zone — after Halas had run ninety-eight yards with a fumble.

He was right, that is, if they could all promote professional football into something more *camp* than a twenty-two-man wrestling match on grass. But the public's passion, to say noth-

ing of the public's money, was aimed in other directions. Curly
Lambeau even put the bite on a friend in Green Bay, who sold
his Marmon roadster for $1500 in order to stake Lambeau when
the going got exceptionally rough. (Lambeau showed his grati-
tude by allowing his "angel" to play tackle in the Packers' opening game — for one minute.)

But in spite of sacrifices like these, and in spite of Halas's
smart decision to move the Bears from Decatur to Chicago and
into Wrigley Field, the league was still hanging by a thread.
The players traveled in day coaches and even ate bananas for
nourishment on days when the menu was necessarily skimpy.
New owners like Jimmy Conzelman shelled out $1000 a game
to rent big-league parks like Detroit's Navin Field — only to see
it rain on all ten home dates. Three franchises failed in Cleveland in the first decade of the league, and three failed in Detroit.
What they needed was money, and to get it they needed the
magic of a name. A name like Red Grange.

They got it in November, 1925, Grange's senior year at
Halas's old school, Illinois. The league was then in its fifth season of struggling, and it numbered twenty teams sprawled
around the landscape from Providence to Kansas City. The
only hometowns of any economic consequence were Chicago,
which had the Bears and the Cardinals, and New York, which
joined the bucket brigade of "postgraduate football" that year.
New York had been offered a franchise three years earlier for
$50, but had declined. Now the price was up to $500, and a
bookmaker named Timothy J. Mara — a legal bookmaker —
calculated that the odds on success were worth risking, especially at that price. "Any New York franchise ought to be worth
that much," he observed. "I'll buy."

A few months later, though, his football expenses had spiraled
to $40,000. So Mara joined the search for a "name" too, and his
search also led directly to the Galloping Ghost of Illinois, Harold "Red" Grange. But Halas got there first. Four days after

Grange's final college game for Illinois, he was signed, sealed, and delivered — signed by Halas; sealed by C. C. Pyle, a theater operator in Champaign, Illinois, who became Grange's agent and who later became legendary in the economics of sports as Cash & Carry Pyle; and delivered to Wrigley Field, where the Bears played the Cardinals on Thanksgiving Day.

The result was a full house of 36,000 persons, probably the first sellout crowd ever drawn by pro football. The net result was $14,000 in receipts, with Grange and Pyle pocketing $9300. The actual result on the field was a scoreless tie. But they were the only ciphers that football's merger with Grange produced, as Halas took his team and its new prize performer on a whirlwind tour. It started three days after Thanksgiving, and these were the mathematical results:

City	Opponent	Grange	Crowd
Chicago	Columbus	—	28,000
St. Louis	St. Louis	4 touchdowns	8000
Philadelphia	Frankford	2 touchdowns	35,000
New York	Giants	1 touchdown	65,000
Washington	Washington	2 field goals	8000
Boston	Providence	—	25,000
Detroit	Detroit	injured	6000
Chicago	Giants	injured	18,000

All these games, and all that money, were crammed into a two-week schedule that both fatigued Grange and enriched him. But Halas and Pyle were not about to let their bonanza go at that. A month later, they headed the carnival south in knickers, loud socks, and special sweaters with "Bears" embroidered across the front. At Coral Gables, Florida, they charged as much as $19.80 for one ticket; it was an overprice and nobody made any money except Pyle, who lived up to his nickname by taking in his guarantee of $25,000 in cash and carrying it to Red Grange.

It was January of 1926 now and the Bears kept packing them

in wherever they went with the football corporation of Grange & Pyle: in New Orleans, Los Angeles, San Diego, San Francisco, Portland, and Seattle. The crowd in Los Angeles was announced as 70,000, which may have been a slight exaggeration. But it was no exaggeration that in two months, the touring Bears attracted 360,000 customers to twenty games — and cleared a quarter of a million dollars.

"I knew then and there," Halas said, "that Grange was the box-office shot in the arm pro football needed. The publicity established pro football as a national sport."

• • •

They were a strange breed, these people who paid the bills for football teams in the IOU days.

Halas, the onetime ceramics engineer, ran a one-man show through several generations of players. He required them to attend lectures, watch films, and take encyclopedic notes in loose-leaf books. Then during games, he would roam the sidelines flinging his hat onto the ground in frustration whenever something was less than perfect, which was most of the time. He borrowed money to keep the team in business after Grange had put it there, and when the Depression undermined the whole structure, he bought out his old teammate and partner Dutch Sternaman for $38,000 and did the worrying himself. He even wrote letters on Chicago Bears stationery that listed the "night telephone number" of the team, which also happened to be the number of the telephone in his own apartment.

Then when the Depression struck and the entire country started to learn about deficit financing, and when his own league retrenched to eight teams, he suddenly had company.

There was Arthur J. Rooney, the son of a Pittsburgh saloon-keeper, who paid $2500 for the right to fret over the Pittsburgh Steelers. He was a gambler of renown, though, at the racetrack as well as in the football business and once was reported to have won a quarter of a million dollars over a weekend at Saratoga.

There was also Bert Bell, who took over the Frankford Yellow

Jackets when they folded and moved them a few miles into downtown Philadelphia as the Eagles. Things got so lean, though, that he once pleaded with the Brooklyn Dodgers to call off a game because it was raining hard. It wasn't so much that the Eagles minded the rain as that Bell minded all those empty seats. But he was so determined to stay afloat that on another occasion he transported his club from its training base at Hershey, Pennsylvania, across the country to Colorado Springs for an exhibition game — by bus. They practiced en route in cow fields.

Later he became the commissioner of the league and a sort of Saint George at that, and once he looked back on the horse-and-buggy days without flinching and said: "Weak teams had a hard time building up in those days."

"In the old days," said Art Rooney, "we'd have a meeting — me and Tim Mara, George Halas of the Bears, Bert Bell of the Eagles, Charley Bidwell of the Cardinals, and George Marshall of the Redskins. We'd sit around and discuss what to do, and then we'd do it. Now, every owner comes into a league meeting with one squad of lawyers and one squad of accountants. One man can't run it anymore."

Charles W. Bidwell, who owned a rug-cleaning plant in Chicago, was another dues-paying member of the inner circle. He bought the Cardinals in 1932 at the depth of the Depression from a dentist, Dr. David Jones, who had achieved two coups during his three seasons in red ink: He sent the Cardinals to Coldwater, Michigan, for their training and he hired the celebrated Ernie Nevers of Stanford as his player-coach. Nevers turned out to be an uncommon coach too. On Thanksgiving Day in 1929, he ripped through the Bears for six touchdowns, added four extra points, and wound up with a forty-point afternoon.

Bidwell already had established himself as an entrepreneur before taking up the challenge of running a football team during the Crash. At one time or another, he operated a girls' baseball team, a Negro baseball team, the Hawthorne racetrack at Cicero, the dog track known as the Miami Beach Kennel Club, a dog track at Jacksonville, another horse track known euphemistically as the National Jockey Club, and a number of apartment houses in Chicago. His brother also owned the Bentley-Murray Printing Company in Chicago, and Charley had stock in that.

Then there was the rug-cleaning plant, and one day in 1933 Bidwell tapped it for an employee named Arch Wolfe, who also served as a rent collector for the apartment houses. Wolfe had been scrubbing rugs in the cleaning house, and he recalled that "we'd wash them on both sides for three dollars." But now Bidwell, recognizing his versatility, switched Wolfe into the business office of his new football team and he stayed there until he died in 1971.

"Money was awfully scarce then," Wolfe recalled years later, puffing on a pipe in the Cardinals' elegantly comfortable offices in Busch Memorial Stadium, long after they had migrated south and become the St. Louis Cardinals. "Later that same year, the year Charley fetched me from his rug-cleaning plant, the Chicago players tried to pick up some extra money playing an exhibition game in Saint Louis.

"Charley told me to fly down there and prevent it, because he was afraid somebody would get hurt in the game and the club would be liable. I flew down in a single-engine plane and talked to them. They needed the money so badly, though, that we finally let them play the game, but we made them call themselves something besides the Chicago Cardinals. But after that, the club began to schedule postseason games itself.

"The next year, nineteen thirty-four," he said, "we even went out to the West Coast for postseason games. The deal was that the players would get all the receipts after expenses — or none, depending on how we made out at the gate. We were one of the first teams to travel in some style too; we went out on the Santa Fe. But then we got into a hassle because the railroad wanted its money in advance and the club refused.

"We finally compromised: We'd pay the running expenses after each stop along the way, wherever we played games. Kansas City, San Francisco, right on to the coast and back."

Wolfe was still stung by the railroad's insistence on instant cash though. He was realist enough to collect the Cardinals' share of the receipts in cash at each stop, refusing to accept checks from the pickup teams they played en route. Then he turned around and was human enough to change it into silver, paying off the Santa Fe bagful by bulky bagful.

"We used to feed the players steak and potatoes before games in those days," Wolfe recalled. "Now we feed them steak and strawberries and waffles and peaches and ham. They digest easier, and the syrup for the waffles gives them energy.

"It was rough then. Only one or two teams in the NFL made money. Not even the Bears drew too many people. Green Bay always did. You had to love the game and love sports — it might cost you a lot of money."

In such precarious times, Wolfe reached a peak of imagination one weekend when the Cardinals took the train from Chicago to Pittsburgh to play Rooney's Steelers and discovered that they couldn't charter a team bus for the ride to the ball park. So he chartered a streetcar, herding his heavyweights to the trolley stop and on to Forbes Field. There was a streetcar waiting outside the stadium after the game, the Cardinals clambered back on board, rode straight to the depot for the trip back to Chicago, and Wolfe paid the trolley fare — a nickel a head.

Whenever the Cardinals played Green Bay, they would take the train from Chicago on Saturday, the day before the game. For New York, they set out on Friday. Nobody could afford the hotel and food bills for more than a day or so before a game, and the receipts were sure to be only a fraction of what a famous college team like Notre Dame or Army might command for a similar weekend.

"A team budget then was around one hundred twenty-five

thousand dollars for a full season," Wolfe noted. "Later on, after television came in and the players started to strike it rich, a budget would be maybe fifty times that. We didn't even have medical plans for the players. But we took care of them ourselves — you could get a meal for a buck then.

"The players got paid by the game. You'd have to be a star to make one hundred seventy-five dollars a game, somebody like Mike Mikulak, our fullback, who was the iron man of the club. A lineman might make seventy-five a game. The rule said you had to have at least twenty-two guys in uniform, or else some teams might show up at only half-strength. And anyway, a guy would play until he got tired."

The schedule was drawn by the owners themselves on a kind of common-sense basis related to natural rivalries and the available ball parks. If it rained on the day of a game, the gate suffered because season tickets were still a generation away; and if the rain froze, as it might in Green Bay, a financial and artistic disaster was a possibility. The Cardinals played in either the White Sox or Cubs baseball park, whichever was free, and on some lean Sundays they played before 2000 fans and 45,000 empty seats.

In spite of the loneliness inside the stadium some afternoons, Bidwell would rove around the sidelines during games the way Halas did, totally engrossed in the game, passionately involved in everything from yardage crises to referees' judgments. They may have been down on their luck as owners, but they usually were sky-high as coaches, and both predicaments were forced on them because they principally were fans.

They even resisted any temptation to bail themselves out of their red-ink existence by luring name players off the campuses too early, although their success with Red Grange had provided the hope and the cash to continue. They somehow stuck with "The Pledge" of 1926 — not to induce a college player to turn pro until his class graduated — and they somehow stuck with the penalty of a $1000 fine or the loss of the franchise. And, in some cases, a $1000 fine probably would have meant the end of the franchise.

Between games, they looked after the administrative details of their league with a kind of cracker-barrel wit and wisdom that was one generation removed from the wall-to-wall hierarchy of the Park Avenue era to come.

"At one time," Art Rooney remembered, "the league had an executive committee of three, rotated among the owners, to screen proposed legislation before each league meeting. One year, Charley Bidwell and George Marshall and I were the committee, and we met in Chicago just before the league meeting.

"As usual, Marshall had about a hundred proposals to make to the league. Charley and I agreed with every one of them, and we got finished in less than an hour. Marshall said it was a great thing that the league finally had a progressive executive committee. Charley and I just wanted to get out to the racetrack.

"We did, but the next day we met again with Marshall and just as calmly voted *against* every one of the things he had proposed the day before. And that was the end of the executive committee."

"Bidwell always knew that the National Football League would reach higher ground," Halas said. "He was a man of great vision where the league was concerned, and was actually always ready to put the good of the league before his own team or personal feelings. He even had a standard answer to anyone who was critical of the league or of football in those days, and I heard him give it many times. He'd look at the guy and snap, 'Why, you don't know what you're talking about. It's really a great game.' "

Bidwell was shrewd enough and eager enough to skip the racetrack and throw his support behind Marshall on one administrative occasion in July of 1933, and as a result the league turned a corner of its own in the midst of the Depression. The occasion centered on a suggestion by Marshall, a grandiose person who was a onetime actor and a full-time extrovert. He simply suggested that the league be divided into two sections, east and west; that each division produce a geographic winner for the season; and that the league championship then be settled in a play-off game.

Accordingly, the league was split into five-team divisions and on December 17, 1933, the Chicago Bears of the West outslugged the New York Giants of the East, 23 to 21, before a crowd of 26,000 persons. The pro football play-off had arrived, and with it the cash-carrying customers.

If there was any doubt about the idea, the Bears and Giants settled it the following December in the Polo Grounds. The temperature was nine degrees above zero and the country was even more deeply frozen into the Depression, but 35,059 persons paid their way into the game as the Bears built up a 13 to 3 lead. That's when the Giants created a legend by switching from football cleats to sneakers in the second half and by scoring twenty-seven points in the last period to win the game, 30 to 13.

The sneakers were provided by Gus Mauch, the trainer of the Giants, who already had established himself as a professional masseur whose clients included Jimmy Durante, George Bernard Shaw, and Admiral Richard E. Byrd, the admiral looking "a little pale," Mauch noted, after one of his expeditions to the North Pole. But after Gus provided the sneakers, the points were provided mainly by Ken Strong, who scored eighteen during the splurge and fastened his reputation as perhaps the most talented and durable athlete of his time.

Two innovations in the rules went into effect along with the East-West play-off, and they changed the nature and prosperity of the game too. The goal posts, which had been moved ten yards into the end zone in 1927, were returned to the goal line, and a forward pass now was permitted to be thrown from anywhere behind the line of scrimmage rather than only five yards or more behind it.

The first rule restored the art of kicking field goals since it shortened the distance by ten yards. Jack Manders — "Automatic" Jack Manders, no less — promptly showed the beauties of the change by booting three field goals and two extra points in the first play-off game for half the Bears' points that memorable afternoon. The second rule loosened up the defense by giving the passer more operating room behind the line of scrimmage, which had a way of resembling the Maginot Line anyway. And it led to the advent of fine passers like Arnold Herber of Green Bay and Sammy Baugh of Washington in a game that had traditionally resembled an elephant stampede.

It incidentally helped the elephants too, as in the first play-off game when Bronko Nagurski added the flip pass to an offensive repertory that already included the most devastating straight-ahead charge in football. Nagurski was a magnificent 230-pound fullback, and Grange once described just how magnificent in these words:

"There was something strange about tackling Nagurski. It was like taking an electric shock through your body. If you hit him anywhere above his ankles, you were likely to get killed."

It was not much of an exaggeration, because the Bears took advantage of Nagurski's reputation as a bulldozer, added the ingredient of the new forward-passing rule, and cashed in two touchdowns against the Giants in the first play-off game. Nagurski would plunge straight toward the line of scrimmage, drawing defenders from all sides of the field, but then suddenly would straighten up and flip a pass over their heads. He did it to Bill Karr for Chicago's first touchdown and he did it to Bill Hewitt, who tossed a lateral pass to Karr, for the second. In between, Manders kicked his three field goals, and, as a result, the Bears and Halas literally threw the new rule book at the Giants and Tim Mara.

Halas, who was no longer playing end for his team, was no longer answering its "night telephone" either. But along with his flamboyant friends who steered the NFL out of those lonely Sunday afternoons and on toward better times, he was still a one-man show as he had been in the days of Staley's Corn Products.

He once watched Bobbie Cahn, a 5-foot-11½-inch referee, pace off a penalty against the Bears and shouted injudiciously, "Cahn, you stink." Whereupon the midget martinet marched off fifteen more yards and called back, "How do I smell from here?"

Halas roamed far beyond the twenty-yard radius allowed coaches from their rightful place alongside the bench, and he hurled his hat up and down the sidelines while, from the box seats, his antics were mimicked by his wife Min and his two children, George Jr. and Virginia. He also acquired a reputation as the Sarah Bernhardt of the game because he frequently threatened to retire and in fact did three times — in 1929, in 1942 (to re-enter the Navy), and in 1955.

But whether "retired" as the coach or not, he still held the purse strings and he still held them the way he did in the five-and-dime days. Even after his undefeated Bears charged into New York in 1934 and knocked off the Giants, he reacted from instinct at the height of the team's victory party at the old Hollywood Restaurant. For once, it seemed he let the training rules slide by. That is, until after many hours of wining and dining his tigers, he casually asked a waiter how high the bill had climbed and was told $800.

"Good heavens," roared the Papa Bear, appalled. "These men are athletes. Cut them off."

In 1936, Halas and the other owners made one more change in their game, and, though the results were not startling at first, they eventually laid the foundation for much of pro football's surge after World War II. They instituted the first "draft" of college players. The last team in the league got first choice and so on up the ladder. It was a solid idea based on the principle that the last shall be first, and in time the last did become first. But in the bleak days, the weak teams frequently traded away their draft selections for established players from the stronger clubs and for them "tomorrow" was a long time coming.

It happened in reverse to Halas the first time the teams drafted college men, but it didn't happen often to Halas. The first college player chosen under the new system was Jay Berwanger, the All-America back from the University of Chicago. He was picked by the Philadelphia Eagles, who then traded him to the Bears, who then were caught short when Berwanger decided not to play pro football.

Three years later, though, the shoe was on Halas's other foot. The first selection in the draft fell to his old friend Art Rooney of Pittsburgh, who agreed to trade his choice to the Bears in exchange for an established end, Ed Manske. That is, Halas stipulated, it was a deal so long as Rooney's first selection was Sid Luckman, the quarterback from Columbia. They completed the deal and Halas wound up with a quarterback who led the Bears to their greatest successes.

By the same sort of bartering, Halas also picked up George McAfee, who became his best running back. He also inherited the rights to Tommy Harmon, the spectacular runner and gate attraction from Michigan, though Harmon went into the Army Air Forces and did not return to the Bears. But the Midas touch often stayed with Halas right down to the end of his draft list, as it did in 1936, the inaugural year, when he ran out of familiar names and fished into the manpower pool for an unknown.

"Daniel Fortmann of Colgate," he speculated. "That sounds like a nice name. I'll take him."

He did, and Fortmann became an all-league guard six times while the Bears strengthened their grip on the game they had helped get into business in the old cornstarch days. In fact, starting with the East-West split in 1933 and continuing through the first postwar season in 1946, they won eight western championships. The Green Bay Packers, who had gone bankrupt in 1933 and then were refinanced, won four, and between them the two old rivals dominated the West. The only other teams who broke into their monopoly were the Detroit Lions in 1935 and the Cleveland Rams in 1945. In the East, meanwhile, the New York Giants took eight titles, the Boston/Washington Redskins six, and nobody else cut in.

The most stunning result of all this, though, was reached in 1940 by the Bears as the league and its new rules and new stars headed into the second "wartime decade," completing the cycle started after the first wartime decade in Green Bay and Decatur.

Halas now was surrounded by his richest team, with Luckman at quarterback, Bill Osmanski at fullback, McAfee at halfback, and a line that included Ken Kavanaugh, Lee Artoe, Ed Kolman, Joe Stydahar, and Bulldog Turner. "We hated one another," observed Kolman, uttering two understatements, "but we played together."

They played together most spectacularly on December 8, 1940, in Griffith Stadium, Washington. Their opponents were the Redskins, led by the great passer from Texas Christian, Sammy Baugh — a Texan who had never worn cowboy boots or a ten-gallon hat but who had arrived in town on Marshall's orders three years earlier bedecked in both.

Three weeks before their championship match, the Redskins had edged past the Bears, 7 to 3, and Marshall had baited his old crony by deriding the Bears as "a first-half team" and "a bunch of cry-babies." Halas duly posted newspaper clippings carrying these compliments on the Bears' locker-room wall and Marshall began to regret them when Osmanski ran sixty-eight yards for a touchdown on the second play of the game.

By the end of the first half, exploding in all directions out of the T formation, Chicago expanded its lead to twenty-eight points. Then, during the intermission, instead of cooling things, Halas reminded his players of Marshall's description of them as "a first-half team." So they added seven more touchdowns in the second half and walked off the field with a 73 to 0 decision and all kinds of gratification.

When it was over, they left 36,034 spectators pondering man's inhumanity to man and they left Sammy Baugh sitting painfully in front of his cubicle answering impossible questions from the writers, such as: If one of his passes had been caught in the end zone by Charley Malone, would there have been a difference in the outcome?

"Yes," said Sammy in total candor, "there would have been a difference. The score would have been seventy-three to seven."

To people who complained that he had "poured it on" the Redskins, Halas noted that ten different Bears had scored a total of eleven touchdowns. Then the Papa Bear, reflecting on the days past when he had sold the tickets, printed the programs, and answered the telephones while Dutch Sternaman pumped the gas for meal money, added without apology:

"We used thirty-three men and the thirty-third scored a touchdown. Should I have rushed out and tackled him myself?"

A few days later, he and his Bears received winners' checks for $873 apiece. The Redskins, for their share in the bloody history of professional football, collected lumps and $606 apiece.

3
The Solid Gold Game

WHEN WORLD WAR II ended in 1945, the United States plunged into another time of transition and inflation, but there were some distinctive differences from the postwar landscape of 1918.

There was no Prohibition problem, nor were there suffragettes, reparations commissions, or Chicago Black Sox. But there was an enormous public hungering for white shirts, nylon stockings, and new automobiles, plus other necessities that had been sacrificed to the war effort, and there was an economic boom that provided the money to feed the hungering. And finally, there was something called television.

The impact of these crosscurrents was instantaneous and fairly staggering. In no time, people began to indulge their long-lost fancy for the blessings of leisure, and it was no longer necessary, either, to make the difficult choice between an outdoor pastime and an indoor speakeasy. They sold the stuff right on the premises. Or, at home, during interludes known as commercials, a man could divert himself by darting into the kitchen and treating himself to a brimming goblet in the comfort of his own estate. And, in fact, the commercial on the squared screen was probably *urging* him to do precisely that.

In professional sports, which were nationally organized by now compared with the Hagemeister Brewery days after World War I, the public's hungering led the mob straight from threshold to turnstile.

The New York Yankees, with Joe DiMaggio back in pin-stripes after four years in olive drab, promptly began to pick up the threads of life before two million spectators a season — double the number that used to watch them before the war — and paying spectators, at that. The Brooklyn Dodgers, in a ramshackle old ball park, played one entire season before crowds that *averaged* 28,000 persons in a stadium that seated only 32,000. Nearby, the semipro Bushwicks packed in the overflow, and even outdrew the St. Louis Browns of the American League, playing only three days a week in most cases and often playing against teams from the Negro National League. And in 1948, in a financial coup that had no equal in baseball or any other sport at the time, the Cleveland Indians under Bill Veeck, the Merlin of the major leagues, averaged more than 40,000 admissions for one whole jumping summer.

It was the era of frantic leisure, all right; the era of expansion, even explosion, in sports; the struggle for the recreation buck, the dawning day of the All-American dollar.

In professional football, it was a time when the founding fathers of the National Football League were lunging to broaden the basic tenet of their own constitution, which read in part:

"The objects of this league are: To promote good fellowship among its members; elevate the standards of football generally; to promote the business and ethical standards of professional football."

That is, they all realized that their teams suddenly had an unobstructed view of an untapped market. They might have been writing their ledgers in red ink for a generation but at least they didn't have to wear jerseys inscribed "Indian Packing Company" anymore.

One of the men who appreciated this opportunity more than most was deBenneville Bell, who presided over the fortunes of the National Football League from a bosky office at One Bala Avenue in Bala-Cynwyd, Pennsylvania, just as he presided over the lesser fortunes of the Philadelphia Eagles — the team that had taken a bus cross-country a few years earlier, stopping along the way to Colorado for some light workouts in cow pastures.

Another man who got the message was Dan Reeves, the owner of the Cleveland Rams franchise, and the first thing he did about it was to move the team west in 1946 as the Los Angeles Rams. He found the Golden West pre-empted by the Los Angeles Dons of a rival league known as the All-America Conference, and both teams found the region pre-empted by college teams like Stanford, California, and UCLA.

But Reeves was not about to let either the Dons or the deans keep him from those unmined hills, even though the colleges and their football bowls were entrenched and the Dons were bankrolled by Ben Lindheimer, the Chicago racetrack owner. Lindheimer immediately showed his style by offering Steve Van Buren the heady salary of $25,000 to switch his services (running with a football) to the Dons from Bert Bell's Eagles, where he was making the munificent sum of $15,000.

Reeves needed help for this kind of economic warfare, so he brought in his well-heeled partners from Cleveland. They were headed by Fred Levy Jr., who had been with him in the original purchase of the Cleveland team before the war, and Edwin Pauley, who had merely struck oil. Three years later, the Dons folded.

By then, the Rams were striking oil of their own in Los Angeles. They did this because they had a large stadium, the Coliseum, and because they had taken the precaution of lining up large players to fill it with people on those postwar Sunday afternoons. The secret was that, while the military services had been drafting men during the war, Reeves had been drafting them for service after the war. And when the big boys' college classes finally graduated them between 1947 and 1949, Reeves and his partners were waiting to greet them with open checkbooks.

By 1949, the Rams were loaded. Moreover, they were blessed

with a coach named Clark Shaughnessey, who had modernized
the T formation at Stanford in 1940 and who was now unleash-
ing it in the professional West just as he had helped George
Halas unleash it back East a few years earlier. He also had the
athletes to go with it, notably a pair of uncommon quarterbacks
— Bob Waterfield and, in reserve like a computerized battle-
ship, Norman Van Brocklin. They both pitched footballs to an
enormous end named Tom Fears, who broke all records in the
league by catching seventy-seven passes one year and then broke
his own record by grabbing eighty-four the next.

So it came as no surprise to people that Reeves, Shaughnessey,
& Company started winning games, to say nothing of championships. They won three straight championships, in fact, starting
in 1949. And, more significantly, they won them before incredibly big crowds of people.

They even did it before incredibly big crowds of coaches.
The Rams employed six from 1946 to 1955 (viz., from Clark
Shaughnessey to Sid Gilman), which suggested a certain galloping restlessness in the front office. But, on the field, they became
the first professional football team to cash in on the public's
postwar appetite for action.

There were little setbacks, like the 1949 play-off game, which
was staged before 29,751 fans and 63,000 empty seats. The reason for the nonstampede was something that not even deBenneville Bell could have prevented. It simply rained that day in
southern California. The following year, though, the sun began
to shine on the National Football League's western outpost, and
one day the Rams were watched (and paid) by 90,000 persons
— which was sixty times more than the capacity of the little
park behind Hagemeister's Brewery in Green Bay in the days
when somebody used to pass the hat for Curly Lambeau's Packers.

By the middle of the nineteen fifties, with the help of gimmicks at the gate and great running backs like Jon Arnett, the

Rams were in business to stay. They hit the skids on the field for a while, and even lost twenty out of thirty-six games starting in 1957. But more than a million persons saw them play at home and away during three thriving years in the counting-house. And in that time, they attracted three crowds of more than 100,000 customers, five greater than 90,000, and seven above 80,000.

The visiting teams shared the wealth too. One day in 1958, the San Francisco 49ers played to 90,833 paying fans in Los Angeles and went home with $90,000. And so the cash, in addition to the message, was being spread around.

Dan Reeves made one other contribution to the economics of pro football — maybe two, counting Alvin Ray Rozelle. The first contribution was an experiment in television, which Reeves undertook in 1950, the year Rozelle was getting his bachelor's degree at the University of San Francisco. Rozelle spent the next two years at his alma mater as an assistant athletic director at $4400 a year while Reeves was trying to learn what would happen if he presented his football team on home television screens while trying to fill the home stadium the same afternoon. He found out: People stayed home.

That was good enough for Reeves, and for Bert Bell too. So they next searched for a way to protect the football goose while preserving the golden egg of television. Their solution was the seventy-five-mile blackout: No television would be shown within a radius of seventy-five miles of a home game. The people within the magic circle could drive to the stadium and watch; those beyond it could stay home and watch. Both the spectators and the sponsors were reasonably happy with this arrangement, and so were the athletes when the first play-off game was televised nationally in 1951 and each player's share of the prize money leaped from $1113 to $2108.

The colleges were quick to learn the lesson in economics too. And their solution, spelled out by the National Collegiate Ath-

letic Association, was this: Only one game a week on one network, with local stations blacked out. There were more than
one million television sets in the country by now, and as much
as the pros and the professors nourished the notion of coaxial-
cable treasure, they were panicked by the twin possibility of
empty stadiums. So the lines were drawn.

They were drawn so strictly, in fact, that in 1952 the Justice
Department brought suit against the NFL, charging that the
TV blackout system was illegal under the Sherman Antitrust
Act as a restraint of trade.

Bell corralled the other owners into line with the unassailable
argument that they needed TV rules "to protect our home
gate." He was so convincing that they dug down and paid
$200,000 to finance the league's defense against the suit. And it
became a defense that every coach in the league might envy. On
November 12, 1953, Judge Alan K. Grim in the Federal District
Court for Eastern Pennsylvania upheld the blackout, denied the
government's suit, and cleared the path for an entire new pattern
of playing for pay.

Far from killing the home gate, television under these new
rules helped to whet the people's appetite for the violent world
of Sam Huff, Andy Robustelli, and all the other new padded
public heroes who came bursting into living-room gatherings on
Sunday afternoons. In 1950, as TV made its mark, the NFL
played its games before 1,977,556 spectators on the scene, an
average of 25,353 a game; in 1960, the total draw was 3,128,296,
an average of 40,106. So, by the time Bert Bell collapsed and
died during an Eagles game in 1959, his league and his game
were becoming big business.

By this time, Pete Rozelle was making a few astronomical
moves of his own, and, before the next decade began to multiply
all these plus signs, he was becoming big business too.

In 1952, he was hired from his alma mater by Reeves as publicity director of the Los Angeles Rams and improved his earn-

ings situation from $4400 at San Francisco to $5500. In 1955, he left the Rams to join a public-relations company at $13,500. In 1957, at Bell's urging, he rejoined the Rams as general manager at $25,000. And in 1960, he succeeded Bell as the commissioner at $40,000, which was, he conceded, "the most ludicrous thing I ever heard of — there I was, thirty-three years old."

There he was, all right; thirty-three years old with a tiger by the tail, on the threshold of the nineteen sixties. It was forty years after the charter members of the league had stood around on running boards in the automobile agency in Canton, Ohio, and had ordained an entry fee of $100 per franchise. And it was almost forty years since they had reconsidered and sliced the fee down to $50. Now their football heirs were about to cash in, and the numbers were indeed astronomical.

They suddenly owned the postwar players to match the postwar appetite for action, and the postwar medium of television to stoke both. There were the Detroit Lions, for example, with stars like Doak Walker and Bobby Layne, and an imaginative scheme for exploiting them: sell tickets for the whole season, rather than just for a whole afternoon.

In 1952, when Pete Rozelle was just starting up the ladder to Park Avenue, the Lions sold 17,554 season tickets and won a championship for their faithful followers. The Lions now were providing an entertainment package for the full season of autumn; they guaranteed the same seats in the stadium for all home games, and their fans in return guaranteed them a hard-core budget at the gate. Three years later, they had sold the package to 36,434 customers, and by 1958 the Lions were floating 42,154 season tickets in a stadium that seated 45,555.

In Baltimore, the Colts reached a similar peak of financial security just as they were reaching their senses over John Unitas, a crew-cut quarterback who had been dropped by the Pittsburgh Steelers in 1955 because he was considered a little "too dumb." Unitas proved so dumb that he immediately switched to semipro football to console himself at six dollars a game, which was a little like boxing a polar bear every weekend for doughnuts.

But the next year, the general manager of the Baltimore club, Don Kellett, spotted his name on an old waiver list, paid eighty cents to telephone him long-distance, and invited him to the Colts' camp. Unitas went and, when George Shaw was injured the following season, 1957, he became the starting quarterback — and the Colts became wealthy. They promptly won two championships, in 1958 and 1959, behind the absolute wizardry of their new quarterback. And, more to the point perhaps, attendance in Memorial Stadium reached a chronic sellout level of 57,555 and stayed there.

In Green Bay, Wisconsin, the smallest city in the league, a small revolution was being worked by a king-sized dictator, Vince Lombardi, the son of an Italian butcher who had started his coaching career at St. Cecelia High School in Englewood, New Jersey. He got $1700 a year for that job: assistant football coach *and* teacher of physics, algebra, chemistry, and Latin.

He was forty-six when he took charge of the Packers in 1959, one year after they had lost eleven of twelve games, and within two seasons he drove them into first place. By the time the sixties were over, they had won five league titles and two Super Bowl games, and the street outside their new stadium was named "Lombardi Avenue."

"The teams that win the most," he said, putting his cards on the table, "make the most money."

As if to punctuate that fact of life, Lombardi rewarded his players after their first championship by buying their wives mink stoles. In return, when the Los Angeles Rams tried to lure Lombardi to the West Coast, the board of directors of the Packers sweetened his job with a gift: 320 acres of apple orchards in nearby Door County. And when the rookie running back Donny Anderson was being courted by the rival American League, he untied the purse strings long enough to pay Anderson a record bonus of $600,000. His reasoning was characteristic: The Packers were a nonprofit co-op with a cash surplus and no place to spend it, while Anderson was a young man with a price. So Lombardi applied one problem (the surplus) against another (Anderson's demand) and solved both.

With other players, though, he was unrelenting both on the field and in the office. Jim Ringo, a center who once played a game with fourteen painful boils, held out for more money one season and was traded the next. Another time, the celebrated fullback Jim Taylor exercised the option clause in his contract and became a free agent so that he could sign with another team for more money. The other celebrated running back then was Paul Hornung, who had both talent and favor with the coach and who retired the same year.

"We'll miss Hornung," Lombardi said, signaling the end of an era behind Hagemeister's Brewery. "The other fellow we'll replace."

In New York, the Giants — who had lost those two championship games to Unitas and the Colts — were piecing together an empire too. They had moved from the Polo Grounds to Yankee Stadium in 1956, assuring themselves a bigger and more modern park, and then they began to fill it regularly during one of the great streaks of winning in NFL history. With Jim Lee Howell as their coach, and Vince Lombardi as their offensive coach, they revived interest in pro football in New York, the biggest market on the map.

They were blessed with durable players like Jim Katcavage, Roosevelt Grier, Andy Robustelli, Dick Modzelewski, Sam Huff, Swede Svare, Roosevelt Brown, and Jimmy Patton, plus Kyle Rote, Alex Webster, Frank Gifford, Pat Summerall, and Ray Wietecha — a center who performed in 133 consecutive games. Starting in 1958, while Unitas was moving Baltimore up in the Western half of the league, the Giants were winning five out of six titles in the Eastern half. And by 1962 and 1963,

when the entire league was turning a corner, they were selling
out every home game and were marketing 45,000 seats on a season basis in a park that held 62,800.

By now, the whole league was dealing in something like 400,-
000 season tickets a year. It had fourteen teams playing in stadiums with a capacity of 802,515, and it was playing before
4,000,000 persons every season. By now, the American Football
League was joining the gold rush too, with eight teams appearing in parks that seated 307,657 persons.

The margin for profit was still scant enough to make prudent
businessmen cautious, but the outlook for success was growing
rosy enough to make prudent investors bold — even before television began to tip the balance as the nineteen sixties started.

As the decade opened, for instance, the Detroit Lions — who
had operated in red ink continually until the nineteen fifties —
showed this dollars-and-cents posture:

Operating income = $1,923,836
Operating expense =   1,760,940
Net (after taxes)   =   121,512

Not much, but a start. The Lions' income trickled in from all
points of the compass, and the chief items were these:

Ticket sales   = $1,100,000
Exhibitions   =   275,000
Road income
  (40% of net) =   335,000
TV and radio   =   200,000
Sale of players =   37,500
Programs, ads =   25,000
Securities   =   21,000

There was no income from hot dogs and coffee, because *all*
the concessions revenue was turned over to the Detroit Tigers
baseball team, which owned Tiger Stadium and which also took
15 per cent of the gross game receipts for rent. In addition to

those initial outlays, the Lions forked over widely varying amounts for other expenses, all the way from $8600 for clerical salaries and telephones to $9000 for motion pictures of the team in action. The chief items of expense were these:

Stadium rent, visiting-team shares, and travel costs	= $700,000
Player salaries, uniforms, medical expenses	= 527,000
Coaches' salaries	= 100,000
Trainers, equipment men	= 16,000
Scouting costs	= 10,000
Stadium police, groundskeepers	= 28,000
Publicity and promotion	= 35,000
Ticket-office expenses	= 33,000
Camp, payroll tax, insurance	= 103,000
Business and income taxes	= 111,000

By the time the money stopped changing hands at the end of the season (during which the team won seven out of twelve games), the money left on hand was just under $122,000 — which was $122,000 more than the team had kept during most of its first twenty years in business, but which was a small fortune *less* than prize rookies like Joe Namath and O. J. Simpson were commanding before the decade ended.

It was a risky proposition all right. Barron Hilton reported that his Los Angeles Rams of 1960 were losing $900,000 while the Lions were eking out their $122,000. Harry Wismer said he lost $1,340,000 on his New York Titans in the new American Football League between 1960 and 1962, though his fame as a juggler of statistics made his testimony questionable. And the Dallas Texans in 1962 won the AFL title but lost $200,000 and promptly moved to Kansas City.

Even locked-in teams like the Green Bay Packers were not yet on Easy Street. The Packers had 1678 stockholders who owned 4738½ shares in the team's fortunes, but their ticket sales of $1,348,984 were almost canceled out by expenses of $1,173,351 (half of which went for salaries), and after taxes the net return was only $175,075.

But help was just around the corner, big help, in the form of the young new commissioner of the NFL, Pete Rozelle, who now was getting used to big numbers, even in his own salary. To Rozelle, the lessons that Bert Bell had taught about the value of television were clear.

"We have a heavy male audience," he observed, getting right down to business. "Youthful, high-income, extraordinary. Not only that, there are intangibles. If Ford sponsored 'Lassie,' it would be unlikely that someone would come into the local Ford dealer the next day and say, 'Gee, I saw "Lassie" last night. That sure was great how she put out that fire.' But football does generate an awful lot of conversation. You don't have columns written about Lassie on Monday. You do on football. The sponsors see a great value in that."

The arrival of TV onto the scene, heralded by Judge Grim's favorable decision in the antitrust suit in 1953, was probably guaranteed in 1956: the Columbia Broadcasting System negotiated TV rights with eleven of the twelve teams in the NFL. The whole package cost the network less than $750,000, with top dollar ($85,000) going to the New York Giants because of their top "market," while the Green Bay Packers settled for potatoes ($35,000) because they played their home games in the boondocks.

But the rout was on. By 1961, the Packers' share was up to $113,000 and the next year it doubled to $255,501. By then, Rozelle reported, only four clubs in the league could turn a profit without the new consolation of television loot.

"What Rozelle did with television receipts probably saved football in Green Bay," commented Vince Lombardi, who most people thought had saved football in Green Bay himself.

"Bert Bell put us on an even keel," said Wellington Mara of the Giants. "Rozelle kept us there."

"Pete Rozelle," said Art Rooney of the Pittsburgh Steelers, "is a gift from the hand of Providence."

The wise old heads of the league were moved to rapture by a dazzling series of TV contracts signed by the new czar of the league, and their rapture was not dimmed by his insistence that the teams ought to share the new revenue and share alike. So, as the sixties unfolded, the money skyrocketed and the least of the brethren began to cut into the pie with the best.

In 1961, the National Broadcasting Company shelled out $615,000 for the championship game alone; the same in 1962; $925,000 in 1963. By the time the Super Bowl arrived in 1966, the one-game fee was $1,000,000 and two years later it had zoomed to $2,500,000.

For the regular-season games, the bidding went through the roof. In 1964, CBS beat out the other big spenders by pledging $28,200,000 for ninety-eight games over two years. In 1965, NBC paid $42,000,000 to the American Football League for five years. And in 1970, both networks reached a four-year agreement with both leagues — now combined into one merged family — for something like $142,000,000. The Age of Aquarius was here, wrapped in a dollar sign.

• • •

Something else was here too — people with cash wanting to invest in professional football teams — and they were drawn not so much by the Age of Aquarius as by the dollar signs.

First in line was a Texas oil man, Lamar Hunt of Dallas, a onetime end at Southern Methodist University, who was so well-heeled that at the age of twenty-six he had offered to buy the Chicago Cardinals from Charley and Bill Bidwell and move them to Dallas. The Bidwells countered by offering to sell him minority shares, which did not interest Hunt very much, and then they moved their team to St. Louis while the Texas oil man went looking for a piece of the action someplace else.

He next offered to set up shop with a new team in Dallas, but that didn't exactly grip the imagination of the NFL either. So then Hunt did the only sensible thing left for a man who had inherited a couple of hundred million dollars: he decided to finance his own *league*.

His idea, which may have seemed radical at the time to some souls, actually was merely an expansion of the game of musical chairs that was taking hold in sports. Baseball already was adept at it. The Boston Braves had switched in 1953 to Milwaukee in the first franchise raid in half a century, and the St. Louis Browns migrated to Baltimore. A year later, the Philadelphia Athletics hopped to Kansas City, and four years after that the Brooklyn Dodgers went to Los Angeles and the New York Giants to San Francisco in a couple of really big leaps. And by the beginning of the nineteen sixties, the National League opened its doors to the New York Mets while the American admitted the Los Angeles Angels and Minnesota Twins.

The aim in all cases was to mine new gold, and it was right about then that Lamar Hunt ambled onto the scene from Texas.

Hunt, a mild-mannered young man, arrived just as a whole new frontier was being opened up to the gold rush: the upper Middle West. Not long after nearby Milwaukee had spirited away the Boston baseball franchise, some of the shrewder citizens of Minneapolis and St. Paul began to plan ahead for their own turn at bat in the franchise market. They constructed a modern stadium on the rolling cornfields halfway between the Twin Cities (supported by the public sale of bonds), and by 1956 they had a ball park but no team. They almost lured Horace Stoneham's New York Giants to town, especially since Stoneham had a top farm club in Minneapolis. But, even though that ploy failed, they were soon catapulted into business by the creation of the Continental League in baseball and the American League in football — both loaded with sponsors, both looking for markets.

It was 1960, the start of the decade of the dollar sign in sports, and the Twin Cities crashed both sports at once. But the established major leagues in both sports promptly moved to pre-empt the territory. Baseball absorbed the Continental League and expanded, with the Washington franchise transferring to Minnesota, and football rolled out the red carpet to Minnesota and its empty new stadium too, granting a franchise to the new territory in the NFL.

So far, the entrenched leagues had managed to hold off the invaders and their new leagues. But Lamar Hunt still was left holding his moneybag, and he still had Texas, and he immediately started to spend the former in the latter. He pushed forward with his new thing, calling it the American Football League, and the first ally he signed up was K. S. (Bud) Adams of Houston, also eager, also Texan, also rich.

They expanded rapidly to Denver, Los Angeles, and Oakland in the West and to Boston, Buffalo, and New York in the East. And when they kicked off in 1960, they numbered eight. True, they were "major league" in name only. True, they were soon outhustled for players by the NFL, which controlled the big stadiums and the big TV contracts. And it was true that they were afflicted for a while by tycoons like Harry Wismer, the high-decibel radio announcer, who first had married the niece of Henry Ford and later the widow of Abner (Longy) Zwillman, the New Jersey racketeer.

But it was also true that they had bankrolls sufficient to the day, plus Lamar Hunt as president, former Marine air ace Joe Foss as commissioner, and a five-year television contract with the American Broadcasting Company that provided $1,785,000 the first year alone.

It was a start. A kind of raggedy start maybe. The New York Titans even conducted their business operations from Wismer's apartment on Park Avenue. And they keyed their team on players like Al Dorow, a quarterback who had been earning a living

in Canada, and Don Maynard, a pass catcher who wore cowboy
boots and long sideburns and who had been cut by the New
York Giants after Allie Sherman had criticized his long strides.
But it was a start of sorts, even though the entire league drew
only 926,156 customers the first season while the NFL was
counting 3,128,296.

The New York franchise, which was supposed to be the front-
window display in any professional sport, showed the rigors of
big-league cutthroat competition better than anybody else. In
1960, the Titans played before 114,628 fans; the next year, 106,-
619; and the year after that, only 36,161, based on these home
"crowds":

Denver	5729
Boston	4719
San Diego	7175
Oakland	4728
Dallas	5974
Buffalo	4011
Houston	3828

By contrast, the NFL franchise at Los Angeles was valued that
season (1962) at $7,000,000 and, indeed, the Rams occasionally
had drawn almost as many people into the Coliseum on one
afternoon as the Titans did all season. And the sixty-five stockholders of the Philadelphia Eagles, who paid $3000 a share for
their risk in 1949, now were collecting more than $50,000 a
share less than fifteen years later.

So, while the National League under Rozelle was striking
gold with each TV commercial in each new market area, the
American League was learning the hard way why economics was
called "the dismal science." Wismer, bumbling from one ad hoc
ruling to the next in an effort to float his Titans, once demoted
Sammy Baugh from head coach to "kicking consultant" — the
same Sammy Baugh who had withstood with honor, though not

with success, the rampage of those Chicago Bears of 1940. Another time, he assigned his general manager, George Sauer, to the additional duty of backfield coach.

Wismer also was unusually talented at seeing multitudes where only handfuls existed. To give his stadium the appearance of busyness, he often opened the gates to every neighborhood kid in sight and even then multiplied the crowd figure to produce a respectable, though fictitious, attendance. Alex Kroll, an All-American center at Rutgers, joined this tattered cast for a while and later recalled his favorite newspaper report on Wismer's inflationary weakness:

"The announced attendance of twenty thousand refers to arms and legs. Or else fifteen thousand of the twenty thousand people came disguised as empty seats."

Things grew so desperate that the players once met in emergency session and then advised Wismer that the payroll was "194 hours late." Another time, the locker room was briefly enthralled by the rumor that Harry was offering $100 extra for every touchdown scored against San Diego. The Titans duly rose to the occasion and shattered the Chargers, 23 to 3, but were rewarded with neither $100 bonuses *nor* regular paychecks. But the essence of the dollar squeeze was best measured by the fact that only one teller at the team's bank was authorized to cash paychecks and, Kroll recalled, as each player submitted his occasional check, the teller would subtract the amount from Wismer's dwindling balance.

The team — in fact, the whole league — urgently needed a vision and a bankroll. And both were supplied in March of 1963 by David A. (Sonny) Werblin, the impresario of the Music Corporation of America, whose chief *business* was *entertainment*. From the debris of Wismer's Titans, he rebuilt the team as the New York Jets along with a syndicate of money men that included Leon Hess, an oil man; Townsend B. Martin, a banker and horse breeder; Philip H. Iselin, one of the giants of the garment industry; and Donald C. Lillis, a stockbroker who was president of the Bowie Race Course in Maryland.

Werblin, who had been born on St. Patrick's Day in 1910, promptly made green the official color of the team — and, more significantly, of its money.

He hired a new head coach — Weeb Ewbank, who had led the Baltimore Colts through some of their finest hours in the NFL but who now was sitting out an enforced two-year sabbatical at full pay. That is, he had been fired. Between them, they signed a bright new coaching staff, held tryouts for players in Van Cortlandt Park in the Bronx, severed all public ties with the bankrupt Titans, and moved their new show into Shea Stadium, which was opened in 1964 as the home of the baseball Mets and which soon became the citadel of the nouveau riche of professional sports.

But the wisest move they made was to open their roster and their purse strings to a quarterback from the University of Alabama named Joe Willie Namath. The talent hunt for quarterbacks was especially ripe that year for teams in both leagues, with John Huarte of Notre Dame, Craig Morton of California, Archie Roberts of Columbia, and Steve Tensi of Florida State. But the high command of the Jets was convinced that their man was Namath, despite damaged knees, despite a growing reputation as a swinger, despite a price tag that was certain to soar once the NFL joined the bidding.

Namath, though, already was being labeled "the best athlete I've ever coached" by Bear Bryant, the ringmaster of Alabama football. And George Sauer's scouting report, based on ratings of 1 down to 5 in football skills, gave Namath these grades: quickness – 1, agility – 1, strength – 2, reaction time –1, coordination – 1, size potential – 1, durability – 2, speed for position – 2, intelligence – 1, character – 2, aggressiveness – 1, pride – 1. In short, Sauer wrote, "will be everybody's Number One draft choice."

The prediction was not quite accurate, because when the

NFL held its draft on the same day as the AFL, the New York Giants got first pick in tribute to their record of two victories, ten defeats, and two ties, and although they were losing the great Y. A. Tittle at quarterback they nevertheless drafted a running back — Tucker Frederickson of Auburn. Later in the first round, the St. Louis Cardinals made Namath their number one selection, and so the auction lines were drawn.

The actual bidding took place in Birmingham, Alabama, with Namath represented by a young lawyer named Mike Bite, who shuttled between Werblin on the one hand and Bill Bidwell of the Cardinals on the other. There was some suspicion that the Cardinals were acting as a stalking-horse for another NFL club, maybe even the Giants. But at any rate, when the bidding reached $389,000, they dropped out.

Namath still had one game left to play as a college senior, the Orange Bowl game on New Year's Day against Texas, and he had to play it on a collapsing right knee. But even before that last fling, he and Werblin shook hands on an agreement that shook the football firmament — financially, at least. For a three-year contract plus a fourth optional year, the Jets promised the twenty-year-old senior these considerations:

Salary (4 seasons @ $25,000)	=	$100,000
Bonus for signing with them	=	200,000
"Scouting" jobs for his three brothers and brother-in-law (@ $10,000 a year each)	=	120,000
Lincoln Continental (green)	=	7000

The package was worth something like $427,000, and it included little economic wrinkles like a deferred payment on the bonus so that it could be spread out for several years *after* his playing career had ended. As things turned out, his playing career almost ended then and there, because his collapsing knee collapsed again during practice for the Orange Bowl game.

But on the big night, Joe Willie appeared in sneakers before a crowd of 72,000 persons and he came within an ace of pulling the game out by driving Alabama the length of the field during the closing minutes. He completed eighteen of thirty-seven passes for 255 yards and two touchdowns, just missed scoring another on a quarterback sneak at the end, and lost to Texas, 21 to 17. But the game was a milestone for the class of 1965, which included Paul Crane of Alabama and Jim Hudson, George Sauer Jr., Pete Lammons, and John Elliott of Texas, all of whom wound up with Werblin's Jets.

It also became a milestone for Werblin, because it was the first Orange Bowl game played at night and it suffered from absolutely no competition that evening on national TV. And for the American Football League, it became a milestone too, because big money finally had been spent to land a big fish in the middle of a big decade for a new big business.

It was almost half a century since Frank Peck had slipped Curly Lambeau $500 for sweaters and stockings for the Indian Packing Company club in Green Bay, Wisconsin. But the plot line was clear. When Sonny Werblin retired from MCA–TV in 1965 to lavish full time on his horses and his football players, he was lionized by the show-biz journal *Variety* as the industry's "greatest promoter and salesman." And nobody bothered to pass the hat anymore during the football games on Sunday afternoon.

4

The Sport of Kings and Conglomerates

HAVING BROUGHT JOE NAMATH to the television screens of America in 1965, there was probably no direction for Sonny Werblin to whirl but downhill, especially after he was bought out by his football partners two years later. They were afraid that Sonny's imagination would prove too big for everybody else's pocketbook. Disappointed, but not dismayed, Werblin immediately began to reinvest his imagination — and his cash — into horse racing, a sport that had long since caught his fancy, and he was promptly back in another revolution in the galloping business of entertaining people and sometimes enriching himself.

At the Saratoga sales in 1967 he paid $11,500 for a filly named Process Shot, which was $415,500 less than he had paid for Namath. And the filly promptly justified his confidence, and probably exceeded his expectations, by going out and winning a quarter of a million dollars.

Entering into the spirit of things, Werblin then invested $39,000 into a yearling named Silent Screen, which entered into the spirit of things by winning the $366,075 Arlington-Washington Futurity in his third start. The distance was seven furlongs, the winning margin was eight lengths, the return for every $2 bettor was $10.40, and the prize for Werblin was $206,-075 — which was five times what he had paid for the horse and about half as much as he had promised Namath for four years of violent Sunday afternoons.

Not only that, but Silent Screen won more money in 1 minute 22 and four-fifths seconds than Man o' War won all year in 1920 and almost twice as much as Bimelech earned in 1940, when New York State joined the switch to pari-mutuel betting and every major racing state in the Union started sharing the wealth of the flat tracks.

What had happened, in a nutshell, was that Sonny Werblin's two-year-old colt, in his first stakes race, had won the world's richest race for thoroughbreds. It was September 6, 1969, almost the end of the gold-rush decade for all professional sports, almost the beginning of the new decade when the purses and the tax rake-offs would grow even bigger. So when a friend asked, "Would you rather own Namath or Silent Screen?" it was no problem for Werblin to answer:

"I'd much rather own the horse than Namath. Silent Screen has four good legs."

What he meant was that, sentimentality aside, Namath had two bad legs — and in this era of big-business bucks in sports, sentimentality more and more was being put aside.

Still, of all the stunning statistics surrounding Silent Screen's coup at Arlington Park, none was more significant, not even the treasure involved, than the time the horses left the starting gate: 11:26 P.M. It was the first stakes race ever run under lights at a major thoroughbred track in the United States and, Steve Cady reported in the *New York Times,* the Elberon Farm colt carrying Werblin's colors proved that "money looks just as green at night as in the daytime."

In fact, four of the jockeys in the big race had opened their working day 750 miles to the east at Belmont Park in New York. They were Eddie Belmonte, Angel Cordero Jr., Braulio Baeza, and John Rotz, who rode in the afternoon in New York, caught the six o'clock plane to Chicago from La Guardia Airport, and checked into the Arlington jockey room outside Chicago at 8:05. Another rider, Jim Nichols, finished second in a stakes race at River Downs near Cincinnati and made it too.

Their itinerary was so exact that Belmonte wasted absolutely no time reaching the winner's circle in Chicago, just as he had reached it twice earlier in New York that day. He brought home a horse named Fancy Knave at $16.80 in the second race at Arlington just after arriving from the East. And if the road traffic from O'Hare Airport hadn't been so heavy, he even would have arrived in time to ride the daily double — at $61.00. His scheduled mount in the first race won easily, but that race went off just ten minutes after Belmonte and the other globe-trotters arrived at the track and they were momentarily delayed in their scramble for gold.

But the delay was only momentary. Before midnight, Rotz earned $20,000 as his 10 per cent share for steering Silent Screen across the seven furlongs and Willie Shoemaker — who already had earned $4,000,000 riding horses as perhaps the highest-paid athlete in the world — took down $7000 more as his wage for finishing second aboard Insubordination.

Not everybody was as enthusiastic about the debut of night-time racing as Rotz, Shoemaker, and Werblin, nor as rich. The grooms and the other "backstretch" people in the stables were forced to work eighteen-hour days in order to saddle horses at odd times of the morning, noon, and night. And racing at 11 P.M. was bound to intensify the labor disputes that had accompanied big money to the racetracks.

"They will have to adjust like baseball players adjusted," Werblin suggested, giving the innovation its long-range due. "When they first started putting air conditioners in movie theaters, there was hell to pay. Customers complained it gave them all kinds of aches and pains. Ushers and usherettes protested they couldn't work in the freezing atmosphere. Now nobody will go near a movie house that isn't air-conditioned."

"We're making new fans," said Mrs. Marjorie Lindheimer Everett, the mistress of the track. "We talk about educating the public and bringing in new people — well, here they are. As soon as they find out what it's all about, they'll begin betting. Somebody has to pioneer. When they put night baseball into Cincinnati, many thought Crosley was nuts. But he was proved right. I'll be proved right.

"All the supermarkets stay open nights and lots of department stores. And there's plenty of night football, and night harness racing. So why not thoroughbred racing under the lights?"

Werblin agreed, and not just because Marge Lindheimer had just handed him a check for $206,075 for his part in pioneering the project. He had some reservations though. Resort tracks like Monmouth Park in New Jersey, his northern headquarters, were likely to stay with daytime racing. And so were tracks in states where the nighttime hours had been pre-empted by the trotters — states like New York, where Aqueduct and Belmont Park produced something like $72,000,000 a year for the state in tax revenues (daytime) while Roosevelt and Yonkers Raceways contributed close to $60,000,000 (nighttime). No governor worth his salt would queer a deal like that.

But the lesson of that night was not lost on anybody, from governors to grooms to jet-set jockeys: More racing means more business, more business means even more racing, more racing means more betting, and more betting means more taxing. As long as a $2 bettor could stagger to the window, the wheel of fortune would spin away.

And just in case some potential $2 bettors were hanging back on those summer afternoons — or evenings, for that matter — to pass the time staring at TV screens, the race courses of America were gathering themselves for the "big sell" as the seventies arrived.

Racing after dark on Saturday night, that was one way to shake them loose. But from Boston to Bay Meadows, the one-time purists of the sport of kings were broadening their viewpoints and their sales pitches in order to broaden their beach-

head on the famous old "recreation dollar," and the trick
seemed to be this: make a day at the races something that even
the Marx Brothers would appreciate.

Louisville Downs in Kentucky tried it with a baby-sitting
service, making it possible for young mothers to visit the track
without abandoning their kids. Batavia Downs in Buffalo did it
by scheduling storytelling sessions for young and old alike. Au-
dubon Raceway in Kentucky, another harness track, went a step
beyond and built a playground with a carousel. And Monticello
in the Catskill area of New York State hung out an art gallery,
complete with paintings by Salvador Dali, and if that didn't
work there was always the $3 perfecta — pick the one-two finish
in the race and back your choice with three bucks instead of the
traditional two.

Santa Anita, at the foot of the San Gabriel Mountains in California, went even further: It drew plans for converting 65 of its
400 acres into a $30,000,000 shopping center and made no bones
about it — economic diversification was the only answer for
both the track and the surrounding community of Arcadia. The
idea was that the track had opened in 1934 when Arcadia's population totaled 7000; now it was nearing 50,000. The shopping
center presumably would provide 1700 new jobs, a $7,000,000-a-
year payroll, and sales up to $50,000,000. And why did the track
have to turn "square" to such a degree, after thirty-seven years
of just staging horse races? Because the high cost of everything,
from money to pari-mutuel clerks, was putting a crimp in its
budget. (One thing that furrowed the brows of the horsemen,
though, was that the proposed shopping center would wipe out
their *training track*.)

At Tropical Park in Miami, the track decided that man does
not live by bread alone and accordingly diversified in another
direction. It installed two Lutheran ministers to provide comfort, and sometimes consolation, to the stable workers. The
ministers were David Kruekenberg, who also had given spiritual

succor at Sportsman, Hawthorne, and Arlington the summer before, and Edward Homrighausen, who said he had been "specializing" in racing since 1965 when a parishioner thoughtfully took him to the Fair Grounds in New Orleans.

Their first service at Tropical was held on a Sunday and twenty-seven grooms showed up, which made the experiment a resounding success. Dr. Ed, as Mr. Homrighausen was called, even fielded a question on morals and racing: How, for example, did he feel when he saw a jockey holding up a horse in a race?

"Well," he replied, cementing his reputation as the theologian of the track, "I must admit that I've seen it happen, and I do find it quite disturbing when the horse being held is one that I've bet on."

One of the more spectacular moments in bringing the public to the track, or at least bringing the track to the public, came about in a transatlantic horse auction between two distinguished offices: Parke-Bernet in New York and Sotheby & Co. in London. The auction involved thirty-five head of horses, and the bids — carried across the sea by telephone, with groups of bidders gathered at each end — got up to $669,780. The owners represented in the long-distance sale included the Begum Aga Khan, Baron Guy de Rothschild, and Madame Volterra. One horse, Pandora Bay, went for 390,000 francs, which was $70,300 in any language.

"It's a low-key experiment in diversification," noted a spokesman for the Parke-Bernet Galleries, which in its pre-horsy days had sold a Rembrandt for $2,300,000.

Still, with all these attractions, gimmicks, and economic spurs, some of the most memorable and avant-garde moments on the "new" racing scene of the late sixties were furnished by the exile from baseball wizardry, Bill Veeck. Having sent tremors through the board rooms of the major leagues for two decades by the range of his business imagination, Veeck sought new fields to conquer and for a while roosted with his imagination at the Suffolk Downs racing strip near Boston. He promptly staged something called Joe Fan Day, stashed a prize-winning certificate under one chair in the park, and awarded the lucky seat holder the pièce de résistance: a three-year-old filly named Buck's Delight.

But that was only the beginning. On Flag Day, he treated the early arrivals to 3600 American flags, stashed more gift certificates around the grandstand (each one was worth a case of champagne), and granted free admission to anyone named John Alden or Priscilla in honor of the John Alden Handicap. And if that didn't jostle the customers, Veeck scattered "suggestion boxes" around the track and, on the afternoon of a race called the Beef Stake Handicap, opened the boxes and reviewed the 2500 "beefs" submitted by the long-suffering fans. (The chief complaint: the food and service at concession stands.)

"We're going to keep doing things, one by one," he announced, "until this track gets back the prestige it used to have."

What he meant was that he would keep doing things to attract customers to Suffolk Downs, to the pari-mutuel windows, to the clubhouse dining room — yes, even to those rundown hot-dog stands. The sport of kings, Veeck reasoned flawlessly, was not so much a sport as a business, and it depended, in the late twentieth century, not so much on kings as on commoners.

He was well aware that the competition for the customers' attention, and dollars, ranged all the way from the Boston Symphony to Hawk Harrelson, the ballplayer who had recently been traded from the Red Sox to the Cleveland Indians and who was conducting his own business campaign by threatening to retire unless the baseball establishment paid him large new sums of money, which it did. But Veeck was shrewd enough to realize that people went to the track to dote on, and to bet on, horses — not just to dine on frankfurters. So he also beefed up the purses, reaching a zenith of sorts with his $254,750 Yankee Gold Cup Handicap in June of 1969, the richest grass event in the history of American racing — at least the richest until Arlington Park raised the ante three months later.

"Tradition," observed Veeck, in the kind of pronouncement that used to make the baseball people shudder, "is the stinking albatross around the neck of progress. The only similarity I've found between baseball and racing is the hesitancy to try new things."

Getting down to economic cases, he put it this way: "There are such things as good and bad sports towns, depending to some degree on geographical location, population, and competition. While there generally isn't, I don't think, much conscious budgeting, there is in everybody's case an unconscious budgeting for sports activities. When you have many events going on in one city, you will find that they will all be adversely affected by the addition of others if the potential market isn't there to start with.

"When hockey came to St. Louis and did such a tremendous job of promotion, the Blues took over winter activities and virtually put the basketball team out of business, so the Hawks moved to Atlanta and it seemed very definite at the time they were leaving that they were being chased out of town by the competition for the dollar of professional hockey.

"Sports are also competing for space in newspapers and on radio and television. It's just that everyone finds it difficult to go every night or afternoon to some different event. But also in quest for newspaper space, there are only a certain number of columns, and how they are divided depends on what is happening at any particular moment. For instance, the start of the nineteen sixty-nine baseball season was probably unprecedented in the feverish activities of the Red Sox. First, the return of Tony Conigliaro; second, the emotional departure of Harrelson; and third, the equally emotional return of Ted Williams.

"Now, I've spent the greater part of my life in baseball and I can't remember a similar series of events, each of which was in its own way a gripping drama. So obviously the greater part of newspaper, radio, and television coverage was going to be aimed at these three highly unusual events. Even, I might add, to the exclusion of the game itself. The great stories are of the people involved. Fortunately, we still haven't replaced the interest in the human animal completely with the machine."

The place of spectator sports in the body politic, Veeck went on, was established two thousand years earlier in Rome, when the mob was kept docile by the unbeatable formula of bread and the Circus Maximus. But as the modern promoter of the Circus Maximus, he was not just going to take any bows for being a social servant.

"Altruism," he confessed, "is not one of my great gifts. The average racing fan is slightly over fifty years of age. If you don't create new fans, how do you insure future growth, or even future existence?"

In pursuit of that nonaltruistic goal, he opened the gates of his racetrack to children, pointing out that racing originally had been a family affair and a Sunday family affair at that. And just in case that argument didn't catch on as a topic at Sunday morning church sermons, he backed it up with an outright appeal to political self-interest with a plug for more racing days.

"I'm not altruistic, as I've said," he repeated, "and while the state and the taxpayers would be beneficiaries of this, so would I — and my principal interest is myself. I do think that it is a strange set of circumstances in which a state needing money allows it to go to Rhode Island and to New Hampshire: the greatest amount of attendance in those areas comes from Massachusetts but none of the dollars filter back. And we, by running extra dates, would provide additional income for ourselves and in the process would provide additional entertainment and I think an opportunity for the fans to have some fun, and would provide additional revenue to the state."

Veeck, who lost a leg from wounds suffered during World

War II while serving in the South Pacific as a Marine, showed that he was no piker in making these twin aims a full-time business. While his wife and six young children kept their home in Maryland, or shuttled to the track in Boston on vacations, he took up residence in an apartment over the clubhouse at Suffolk Downs. And one November morning at five o'clock, he smelled smoke, found his exit routes to an inside stairway and an elevator blocked by fire, climbed out a window, bad leg and all, escaped by way of a ledge to an outside window, and later reported: "It does pay to live on the premises."

• • •

Long before Bill Veeck started climbing across clubhouse ledges, long before racetrack purses reached $100,000 and up, long before state governments began regulating bets on horses and certainly before they began taxing bets on horses — it had all been a simpler sport, and a smaller business.

Before the United States entered World War I, in fact, August Belmont bred the mare Mahubah to a horse named Fair Play, and on March 29, 1917, Mahubah foaled a chestnut colt who was given the name Man o' War. He was bought at the Saratoga yearling sales in 1918 by Samuel Riddle, chiefly because Riddle's trainer, Sam Hildreth, had clocked Man o' War's sister Masda and had come to the popeyed conclusion that something was up. He was right. The price was $5000, and during the next two seasons, Man o' War went to the post twenty-one times, won twenty times, and earned $249,465.

The first day he went to the races, Man o' War made a fairly modest start toward his destiny as the first great capitalist of the turf. It was June 6, 1919, and he ran five furlongs at Belmont Park in New York, won by six lengths, and took home the purse of $500. Within a month, though, he had a winning streak of four and a bankroll of $12,000. By the end of the year, he won nine of ten starts and the bankroll had reached $83,325, and the only time he lost — ever — was in his seventh outing, a five-furlong sprint at Saratoga in which he got off badly, passed five of the six other horses with his late rush, and just missed catching the sixth, who appropriately was named Upset.

The following year, Man o' War was undefeated and even had the human satisfaction of trouncing Upset in the Preakness. He captured every other important event for three-year-olds that summer, except the Kentucky Derby, because his owner somehow had neglected to enter him. But he broke either the track record or the world record in eight of his eleven starts, three times went to the post as the 1 to 100 favorite, and did not run that summer at any odds longer than 4 to 5.

As a breadwinner, Man o' War took down his quarter of a million dollars in two seasons at a time of token purses. If he

Horse Dollars and Cents

Year	Racing Days	Races	Starters	Purses
1910	1063	6501	4180	$2,942,333
1920	1022	6897	4032	7,773,407
1930	1653	11,477	8791	13,674,160
1940	2096	16,401	13,257	15,911,167
1950	3290	26,932	22,954	50,102,099
1960	4304	37,661	29,773	93,741,552
1965	5283	47,335	38,502	126,463,984
1969	5825	52,315	45,808	168,713,911

Revenue to the States

Year	Revenue
1934	$6,024,193
1940	16,145,182
1950	98,366,166
1960	257,510,069
1965	369,892,036
1969	461,498,896

had raced twenty years later, it was calculated, he would have won $1,000,000. However, he showed the later generations where the big money really was: As a stud, he drew a fee of $5000, was booked twenty-five times a year, averaged $125,000 a year for two decades, and sired more than 300 colts and fillies who won more than 1200 races and earned more than $3,200,-000. Even when he was eighteen years old, he ran eight miles every morning for exercise, and he was still a producing stud in 1943 when Riddle retired him to the Blue Grass Pasturage of the Faraway Farm in Kentucky at the age of twenty-six.

Once, when W. T. Waggoner tried to buy him, Riddle put a price on his great horse in these unmistakable terms: "You go over to France and buy the Invalides, which contains the tomb of Napoleon. Then stop off in England and buy the Koh-i-noor Diamond. When you have done that, come back to me and I'll set a price on Man o' War."

Still, it was Man o' War's luck, or destiny, to be running in the era before inflation fattened the purses at the racetracks. In 1920, his three-year-old season, he won eleven straight races and brought home prizes totaling $166,140, which he might have earned in one afternoon by the time Bill Veeck began throwing money around the stables half a century later. In fact, all the prize money in the country from the 6897 thoroughbred races that year totaled only $7,773,409, and in later years some horses like Kelso and Round Table won 25 per cent of that amount in their own careers.

But as the boom of the twenties spiraled along so did the value of the purses. Three years later, the great colt Zev earned $272,008 for twelve victories and one second-place finish in fourteen starts. In 1930, Gallant Fox took down $308,275 for nine victories and one second place in ten starts. And, once World War II had ended and all professional sports began their big, boisterous boom, Assault finished in the money thirteen times and was paid $424,195, the greatest one-year haul in track history at the time.

After that, everybody ran onward and upward to the bank, and these were the money milestones they passed:

Year	Horse	Starts	1st	2nd	3rd	Won
1948	Citation	20	19	1	0	$709,470
1953	Native Dancer	10	9	1	0	513,425
1955	Nashua	12	10	1	1	752,550
1957	Round Table	22	15	1	3	600,383
1958	Round Table	20	14	4	0	662,780
1959	Sword Dancer	13	8	4	0	537,004
1960	Bally Ache	15	10	3	1	455,045
1961	Carry Back	16	9	1	3	565,349
1962	Never Bend	10	7	1	2	402,969
1963	Candy Spots	12	7	2	1	604,481
1964	Gun Bow	16	8	4	2	580,100
1965	Buckpasser	11	9	1	0	568,096
1966	Buckpasser	14	13	1	0	669,078
1967	Damascus	16	12	3	1	817,941
1968	Forward Pass	13	7	2	0	546,674
1969	Arts and Letters	14	8	5	1	555,054

What it meant, as the seventies arrived, was that the purses had become as significant as the prestige. Not every colt was a Round Table, strutting to the post forty-two times in two years in the late fifties and racing in the money thirty-seven times and earning a million and a quarter dollars in that prosperous spell. Nor was every horse a Buckpasser, the speedball of the sixties, who also led the earnings list two years in a row by running in the money twenty-four out of twenty-five times. But more and more thoroughbreds were getting a piece of the big action and, in the final season of the sixties, no fewer than eight horses won a quarter of a million dollars and forty topped $100,000.

Horses like these, and prizes like these, by now were drawing a breed of uncommon owners too. Not just the old landed gentry like the Whitneys, Phippses, Riddles, and Belmonts, but the business conglomerates like Charles Engelhard, the international oil millionaires like Frank McMahon, and the public

lions like Paul Mellon — banker, art connoisseur, the only son
of the three-time secretary of the treasury, Andrew W. Mellon,
and the appreciative owner of Arts and Letters.

They had one thing in common besides renowned race horses,
namely, money. But they also possessed a certain amount of
public involvement, as did the owners in other sports at a time
when privacy was disappearing, television was prying, and government generally was increasing its interest in the business of
sports entertainment.

Engelhard, whose fortune stemmed primarily from platinum, gold, and other metals, was a confidant of presidents and
prime ministers in addition to jockeys and grooms until he died
unexpectedly in 1971 at the age of fifty-four. He once had a
guest list of 1700 persons for a garden tea in honor of Eunice
Kennedy Shriver. On another occasion, he served a barbecue of
ribs, beans, and hog jowls for Lynda Bird Johnson and the guest
list reached 3500. But his wife Jane, a regular on the list of Ten
Best-Dressed Women in America, just as casually and graciously
kept their eight homes open and fully staffed and showed no
qualms over luncheons for eighty persons.

The Engelhards' charities were as impressive as their dinner
parties: half a million dollars to Boys Town, a million and a
quarter to Rutgers University, gifts of antique furniture to the
White House, and frequent support of the New Jersey Symphony, the Bronx Zoo, and the World Wildlife Fund. Their
passion for animals also extended to salmon, notably on the
Gaspé in Canada, where they spent perhaps a million dollars
cultivating fifteen miles of fishing waters, and to horses, which
included something like $15,000,000 worth of yearlings, racers,
mares, and studs.

With all this behind him, Engelhard spent his money un-
flinchingly, took his victories gleefully, and endured his defeats
bravely. He paid $110,000 for the yearling Ribofilio and con-
fessed that the horses was "the last of the cheap Ribots." Another time, he spent $177,000 for a yearling filly at Saratoga,

raced her twenty times before she won a race, then retired her to the broodmare barn without complaint.

But his greatest, and saddest, moments of all came with the great Nijinsky, the super-horse named for the super-ballet dancer. Eleven times Engelhard sent his horse to the post in Europe and eleven times joined him in the winner's circle. That is, until October 4, 1970, when Nijinsky wavered at the finish of the $400,000 Prix de l'Arc de Triomphe in Paris, despite the desperate urgings of the veteran rider Lester Piggott, and finished one head behind Sassafras, which paid $39.80 for every $2 bet.

Afterward, the rider of Sassafras, Yves Saint-Martin, who was France's leading jockey, said simply: "I rode a hell of a race." And Charles Engelhard, who got $86,486 and a heartache, observed simply: "The shifts from delight to disaster in racing are such that I don't see how anyone can become bored with it."

His philosophy of racing life, and sometimes his racing luck, was shared by McMahon — born Francis Murray Patrick McMahon in the mining town of Moyie, British Columbia, in 1902. McMahon started without Engelhard's platinum spoon, attended Gonzaga University, played baseball alongside Bing Crosby, quit school to join an oil-rigging crew, borrowed money to bring in his first oil well in Alberta, and eventually became a multimillionaire and the owner of thoroughbreds.

He once paid $9,800 for a half-share in a colt named Meadow Court in England, saw the horse win $400,000 in purses, then joined his partner Max Bell and Crosby in a million-dollar syndicate that staked Meadow Court to life as a sire. At the other end of the price scale, he paid $250,000 at Keeneland in 1967 for the yearling Majestic Prince, who then won nine races in a row, leading McMahon to report: "Majestic Prince is a very fast horse."

McMahon already had most of the good things in life through his business empire, based on Westcoast Transmission Company Ltd., which has supplied British Columbia and the American

Northwest with natural gas since the middle of the nineteen fifties. If there were any doubts about his "hot hand" in business, they were probably eased in 1969 when one of his subsidiary companies started drilling for oil in the Rainbow Lake region of Alberta and struck it in the first well.

Still, McMahon developed a consuming ambition outside the money market and the oil fields. He first spotted Majestic Prince as a weanling in 1966 at Leslie Combs's Spendthrift Farm in Lexington, Kentucky, and immediately wanted to own him. "Take care of him," he told Combs, "I don't intend to be outbid for him." He promptly showed his colors by bidding $200,-000 at the Keeneland Sales for one of Combs's yearlings named Bold Discovery, a son of the famous Bold Ruler, but the colt never got off the ground, so to speak, and people suspected that McMahon was trying to recover his pride the next summer by going to $250,000 for Majestic Prince.

This time, though, his intuition and his ambition both were satisfied. Majestic Prince grew into a constant winner, scoring nine times in a row. By then, his value had soared, and Combs even offered to buy him back from McMahon for $1,600,000. and that was before Majestic Prince won the Santa Anita Derby, before he won the Kentucky Derby by a neck over Arts and Letters, before he won the Preakness by a head over Arts and Letters. After that, all he had to do to win the Triple Crown was to take the Belmont Stakes, and he was the only one of the 19,832 thoroughbreds foaled in 1966 with that opportunity left. But it proved to be a pretty big "all."

On the fateful afternoon, McMahon learned something about Charles Engelhard's stoicism. His pride and joy finally was beaten in the Belmont — by Arts and Letters, the pride and joy of Paul Mellon.

In Mellon, the racing world boasted a solid citizen that day who rivaled the pillars of other professional sports in meaningful money, and who probably surpassed most of them. Like

John Mecom in football, Joan Whitney Payson in baseball and racing, and Gene Autry, Robert Reynolds, Lamar Hunt, John Galbreath, and August Busch, he was active in a dozen different directions and he invested in sports in an era when only very wealthy individuals — or corporations — could stand the cost. It was an era of tax write-offs, talent depreciation, and franchise switching, and the Old Guard was not so numerous anymore. But win or lose, red ink or black ink, there were still a few like Paul Mellon who ran their banks, their art collections, and their stables as a way of life. A fading way of life maybe, but they were to the manner born and, although the nineteen sixties and seventies thrust them more and more into public life, they still formed a link to the old days of private ruffles and flourishes.

Mellon inherited both his money and his place in the public eye from his father, who was brought to Washington as secretary of the treasury by President Harding in 1921 and who thereupon did the only proper thing to avoid conflicts of interest: He resigned as a director of *sixty* companies.

Andrew Mellon lived through four federal administrations, one colossal depression, a $3,000,000 income-tax suit, and other adventures, and then made a beau geste of unusual dimensions in 1936 by offering Franklin D. Roosevelt a gift to the nation — his $50,000,000 art collection plus $16,000,000 to build the National Gallery plus $5,000,000 to provide for future purchases. The government accepted, the gallery opened in 1941, and after that the Mellon family and its foundations continued to feed in financial support. In 1967, when Arts and Letters was a yearling, Paul and his sister donated $20,000,000 more to add a wing to the gallery and to expand its extension service, which lends paintings and sends traveling exhibitions to communities around the country.

Paul studied at Yale, spent summers in England, served in the Office of Strategic Services in the war, and got into racing heavily soon thereafter. His Rokeby farm in Virginia became a leading stud farm, and his fifty mares included the bountiful All Beautiful, who produced Arts and Letters six weeks after Mellon paid $175,000 for her. On grass, the stable's colors were carried by Fort Marcy, the conqueror of Damascus in the Washington International in 1967 and the Grass Horse of the Year, and on dirt they were carried by Arts and Letters, who won half a million dollars and became the Horse of the Year two seasons later.

Mellon's second wife, Rachel Lambert Lloyd, an heiress to the Listerine fortune, joined him at the track and in their world of culture and civic involvement off the track. At John Kennedy's behest, she supervised the planting of an eighteenth-century American garden near the President's office, the famous Rose Garden, and she later helped to landscape the President's grave with rough fieldstones and wildflowers that were reminiscent of Jack Kennedy's years on Cape Cod.

At art auctions, they were as free-spending and as tasteful as they were at horse auctions, investing $210,000 for Gauguin's *La Ronde des Trois Bretonnes,* $249,000 for Manet's *Madame Gamby,* $317,000 for Manet's *La Rue Mosnier,* and $800,000 for Cézanne's *Houses in Provence.* Their private library included an extraordinary collection of sporting books, some several centuries old, and other treasures like a first edition of Chaucer's *Canterbury Tales.*

At a private-school graduation a few years ago, Mellon expressed his outlook in these words: "There is an inherent duty to be aware, to do something, to care."

In pursuit of his "inherent duty" as a horseman, Mellon enlisted the talents of people like Elliott Burch, an intelligent and educated trainer who had prepared Sword Dancer and Quadrangle for their Belmont Stakes victories in the preceding decade, and Braulio Baeza, a 112-pound genius in the saddle who had won his first race in Panama at the age of fifteen and had finished first in one out of every three races since. Between them, they commanded about one quarter of Mellon's prize money from colts like Arts and Letters, and they already ranked among the highest-paid capitalists in all sports.

In Baeza's case, few athletes were rewarded more lavishly for a day's work — not Wilt Chamberlain, not Lew Alcindor, not even Arnold Palmer. He was not rewarded as handsomely perhaps as Willie Shoemaker, the leading capitalist in silks, whose mounts had won more than $40,000,000 and had made him a rich man at 10 per cent of the purse. But Shoemaker, a neat rider whose "quiet" style aboard a horse contrasted with, say, Bill Hartack's, gave Baeza a sort of official blessing by observing: "He may be the best. He doesn't flop all over a horse."

Braulio Baeza had learned to sit still on a horse's back in Panama, where he grew up close to the Juan Franco track, where President José Antonio Remon had been assassinated in 1955. He was the grandson of a jockey and the son of a jockey, and he started to ride at six, recalling later:

"When my father got too big to be a jockey, he and my mother moved into a little apartment behind the barns at the old Juan Franco track in Panama City, where he worked as a trainer. There was racing all year round. When the time came for me to be born, they just got my mother out of the apartment and into the hospital in time. So I wasn't really born on the track — almost."

When he reached eleven, his father put him on a horse in the starting gate and "the horse broke, and I went on my backside." But he was riding as a professional as a teen-ager "when they raced only on Saturdays and Sundays, and you had to be a winner to make a living." That was in 1955, and four years later he was riding 309 winners in 112 days, often making it five or six times in one day. In 1960, he migrated north and arrived at Keeneland just as the decade of greenbacks was opening at American tracks.

Baeza stood 5 feet 4½ inches with a long, thin torso and had a trace of Oriental blood along with Spanish and Indian. He also had a clock in his head that led him on occasion to work a horse for half a mile and then to announce to the trainer: "Forty-nine seconds." He also was prone to injuries, breaking a collarbone at Hialeah early in his career but returning within two months in a manner that Shoemaker might admire after two decades of his own injuries. His first major victory came aboard a 65 to 1 shot named Sherluck, which defeated Carry Back at Belmont in 1961, causing Baeza to pluck carnations from the victory blanket and toss them to the railbirds with the remark:

"People think this is a Panamian custom, but that is not the truth. Braulio does it because he is a happy boy."

Two years later, the happy boy rode Chateaugay to an upset victory in the Kentucky Derby, cementing his future as one of the big bankrolls of racing, and the horse's trainer commented: "He never ran the same with anybody else on him." By then, Braulio was getting $1000 a month plus his 10 per cent, but he was about to encounter some of the business complications of the life of a sporting capitalist.

It was in April of 1964, almost a year after his Derby ride, that he sat down and addressed a letter to Fred Hooper, for whom he worked under contract. The message was just that Braulio was disaffiliating. But Hooper, in one of the early legal coups in a decade that came to be symbolized by legal coups involving athletes, obtained an injunction restraining Baeza from riding for any other stable. Noting that Baeza was "a jockey of great skill," he reported that the little man between 1960 and 1963 had earned $180,000 with him and half a million overall.

Baeza, trapped by the injunction, countered by offering to buy back his own contract for $75,000, but Hooper declined. The stalemate finally was settled by John W. Galbreath, who wanted Baeza as a contract rider for his Darby Dan Farm and reportedly posted most of the $100,000 that eventually shook the contract loose from Hooper.

In turn, Baeza got himself a new agent, signing with Lenny

Goodman, who also represented Bill Hartack, Bob Ussery, and John Rotz and did all right with his own piece of the action, taking 20 per cent of each jockey's earnings.

By the beginning of the seventies, Baeza was making $200,000 a year and was established alongside Shoemaker, Hartack, and several other jockeys as one of the working millionaires of the sport. But even in that nifty bracket, he found common ground and common sorrow with the other track millionaires like Charles Engelhard and Frank McMahon: When he lost, the $2 bettors squirmed — and booed.

On one October afternoon — his longest afternoon in quite a while — Baeza rode out of the money seven times in a row, giving him a twenty-four-race slump over nine days without a winner. It was as though Willie Mays went 0–for–24, except that the track fans, unlike most baseball fans, were trying to become capitalists too. So they booed the little millionaire all afternoon.

By chance, the jockey fees at Aqueduct that day were rising along with everything else in the inflated economy. Winners still got their 10 per cent of the purse. But the rider's fee for second place went up from $40 to $55; for third place, from $30 to $45, and for also-ran, from $25 to $35. Baeza was an also-ran seven times that afternoon and accordingly collected the loser's pittance of $245. Good times, bad times, it was all in a day's work.

• • •

From Werblin to Veeck to Phipps to Mellon to Baeza to Joan Payson, the sixties were superlative for the horses. They ran faster, they won more, they cost more, they returned more, they were taxed more. There were more programs, more races, more starters, more bettors and, the American Racing Manual observed at the head of the seventies, they all "served as the basis of a business boom of unprecedented proportions at North American thoroughbred tracks."

True, some old-timers like Captain Harry F. Guggenheim

called it quits, disposing of the renowned blue-and-white blocks of his Cain Hoy Stable and all 120 animals in a spectacular, and rather sad, sale. It ended when a man named Humphrey S. Finney picked up a telephone in a tent at Belmont Park, called the Guggenheim estate at Port Washington on the North Shore of Long Island, and said:

"Harry? Finney here. We've just finished. The yearlings brought nine hundred eighty-five thousand dollars, the others eight hundred twenty-one thousand dollars. Your friends bought a lot of them."

And so, in the most glittering dispersal sale ever held at Belmont, the Cain Hoy Stable passed from the otherwise jumping scene. On that one final day alone, thirty yearlings and twenty-seven horses of racing age were auctioned off for a million and three-quarters dollars. A few days earlier, at Lexington, fifty broodmares and twenty-nine weanlings went for nearly three million more, and the entire auction brought in $4,751,000.

The captain, a fixture at the track for thirty years, was retiring for reasons of health at the age of seventy-nine. He had been an aviation pioneer, publisher, art patron, and philanthropist, but he still had waited four years for his first winner after buying his first horse in 1933. He was the senior partner in the Guggenheim Brothers mining and metallurgical concern, the publisher of *Newsday* on Long Island, the builder of the Guggenheim Museum in Manhattan, the resident of a twenty-six-room Norman manor stocked with art treasures, a hunting lodge, and stables. But on this day in 1969, Steve Cady noted in the *New York Times:*

"As with the demolition of any historic landmark, there was a feeling of regret mixed with the hope of new owners. It was heightened by the blue-and-white motif: filmy white clouds against a blue sky, blue-and-white-striped tent poles, blue-and-white blocks on the catalogue cover, even the blue-and-white vending truck of Red the Baker & Son, where bidders could buy coffee, pastry, doughnuts, or hot soup."

The scene also was being left behind by old-timers like Mrs. C. Oliver Iselin, the former Hope Goddard, an unusual woman who had sailed aboard *Defender* and *Columbia* in the America's Cup races of the eighteen nineties and who enjoyed her biggest day at the racetrack in London in 1969 when Wolver Hollow, an 8 to 1 shot, won the Eclipse Stakes and $61,989. It was the last race before *her* stable was dispersed in an auction by Tattersall's at Newmarket — as Mrs. Iselin turned 101.

The ties were cut, too, by the passing of people like Hirsch Jacobs, the little red-haired empire builder from Brooklyn who became the most successful trainer in America with 3596 winners. They included Stymie, claimed for $1500 and later retired with a bankroll of almost $1,000,000, and Searchlight, the $15,000 mare that won more than $300,000. And in the first year of the decade of the seventies, they included Personality, who won the Preakness, and his stablemate High Echelon, who won the Belmont dramatically after Personality had been withdrawn on the eve of the big race by a cough.

The scene that they left, though, was draped in dollar signs — and a few new question marks.

A yearling brother of Majestic Prince was auctioned at Keeneland for a record bid of $510,000 — which was paid by Frank McMahon, who had paid $250,000 four years earlier for Majestic Prince. The Saratoga sales, a month later in August, 1970, brought $5,867,000 and the average price bid was a Saratoga record of $26,790. The top offer was $256,000 by John Jacobs, the son of Hirsch Jacobs, who broke the record set two seasons before by Paul Mellon. And so it went spiraling up.

When the colts finished training and made it to the tracks — the 130 tracks on the continent in 1970 — they were steered along by jockeys like Baeza, Manuel Ycaza, and Shoemaker, who rode his 6033rd winner on September 7, 1970, at Del Mar, California, at the age of thirty-nine. That was one more than Johnny Longden rode when he set the previous world record at George Royal on March 12, 1966, at the age of fifty-nine.

But no jockey was in Shoe's class as a moneyman: a 4-foot-11-inch 100-pounder who won more than eighty stakes races with purses of $100,000, including three Kentucky Derbies, two Preaknesses, and four Belmonts, and who rode six winners on a single card eight times, all the while banking combined paychecks of more than $4,000,000.

Shoemaker, like the owners who hired him, was one of the new conglomerates of the track too. He owned oil wells in Texas, a 33,000-acre ranch in Arizona, and a restaurant. In one year alone, from all these enterprises, he cleared $400,000. And when his younger brother asked why he simply didn't bag it all and retire, he replied: "What else would I do? I enjoy my work."

The races they rode were more numerous too, and the prizes more fantastic. Tracks went from eight events a day to nine, and in some cases to ten. They ran on Saturday night and Wednesday morning as well as every weekday afternoon, and there was no place to go after that but to Sunday. In one year, trainers like Eddie Neloy saddled horses that took home a million and a quarter dollars, and jockeys like Angel Cordero Jr. rode 345 winners and cleared a quarter of a million. On one *day* alone, Labor Day, the liberated laboring class flocked to the railing and saw the $113,850 Lindheimer Stakes in Chicago, the $108,200 Aqueduct Stakes in New York, and the $602,000 sprint for quarter horses at Ruidoso Downs in New Mexico. At Freehold Raceway in New Jersey, on the same day, more than $1,000,000 was bet on the trotters for the first time in the track's history.

Then, if there remained any doubt about the jackpots available, the famous course at Longchamp in Paris offered more than $500,000 in purses for owners and breeders on one rare day in June, 1970, as well as a sweepstakes with several million dollars in prizes for the public. And, as the pièce de résistance, the main event — the Grand Prix de Paris — offered $300,000, with a first prize of $173,000. It was won by an automobile-painting man from Beverly Hills named Earl A. Scheib, who went to the winner's circle in France for the first time to greet his colt Roll of Honour with the remark: "I have almost recovered my total outlay for the horse." He had bought the animal three days earlier.

When the great horses had finally run their last races, they were likely to be "syndicated" as stallions for ransom figures. In 1967, Buckpasser was incorporated as a sire for $4,800,000. In 1968, Dr. Fager — who had gone a mile in 1 minute 32 and one-fifth seconds with 134 pounds on his back — headed for the green pastures at $3,200,000. In 1969, Vaguely Noble went into business for $5,000,000. In 1970, Nijinsky went for $5,440,000.

Nijinsky had been bought by Engelhard two years before for $84,000, and while he was still undefeated early in 1970 had been priced at $4,800,000 by an Anglo-Irish syndicate, a sum that Engelhard refused. When Engelhard set up his own combine, there were thirty-two shares, each worth $170,000, and the partners included E. P. Taylor of Canada, John Hay Whitney, Ogden Phipps, Paul Mellon, and Robert Kleberg Jr., all giants of the racing world. And in case anyone questioned his dollar value, every time he went to the post Mrs. Romolo Nijinsky, the seventy-seven-year-old widow of the Russian ballet master Vaslav Nijinsky, had a standing bet with a British bookmaker for sixty dollars on the matchless nose of the wonder horse.

The breeding farms for such racing prima donnas may not have resembled the Taj Mahal, but they weren't exactly shabby either. North of Miami, for example, Albert and Arnold Winick bought a 435-acre farm and transformed it into the Delray Training Center, one of the most luxurious breeding campuses in the country: eighty stalls for mares, sixty-four for yearlings, overhead feeding in barns that cost $100,000 apiece, a medical-surgical building, "fogging" systems that kept everything insect-free, and pastures seeded in Pensacola Bahia grass.

Money, naturally, attracts money. And the boom in racing

began to touch off a land rush of sizable proportions and rich investors.

The Realty Equities Corporation of New York put $12,000,-000 into Suffolk Downs one year and $550,000 into Berkshire Downs near Pittsfield, Massachusetts, the next year. Gulf & Western Industries took over Arlington Park and Washington Park in Chicago. The Ogden Corporation counted five tracks in its portfolio, Patina Mining of Toronto had two — all seven bought from private owners. National Industries bid $14,400,-000 for Churchill Downs; Campbell's Soup, $56,000,000 for a company that owned Garden State Park and a minority interest in Hialeah.

"A racetrack is just real estate that happens to have horses on it," said an executive of Realty Equities.

"It's like the outdoor movies," noted the realty chief of Gulf & Western. "They were built on the outskirts of town and pretty soon the town grew out around them, making the land more valuable."

"Racing is still the largest spectator sport by many miles," said the chairman of the Ogden Corporation. "We try to go into things with more than one input. A collateral benefit from tracks is the great potential for real-estate complexes."

His company backed this view by spending $25,000,000 to buy and develop Waterford Park near Pittsburgh, Wheeling Downs in West Virginia, Scarborough Downs and Gorham Park in Maine, and the Fairmount Park across the Mississippi from St. Louis. The tracks had 2000 acres of land, and 1400 of them were considered available for "development," such as a motel, golf course, tennis club, marina, mobile-home park, and housing.

"It's getting to the point," said the president of Santa Anita, "where it is hard to justify using the land for racing."

One reason was the racing split: Out of every dollar bet, something like eighty-three to eighty-five cents on the average was returned to the winning customer, eight cents to the state, three cents to the purses — and four cents to the track. And nobody knew for sure what effect off-track betting would have, not even as it began in New York in 1971 in the most important experiment since pari-mutuel betting was installed in the decade before World War II.

By the end of the first year, New York expected to have fifty betting parlors in operation, including one with ten windows in Grand Central and another in Queens that once was a stock-brokerage house. At any window, the bettor got his money down, a clerk punched out the ticket on a computer, another computer was programmed to record the bets from other customers by telephone, all the bets were relayed to a central processing office, code numbers were assigned to each bet to foil counterfeiters, and finally the coded numbers were returned to the local clerk by television.

The state's interest in all this, like the bettor's, was money. Every off-track wager was taxed 16 per cent: 5 for operating expenses, 8 for the city, 2 for the state, and 1 for the track. City officials, drowning in budgetary red ink, guessed that $50,000,-000 might be realized the first year. But Howard J. Samuels, the industrialist and political candidate who was appointed president of the New York City Off-Track Betting Corporation, said — in the midst of confusion and doubt about the whole system — that he felt the estimate was "an unrealistic goal." But to City Hall, a goal nonetheless.

To the horsemen, though, off-track betting was just the final straw in a series of increasing burdens that made the prosperity of the sixties likely to become the devastation of the seventies.

Money already was tighter because of the recession of the late sixties and attendance had started a slight decline. Betting itself was still going up, meaning that fewer people were laying out more money. But in New York State, as elsewhere, the racing people noted that as the tax bite got bigger, their tracks had to depend more and more for revenue on attendance — for programs, concessions, parking fees. Any further drop in attendance might rock the boat, and to the horse people, off-track betting was certain to mean a further drop in attendance.

The state was gathering in more than $80,000,000 a year in pari-mutuel taxes; the New York Racing Association was distributing more than $21,000,000 in purses, yet it was beginning to realize a cash-flow deficit of almost $2,000,000. And, said an official for the association, "The music has stopped here."

The only place left for racing to go, some people insisted, was to Sunday — adding nine or ten more events to the fifty-odd that most tracks already carded during the week. It would be a political hot potato, but then so was off-track betting, until the need for money began to overpower the need for morality in the state legislatures that regulated the tracks.

"Where else are they going to go?" asked Jimmy Jones, the onetime trainer for the Calumet Farm and later the director of racing for Monmouth Park in New Jersey. "The racing season has been extended about as far as it will go, and the taxes are already too high. Football, baseball, you name it, they're all going full blast on Sunday. Even the bars are open on Sunday after church. Why not racing?"

His idea had long since flowered in France, Italy, and South America, to say nothing of Green Mountain Park in Vermont, Long-Acres in Washington, and Turf Paradise in Arizona. But at the major tracks, it was still one problem on a growing list of problems that ranged from taxes to labor contracts to night racing to harness racing.

"The horse-racing situation in the United States is critical," warned Marge Lindheimer Everett, sounding like Cassandra on the walls. "The saturation point has been reached. We are now in the same position as football and major league baseball because of overexpansion. Many states now have year-round racing, and this is unhealthy because of the shortage of horses.

There are more racing operations and more days than ever before, and the supply can't keep up with the demand."

Saturation, indeed. As the tricky decade began, thoroughbred and harness racing were drawing 64,000,000 viewers a year, they in turn were betting $5,500,000,000 a year, and thirty state governments with a finger in the pie were getting nearly $500,000,-000 in taxes. For the thoroughbred alone, the totals were sensational:

> 130 tracks in North America
> 5825 racing days (a gain of 272 in one year)
> 52,315 races run (up 2538)
> 45,808 starters (up 2098)
> $168,713,911 in purses (up $18,069,433)
> $4,103,459,902 in mutuel bets (up $256,883,727)

To keep the horses interested, the purses at all the tracks averaged $27,889 a day. And at Saratoga, the "horsemen's financial paradise," the prizes for the twenty-four-day meeting averaged $89,786 a day. Belmont Park was next as a happy hunting ground with an average of $89,042 for each of forty-two days. And at Aqueduct, the customers were pouring $3,380,421 across the mutuel counters every day during a sixty-three-day stretch at the start of the springtime season.

But the clouds were there on the horizon along with the horses and the money. And it seemed like a long time since the gentle days when racing was just the sport of kings and gentlemen, when Pete Bostwick was listed on the program as Mister Bostwick and when a professional jockey, submerged in the pack at the head of the stretch, found he had a running horse under him and would shout:

"Get out of my way, you sons of bitches, I'm coming through. And you, too, *Mister Bostwick*."

5

The Barons of Baseball

JOAN WHITNEY sat in the Colony one afternoon in 1928 having a spot of tea with Cathleen Vanderbilt. They had one thing in common — money — but they were about to share something else.

"How I envy you your house in town," Joan Whitney said.

"Nothing could be lovelier than your co-op," Cathleen Vanderbilt replied.

They looked at each other, smiled, nodded, and reached the only sensible solution in a dead heat. "Let's trade," they said.

And they did, as neatly and joyfully as though trading the lemon for the sugar across the tea table. Joan Whitney moved out of her place at 1010 Fifth Avenue and Cathleen Vanderbilt left her house at 11 East Sixty-first Street. The New York newspapers even reported the next day that moving vans had duly exchanged belongings between the two nests, and the *New York Journal* printed a full page on the swap under the headline: "Said Cathleen Vanderbilt to Joan Whitney, Let's Swap Houses." The subhead gave it all a wry twist, not being able to resist the temptation to say: "How the two heiresses solved the house-or-flat dilemma which every bride and every husband knows."

All this took place thirty-two years, one depression, and one World War before Joan Whitney just as sensibly bought a baseball team for $3,750,000 and began to trade players instead of houses. But either way she was the least uptight of persons, and she had the breeding, the education, and the cash to back up her choices.

She also had the casual colorfulness to make her one of the last of the big spenders after she did buy the baseball team, the New York Mets, the wonder team of the nineteen sixties. In fact, she became one of the last of the great old entrepreneurs, the people who owned sports teams for the fun of it or for the love of it. As a child, she sat in the Whitney family box near the New York Giants' dugout while John McGraw prowled the premises. As an adult, she sat in the Joan Whitney Payson private box near the Mets' dugout while Casey Stengel prowled. And she was not the least perturbed by the fact that the former privilege cost several hundred dollars and the latter several million dollars.

Either way, Joan Whitney wanted to sit in the stadium.

In that desire, she had much more in common with the early barons of baseball than with most of her contemporaries in the nineteen sixties. In outright cash, she may have been closer to the "barons" of the sixties — epecially since they tended to be corporations, conglomerates, or financial empires to whom a foothold in the major leagues represented a giant leap toward a more favorable tax stance. But in desire — in sheer pride of possession — she related more to the remarkable band of old operators who had run their teams on a shoestring and frequently had run themselves into bankruptcy.

Like Harry Von Der Horst, the beer wholesaler who leased a lot at Huntingdon Avenue near Greenmount in Baltimore of the eighteen eighties, built Union Park with 2600 seats, and found a home for the talented ruffians who became famous (and hated) as the Baltimore Orioles.

True, Von Der Horst did install a beer garden on the premises and his own beer flowed while the Orioles fought. But he spent much of his own time during the next generation trying to make ends meet with admission prices that started at five cents a head (twenty-five cents when he outrageously began to schedule double-headers), and he kept busy jumping back and forth between the National League and the American Association while Willie Keeler and John McGraw battled on the field for a winner's share of $200 in the Temple Cup play-off series.

Then there was Charles H. Ebbets, an architect who sometimes strolled into bars and took a poll of the house on the burning issue of the moment: Who should pitch the next afternoon for his unusual baseball team, the Brooklyn Trolley Dodgers? Ebbets's personal ties to his employees extended even to the ticket booths, where he often stationed himself and sold tickets to the park, and where he had time to ponder the carefree mood of the day that prompted his team to be known also as the Superbas — because his manager, Ned Hanlon, was running a billiard academy on the side with the spectacular name The Superba.

Years later, the Brooklyn Trust Company inherited the team as a kind of standing liability. Such a liability, in fact, that it often required a meeting of the board of directors to decide whether to spend $6000 to meet the waiver price on a utility infielder being peddled by another club. But in the early years, the liability belonged to Ebbets — and to players like Casey Stengel, who arrived one September day in 1912 and made his own financial debut by immediately joining the afternoon crap game on the locker-room floor.

The old entrepreneurs also included John T. Brush, a clothing salesman who bought the New York Giants at the turn of the century. He suffered from rheumatism and spent much of his time in a wheelchair, but the joie de vivre for Brush began with the theater and the baseball diamond, and to him they were the main ingredients of the good life. He opened his stadium to his cronies from the Lambs and knew that many summer afternoons he could watch his team perform under the fond gaze of Julia Sanderson, Ethel Barrymore, Frank Craven, De

Wolf Hopper, and David Warfield before they in turn headed back downtown to perform on the stages of Manhattan.

Brush even bestowed on his actor friends a certain distinctive badge of honor. He consulted the Lambert Brothers jewelry firm each season and devised personalized passes to the Polo Grounds. One year he produced a decorative pack of playing cards with an autographed picture of an actor on each card; another time, a penknife with a magnified peephole picture of the Polo Grounds in the handle.

When the wooden grandstand in the Polo Grounds burned in May of 1911, he drove along Broadway to his ball park with his wife, a former actress named Elsie Lombard. Together they surveyed the ruins, and Brush's daughter Natalie remembers that "he sat in his wheelchair so ill that almost any other man would have taken the insurance and quit." But Brush turned to his wife and said simply: "Elsie, I want to build a concrete stand, the finest that can be constructed. It will mean economy for a time. Are you willing to stand by me?" Elsie was.

"The one sport my father was really interested in," recalled H. L. Mencken, "was baseball, and for that he was a fanatic."

His father was such a fanatic that he once tried to form a syndicate to take over the Baltimore team and, failing that, worked his way into the hierarchy of the Washington team nearby. His command post was the Mencken cigar store at Seventh and G Streets in Washington, and, even as the vice president of the club, Mencken père plunged into the workaday details of baseball so fiercely that he soon was carrying on sustained fights with the railroads over their scandalous demands that he pay thirty dollars apiece for transporting thirteen players from Baltimore to Cincinnati to Columbus to Louisville to St. Louis and back to Baltimore.

Chris Van Der Ahe in St. Louis, another saloon impresario with a weakness for sports, was even pursued and jailed by his creditors and his ball park was sold from the courthouse steps.

And one afternoon in 1898, the Orioles played in Cleveland before exactly seventy-five cash customers and, when the Cleveland team won only 20 of 154 games the next season, the entire club was simply switched to St. Louis in a pauper's frantic effort to start all over again — on a new treadmill.

In Philadelphia, the reins were held by a onetime horsecar driver named Ben Shibe, who made baseballs in his spare time by hiring the neighborhood women to sew the covers by hand. When the World Series would open, Shibe would present himself before Garry Herrmann, the chief of baseball's National Commission, for the ceremony to determine the site of the opening game.

Life may have been more primitive, but it also was more simple: The decision was rendered by the toss of a coin. Somebody would produce a fifty-cent piece and Herrmann would toss it into the air while Shibe called "heads" or "tails."

Shibe's baseball team, as well as his chronic state of being rundown at the heels, passed eventually to his manager, Connie Mack. He was born with the magnificent name of Cornelius McGillicuddy in 1862, the year before the Emancipation Proclamation, and he was still trying to make ends meet with the Philadelphia ball club during World War II.

Mack worked twelve hours a day in a cotton mill when he was eleven years old and he observed later: "It didn't seem so bad. Besides, we got an hour for lunch." When he grew to his full height of 6 feet 4½ inches, and to his full weight of 150 pounds, he rather resembled a dignified ostrich in a high stiff collar. His indoctrination into the primitive "executive" side of baseball left him with no illusions about who did the work. As the manager of the Milwaukee team in the eighteen nineties, he recalled, "I signed players, made the trades, arranged our railroad transportation, found hotels for the players, and paid all the bills."

Half a century later, Mack was still paying all the bills — except by then he was paying them out of his own pocket. Even after his 1931 team won 107 games out of 154, he discovered that the one-man operation in sports was growing risky. Two years later, the Depression convinced him.

"We didn't have a man under ten thousand dollars on the payroll," he said, "and we operated in an industrial city where the Depression hit hard."

It hit hard, all right — the country lost 5000 banks, 12,000,-000 jobs and $50,000,000,000 in stocks. So Mack, who had just spent $700,000 renovating his ball park, started to peddle talent to pay his bills. He got $150,000 for Al Simmons, Mule Haas, and Jimmy Dykes; $100,000 for Mickey Cochrane; $125,000 for Lefty Grove, Max Bishop, and Rube Walberg; and $150,000 for the great Jimmy Foxx. Then he too started all over again.

The only lone-wolf operators who could survive the economic pressures, it seemed, were those who managed other people's money, those who began to pioneer in extravagant promotions to lure the public through the turnstiles, or those who had so much money that they could afford to pick up the tab even while inflation and taxation soared.

Take George Weiss, the son of a "fancy-grocer" in New Haven, Connecticut, and the student manager of the New Haven High School baseball team in 1912. Five years later, while still studying at Yale, he became the manager and major-domo of the New Haven Colonials, a semipro team that started to make life difficult for the full-time professional team in town, the New Haven club of the Eastern League.

Weiss began to beat the high price of doing business by some way-out showmanship. He staged exhibition games with teams of Bloomer Girls, with all-Chinese teams, and with teams reinforced by Harvard football stars like Charlie Brickley and Eddie Mahan. He also noticed that Sunday baseball was forbidden for the professional leagues, like the one the New Haven club played in, so he began to fill the gap with his semipro Colonials.

And just to make certain that piety would not prevail over performance, he began to invite big-league stars to New Haven from Boston, where their teams were passing idle Sunday afternoons.

When Ty Cobb insisted on a $350 guarantee for the one-shot excursion to New Haven, Weiss came through with $800 — and Cobb came back frequently. Another time he imported the entire Boston Red Sox club with Babe Ruth pitching in "the greatest baseball attraction ever offered New Haven fans." The Red Sox were the world champions that year and Ruth was fast becoming the grandest tiger in the jungle. But Weiss fortified his lineup with the hellcat Cobb, who hit a single and double off Ruth while the Colonials executed the coup of the year by tying the world champions, 3 to 3.

The New Haven club in the Eastern League decided before long that it lacked the cash and the ideas to compete with this kind of box-office hoopla. So the owners journeyed crosstown and offered Weiss a clear field for $5000. He borrowed the money and became a baseball monopoly in New Haven.

Ten years later, he moved his imagination to the International League as the general manager at Baltimore, and then one day in 1932 the telephone rang and Jacob Ruppert was on the line inviting him to join the New York Yankees. So, for the next twenty-nine years, he became the power behind the throne of the most successful franchise in professional sports — spending money for a series of owner-fans named Ruppert, Dan Topping, Larry MacPhail, and Del Webb, until the old order finally began to crumble as baseball turned into the sixties.

MacPhail was one of the last of the three-ring-circus masters too. Where Weiss worked in the wings, MacPhail strutted to the center of the stage, wheels spinning. In 1935, he threw the switch at Crosley Field in Cincinnati for the first night game in the major leagues and ushered 30,000 people into the ball park and a new era into baseball. Three years later, having switched his runaway mind to New York as the kingpin of the Brooklyn Dodgers, he bought $72,000 worth of lighting equipment from the General Electric Company — on the cuff — and introduced night games to the big city.

He didn't let any grass grow under his feet during that extravaganza either. He imported the Olympic sprinter, Jesse Owens, and staged foot races before the game. Then he sat back and watched Johnny VanderMeer of his old Cincinnati team pitch a no-hitter against his new Brooklyn team, the second no-hitter in five days for VanderMeer.

MacPhail's shenanigans were not solely the work of an ad-lib genius with unpredictable brainstorms. He based his promotional thunderclaps on a firm premise: You had to entertain people in the ball park or they would go someplace else to be entertained. His premise grew even more urgent after he had taken a survey in the late nineteen thirties and discovered that a season's attendance of one million fans probably meant that you were drawing between 100,000 and 200,000 people and that they came back to the stadium five or ten times. So, entertaining that hard-core group of customers became essential for a club to survive — more so than a generation later when business concerns bought maybe 5000 season's box seats and guaranteed the home team 300,000 admissions before any game was played.

Occasionally a visiting team might blossom into such an attraction that the home club could sit back and simply wait for its appearance. The New York Yankees, in their salad days, beat everybody in sight. But they never wore out their welcome because they also attracted one third of all home attendance in parks around the American League. They demolished you on the field, but brought along the balm for the box office. But most home teams still had to live by their own wits, and it required a Larry MacPhail or a Bill Veeck to provide the wits.

Veeck, for one, provided so many wits that his fellow owners in the years after World War II reacted in absolute terror. Most of them were still plodding along as proprietors in the image of good old Charlie Ebbets, and Veeck caused so many brain ripples that they began to fear that there was something prophetic in his assertion that his name was "Veeck as in wreck."

Actually, the problem was a generation gap. Veeck had followed his father around the Chicago Cubs' holdings twenty years before as a little boy, in the days when the New York Giants would install Casey Stengel as the manager at Toledo with one purpose: to buy players low and sell them high. Man and boy, Bill Veeck had seen the old proprietary system at work, and later as an owner himself he realized that the old system could not work in the new days at midcentury when baseball no longer reigned as the national pastime. So he set out to make the game competitive with other forms of entertainment, and the higher his imagination soared, the more his colleagues worried where it all might end.

It all ended in some pretty lively moments for Veeck's colleagues and customers alike. When he was running the comatose St. Louis Browns, he achieved distinction of sorts by sending the midget Eddie Gaedel to bat one afternoon and had the satisfaction of seeing Gaedel draw a walk on four straight (high) pitches. Another time, he staged a "Grandstand Managers' Day," during which the Browns' strategy was dictated for one game by the people in the grandstand. At critical moments during the game, one of Veeck's assistants would hoist signs asking, "Infield in?" or "Should we walk him?" The crowd, such as it was, would signify its choice by applause, while a municipal judge sat in a rocking chair on the dugout roof to determine the mob's wishes.

A crisis arose once when one of Veeck's pitchers, Ned Garver, refused to pitch with the infield drawn in tight. But Veeck's deputy, Bob Fishel, got busy on a megaphone and influenced the crowd to reverse its signals. The Browns won the game, 1 to 0, and a lot of grandstand managers went home that afternoon with the satisfied feeling of a job well done.

On other occasions, Veeck would give away hundreds of cans of vegetables as prizes — with blank labels, to add a dash of adventure to the winner's dinner hour. At Cleveland in 1948, he even built a good ball team to go with his promotional sparks, and the Indians won the American League pennant and the World Series. But, more significantly, they played before crowds that *averaged* 40,000 for every home game.

But Veeck proved to be too far ahead of his time for the other owners' comfort. And their serenity was not fortified when he issued a kind of revolutionary guide describing his economic theories with the charming, and chilling, title of *The Hustler's Handbook*. They finally isolated him by refusing permission to transfer the St. Louis club to Baltimore, so Veeck — still the unreconstructed hustler — sold out.

Nowhere was Veeck's galloping approach to the business of baseball more lacking than in Chicago, where his father had worked as an executive with the Cubs. The team slipped placidly into the sixties and seventies with the same gentle hand at the helm, and the hand belonged to Philip K. Wrigley, the chewing-gum heir. Even his ball park, Wrigley Field, which was half a century old, had the splendid Victorian look of another time — tiny dugouts, brick walls, ivy vines creeping up the outfield fences. And, in an era of mercury-vapor lamps and color television, it remained staunchly the only stadium in the major leagues without lights.

Wrigley himself was so shy that he sometimes went three years without attending a game in his own park. He noted that "you get pretty good coverage on television" and once confessed: "The only thing I don't like about baseball is the publicity that goes with it."

Thanks to chewing gum, he was one of the last of the old-time entrepreneurs to survive in baseball and, thanks to his courtly manners, he was one of the last of the practitioners of the personal touch. He answered his own office telephone, even when irate fans called with complaints. He held back 22,000 seats for every game for box-office sale so that the fans would not feel shut out. And, while watching the Cubs on TV in his sixteenth-floor office in the Wrigley Building, he would resolutely note when the game reached the home half of the seventh inning — and then he would stand at his desk and take the seventh-inning stretch.

Another survivor of the good old days — thanks to beer — was Gussie Busch, the master of the St. Louis Cardinals. True, he had enough money to coexist with the big corporations that began to infiltrate professional sports after the war. But he also had enough of the baronial manner to rank with the private owners of fifty years before.

At the peak of the Cardinals' fortunes in the nineteen sixties, his picture hung on the wall behind the manager's desk in the stadium — Busch Memorial Stadium. His general headquarters was a couple of dozen blocks away, in the Anheuser-Busch Brewery, but he kept close tabs on the hits, runs, and errors through his right-hand man, Richard Meyer. He also had the habit of consulting his manager, Red Schoendienst, or his general managers, Stan Musial or Bing Devine, either at his office, his stadium, or his farm outside the city. And *they* in turn developed the habit of addressing him as "Boss."

Sometimes a whole week would pass without any communiqué from Busch to the front office of the team. Or he might unexpectedly telephone from Houston during one of his business trips and ask about decisions on cutting the roster to the limit of twenty-five men. Or he might side with Schoendienst on farming out a young infielder, only to let Musial veto the idea during a cruise on one of the Busch boats. After which, Musial would advise his friend Schoendienst gently: "The Boss agrees not to send Jimmy Williams out."

Busch, who appeared a trifle stuffy to most people, nevertheless relished the idea of presiding over things, whether they involved his yacht or a gin rummy game for sizable stakes with

Musial and other friends. In the locker room at Al Lang Field on the St. Petersburg waterfront in Florida, he would appear at a plenary session of coaches and scouts in his favorite spring-training regalia: a double-breasted yachting blazer, slacks, and a commodore's cap. He has been known to take infield practice and he even indulged in the supreme privilege of baseball rank — commandeering the trainer's table and getting a rubdown in the style of Bob Gibson before a World Series game.

Busch's personal touch with his team led to a kind of Greek tragedy for the city of St. Louis in 1964, just when the personal touch in baseball was being replaced by the corporate touch. The Cardinals were floundering somewhat aimlessly most of the summer, and he decided that Devine should be replaced as general manager at once and Johnny Keane should be replaced as field manager when the season ended. He even approached Leo Durocher on the possibility of succeeding Keane the following season, and Leo was willing.

Much to Busch's unbounded joy, though — to say nothing of his unbounded embarrassment — the Cardinals under Keane rallied dramatically in the final weeks of the season and won the National League pennant on the final day. Then they won the World Series from the Yankees on the final day, and there they stood as the world champions.

The only rub was that Keane had realized that the rug was being pulled out from under him. And the day after the World Series, while the skyrockets were still resounding from Kingshighway Boulevard to the Mississippi, he pulled a rug out from under the "Boss." He walked quietly and somberly into the brewery for the news conference at which Busch was supposed to announce his new contract as manager, and instead stunned Busch by announcing his resignation. Three days later, the "Boss" was further devastated when Keane became manager of the Yankees.

Still, Busch recovered from the shocks of 1964 by adjusting to

the new economic tide that was sweeping in. He bought
$5,000,000 worth of bonds in a massive project financed by a
private group, the Civic Center Redevelopment Corporation,
which was transforming the riverfront. The corporation sold
$15,000,000 more in bonds and borrowed $31,000,000 more.
And the gleaming new Busch Stadium rose near the Gateway
Arch on the Mississippi, while the city put up $6,000,000 for
streets, lighting, and other improvements.

The city, and the "Boss," were edging toward modern times.

• • •

When Joan Whitney was born in New York in the first decade
of the century, the population of the United States was 76,000,-
000 and major league baseball drew about 3,600,000 customers
each season. That meant one in every twenty-one persons paid
to see a ball game. By the twenties, when she was blithely swap-
ping houses with Cathleen Vanderbilt, the population had increased past 110,000,000, and the baseball turnstiles were click-
ing 8,600,000 times every season. That meant one person in
every thirteen was making the baseball scene.

By 1960, the population had "exploded" to 180,000,000 and
baseball was counting close to 20,000,000 admissions a season —
one in every nine.

The prosperity suggested by these figures, though, was elusive
because everything else was going up too — taxes, salaries, public interest in football and other leisure-time activities, and in
general the cost of doing business from peanuts to pavement
blocks. In fact, the margin for error was growing steadily
smaller, and that statistic was becoming far more important than
any of the others.

In fact, the Brooklyn Dodgers and New York Giants decided
in 1957 that the margin was growing unbearably small, and they
migrated to the Pacific Coast, leaving New York to the Yankees
and to anybody else who could pay the tab. They also left Joan
Payson in the lurch as a practicing baseball fan, and that emo-

tional gap meant more to her than the financial gap. So she bought her way into the National League as the number one sponsor, and number one fan, of the New York Mets.

In both capacities, she was an anachronism. In the old tradition of Ebbets, Brush, Shibe, Ruppert, Dreyfuss, Mack, and Wrigley, she was one of the barons of baseball — involved, compulsive, enamored. But in the evolving pattern of the day, in the switch to big business in professional sports, she stood alongside the conglomerates that were buying their way in too. She had the personal stake of the former and the personal fortune of the latter. The only question was how much longer the barons could survive in the era of systems analysis, electronic computers, and depreciation of capital assets.

Still, she was an elegant anachronism. Her mother was Helen Hay Whitney, the daughter of John Hay, onetime aide to Abraham Lincoln and secretary of state for both William McKinley and Theodore Roosevelt. Her father was Payne Whitney, a man who in 1924 paid $2,041,951 in income taxes — in a time when income taxes were not altogether fashionable. Only Henry Ford and John D. Rockefeller paid more that year, the year Joan Whitney was married to Charles Shipman Payson of an old family from Portland, Maine. Three years later, Payne Whitney died, leaving an estate that was calculated at $239,301,-017.

Joan's schooling for her future role as one of the last barons of baseball was many-splendored. She attended Miss Chapin's classes in New York and Barnard College and grew into a chubby, merry, cherubic woman with blond hair, hordes of pets, and priceless art collections. "I was brought up on the Giants," she recalled, and she had the scorecards to prove it, though her personal system of keeping score at ball games defied even George Weiss, who once looked over her shoulder and said with a shrug: "I can't understand any of it."

The family trait of involvement extended to her brother,

John Hay Whitney, who became the publisher of the *New York Herald Tribune,* ambassador to the Court of St. James's, co-owner (with Joan) of the Greentree Stable, and the fortunate financial backer of the film, *Gone with the Wind.* Joan possessed the Midas touch too, having been one of the original angels for the long-running *Life with Father.* But even when Greentree champions like Tom Fool were making track history, her zest for baseball kept crowding into the picture.

She adopted the Greentree Stable's colors, watermelon and black, from a favorite evening gown and promptly attached baseball names to the sleek animals who carried the colors to the post. At one time or another, she named her horses Hall of Fame, Jolly Roger, Shut Out, One-Hitter, Third League, and even Gashouse Gang, in tribute to the rollicking St. Louis Cardinals of the nineteen thirties.

She cheerfully followed the superstitions of baseball people too. No hats allowed on beds, and if her team seemed to be on a hot streak while she was eating candy, ice cream, chocolate bars, or Cokes, she kept on eating and drinking them until the team had cooled off. And whether they were hot or cold, she kept crossing her fingers to invoke good luck.

For years, she was a minority stockholder in the Giants. She tried unsuccessfully to buy the club before it moved to San Francisco, then she tried to retain one share in it as a memento after she had bought the Mets, and she even crossed the continent to attend opening day in San Francisco after all her maneuvers had failed to keep the team in the East. She insisted on hiring Weiss and Stengel for the Mets, and prevailed. She suggested on naming the new team the Meadow Larks because they played on Flushing Meadow, but fortunately did not prevail. Then, while Stengel was adding a spectacular touch of splendor and legend to her team, she would sit next to the dugout in either a floppy hat or a blue-and-orange baseball cap and say: "If only I knew what he was talking about."

When she traveled about on the trail of her horses or her baseball team, she went in regal trappings within her personal Pullman car, which was named Adios II. She always took two or three pet dachshunds along and made certain that the Mets' insignia had been sewn on everything in sight, including her felt turtle. And yet, when she was asked once how great a share of stock she held in the Mets, she replied with a kind of innocent wonder: "Oh, I have no idea. I think it's eighty or eighty-five per cent." And when asked how much money she had spent on the team, she replied with equal innocent wonder and truth: "Oh, I have absolutely no idea of that."

Her principal homes at Hobe Sound, Florida, and Manhasset, Long Island, were filled with masterpieces by Goya, Matisse, Toulouse-Lautrec, El Greco, Cézanne, and Corot. And if she tired of those treasures, she could behold others at the Museum of Modern Art, where she was a trustee, or at the Country Art Gallery in Westbury and Locust Valley on Long Island, where she was the founding owner.

When she traveled in the winter to Hobe Sound, she became the mistress of her mansion on Jupiter Island off Palm Beach and was surrounded by neighbors like Douglas Dillon, General James A. Van Fleet, John B. Ford, Averell Harriman, Joseph Verner Reed, Gordon Gray, and Donald Grant, the stockbroker who became her financial deputy and chairman of the board of the Mets. Grant was a long-time baseball fan too, who often prowled Shea Stadium to the highest and emptiest seat in the fifth deck of the left-field grandstand simply to see what they had wrought. He had been born in Montreal and, when the first Canadian team in the big leagues appeared in New York, he stood during the playing of the anthems and sang "O Canada" — in French.

Joan was a Republican and a valuable one. She once gave $65,050 to the party during the national election campaign of Dwight D. Eisenhower. But her largess reached in all directions.

She and her brother founded the North Shore Hospital on the original Whitney estate on Long Island. She contributed $50,-000 in 1931 to the Emergency Unemployment Relief Committee, which was trying to raise $12,000,000 to finance jobs and direct relief work in New York during the early days of the Depression. And in 1939, she financed and directed the Children's World at the World's Fair, a project that prompted Grover Whalen to extol "the largest, most elaborate children's entertainment center in exposition or amusement park history."

Whalen's estimate was probably accurate, at least until Joan Payson established the Mets in 1961 and made *them* the center of the largest, most elaborate children's entertainment center in history. She did it with the same sense of civic zeal too. When the Giants and Dodgers left town in 1957, Mayor Robert F. Wagner decided that it was unthinkable for New York not to have a team in the National League, so he asked his friend, William A. Shea, an energetic and successful lawyer, to start thinking about the unthinkable.

Shea tried to inveigle the Cincinnati Reds, Pittsburgh Pirates, and Philadelphia Phillies to take up residence in New York. Then he enlisted Branch Rickey, the old deacon of baseball in St. Louis, Brooklyn, and Pittsburgh, to join him in forming a third league, the Continental League.

That's when Joan Payson entered the picture, not only with a race horse named Third League but also with a checkbook. She had allies too — Mrs. Dorothy Killam of Montreal and Dwight F. Davis Jr. of Southampton, the son of the original donor of the Davis Cup in tennis. They in turn were joined by Grant and Herbert Walker, the son of the original donor of the Walker Cup in golf. By the time the Mets took the field in 1962 and began making theatrical history, Joan Payson was four or five million dollars lighter but she was regularly keeping score in her indecipherable scrawl from the owner's box behind first base.

The mood of old-syle elegance extended even to Stengel, who had just been unceremoniously dumped by the Yankees after a

dozen seasons during which the team won ten American League
pennants and seven world championships. After brooding by
the side of his swimming pool near his orange and lemon trees
in Glendale, he was returned to baseball by Joan Payson just as
he was entering his seventy-third year. And when he and his
wife Edna reached New York to join the Mets, Edna remembered the splendor of the occasion:

"We were driven from the airport," she said, "in a Rolls-
Royce. Casey wondered about it, so I said to him: 'You're returning to baseball in New York, Casey. We might as well go
first-class.' "

They were arriving first-class chiefly because they shared Joan
Payson's taste for elegance, and they probably were more aware
than she was that they were savoring a lost art. They were working now for a woman who just as happily entertained Princess
Margaret at the 500-acre Greentree estate in Manhasset, and
who once pitched an anniversary party for 1000 guests while a
specially constructed replica of Niagara Falls emptied grandly
into the swimming pool within the family compound.

The Stengels had money too, from real estate, oil, and bank-
ing — but nothing like the treasure of the mistress of the Mets.
Nor did many people rival her fanaticism for the ball club.
When she was abroad, her chauffeur would mail her the Mets'
box scores. Once on a trip to the Greek isles, she arranged a
daily telephone call from a friend, just to keep up with the
team's adventures. If she had to attend a major race at Aqueduct, she would hang on at the ball park until the fourth inning
before driving fifteen minutes to the track.

When the Mets began their careers by losing nine straight
games in 1962, she was distressed but not defeated. The next
day, they finally won a game and champagne flowed in the
locker room, while Joan Payson sat with a portable radio pressed
to her ear at the racetrack and murmured, "I can't believe it's
true."

The day after that, the Mets won again, and she was again in her box at the finish line watching the races. Moreover, her horse, No Robbery, was winning his fifth straight race by taking the Wood Memorial Stakes and was earning $59,020. But Joan Payson was almost too busy to notice, the portable radio crammed against her ear, listening to the play-by-play report of her favorite baseball team.

•   •   •

Two things happened in the nineteen sixties that marked the passing of the barons of baseball and the glory of their times, though not the trouble of their times.

One was the election of a Wall Street lawyer named Bowie Kuhn as the fifth commissioner of baseball. He succeeded William D. Eckert, a retired Air Force general, who had been hired in 1965 for seven years but who then had been fired in 1968 because the world suddenly seemed like a very hostile place for the "national pastime." In short, the game was beginning to lose prestige, fans, and money. The task of reviving it was entrusted to Kuhn because the task clearly belonged to a man with the legal and financial background to wrestle with the new problems of the new time.

The other thing was the sale of the New York Yankees to the Columbia Broadcasting System. The Yankees of Jake Ruppert and Dan Topping were now the Yankees of a television network. They were now a subsidiary of a financial empire, and not a particularly important subsidiary, at that.

Charlie Ebbets, conducting his pitcher-of-the-day poll in the taverns of Brooklyn, might have had trouble puzzling out the significance of the change. But Joan Payson, Gussie Busch, Thomas Yawkey, Philip Wrigley, and the other survivors of the old days could see the handwriting on the walls of the twenty-four major-league parks. Joan Payson had an especially clear view of the transition from Shea Stadium, across the river from Yankee Stadium. And Bowie Kuhn could see it all from his office at 680 Fifth Avenue.

What it meant was that professional baseball — like football, golf, basketball, hockey, automobile racing, horse racing, and all the other "sports" in the land — was starting to share the resources and the pressures of high finance. It meant that CBS, for one thing, now controlled a diversified portfolio of the things that entertained people for money. Everything from *My Fair Lady* to Joe Pepitone.

6

Due to Circumstances Beyond Their Control

RONALD WESLEY TAYLOR was one of those rare things, like an American in professional hockey. He was a Canadian in professional baseball. He was even rarer than that too, because he was a relief pitcher, an electrical engineer, and a student of literature who could quote Emerson.

Still, he did not seem especially significant until he walked out of the St. Louis Cardinals' bullpen during the World Series of 1964 and pitched four and two-thirds hitless innings against the New York Yankees, who had just been bought by the Columbia Broadcasting System. And Taylor's tour de force was watched by a rare bird on the *other* side of the corporate fence, Michael Burke, a wartime secret agent, onetime circus director, Hollywood scriptwriter, network television executive, Madison Avenue Beatle, the avant garde of the new owners as Taylor was of the new employees. And Burke could quote Emerson too.

Taylor had a lot of time to brush up on his literature and his electrical engineering before he crossed Burke's horizon. He had meandered through baseball's minor leagues like an itinerant, with stops at Daytona Beach, Fargo, Moorhead, Minot, Reading, Salt Lake City, and Jacksonville before reaching St. Louis by way of Cleveland.

"The year after the World Series," he recalled later, "I was traded to Houston, and a year and a half after that, Houston wrote me off. It was nineteen sixty-six, and they sent me a minor-league contract for ten thousand dollars. They promised me more if I made the team. I was going on thirty and had a bad back.

"The next spring, I was at Cocoa Beach for spring training and one day the phone rang. It was Bing Devine, my old boss in St. Louis, who now was running the New York Mets. 'How do you feel?' he asked. And I said, 'Great. Buy me. These guys have given up on me. They're switching to young players, and I'm just mopping up.'

"He did buy me — for Jacksonville. Ten thousand dollars, and fifteen if I made the team. It was the same old 'if' proposition. Besides, the Mets were a last-place team. But I couldn't give up on myself — I needed that one more year in the big leagues, that fifth year, to qualify for my *pension*."

Taylor, proving that he was something of an economist as well as an engineer, cast a kind of fugitive look, like a man reprieved but not quite certain that he has been reprieved.

"Two years later," he said, "I doubled my pay, the Mets won the pennant, and we got eighteen thousand three hundred thirty-eight dollars apiece for winning the World Series."

"Kipling said your life is determined by the flip of a coin," he added, switching neatly back from economics to literature and philosophy in a way that Michael Burke might admire. "That was *my* flip of the coin."

• • •

Mike Burke rode the elevator to the private dining room in the CBS Building, shook hands with Frank Stanton, the president of the company, and William Paley, the chairman of the board, and then knuckled down to a corned-beef-and-cabbage luncheon and the investment portfolio that CBS had entrusted to him. They were sitting around over coffee later when he leaned back in his chair and, mentally flipping a coin of his own, asked:

"How about the New York Yankees?"

His question cost CBS $14,000,000 and a lot of headaches, but it brought new brains, new people, and new money into professional baseball at a time when athletes like Ron Taylor were arriving with new brains and new advisers in search of that new money. Joan Payson and a few of the old-line barons still might be able to foot the bill, but more and more the new economics needed new bankrolls. Burke did not fully realize that he was temporarily bankrolling a pig in a poke, but Kipling and Ron Taylor would have approved his guts.

The first public reaction, though, was surprise tinged with suspicion. After all, people reasoned, the Columbia Broadcasting System probably had not bought the Yankees just to own a baseball team, the way Joan Payson had done — to possess it the way one possesses a motorboat or a Modigliani. Only two reasons seemed to justify the step: either CBS expected to operate (or eventually sell) the Yankees at a profit, or CBS expected to operate the Yankees as part of its network pool of talent, showcasing Joe Pepitone alongside Lassie.

The network promptly denied that it was grabbing "talent" for future programming. But no one could deny that the idea had merit. As far back as the eighteen eighties, the new National League berated the even newer American Association as a "beer-and-whiskey" organization, a league that included teams in Baltimore and Louisville that were owned by breweries and distilleries and in St. Louis by a prosperous saloonkeeper named Chris Van Der Ahe — and that charged only twenty-five cents for a ball game.

If the Yankees *had* been a television show, however, they would hardly have survived another season once the ratings rolled by. There had been two great box-office boosts in Yankee history: Babe Ruth and World War II. The first arrived in 1920, when Colonel Jacob Ruppert bought him from the Boston Red Sox for $525,000 in cash — $400,000 of which was considered a loan to help rescue the Boston club's owner, Harry

Frazee, from the financial narrows. The venture into high finance immediately paid off. Ruth popped fifty-four home runs over fences the first year he played in New York and attendance at Yankee games soared from 619,164 to a record of 1,289,422. Moreover, he kept the club over the million mark in nine of his first eleven seasons before the Great Depression fastened over the economy.

An even more spectacular bonanza arrived in 1946, when the end of the war rocketed the economy into a kind of long-range orbit of inflation. People suddenly were hungry for "release," they had the money to choose the particular leisure they craved — and along came television. Yankee attendance this time roared from 881,846 in 1945, the year the war ended, to the astronomical total of 2,265,512 the next year — while the Yankees ran third in an eight-team league.

By the time the nineteen sixties dawned, television crews were climbing all over the new stadiums that were being built by cities and counties to handle the huge crowds of cash customers, and television money was pouring into the bank accounts of franchises. They needed it too, because everything was more expensive, from electricians to outfielders.

Things grew so expensive, in fact, that rich angels with fat bankrolls became very desirable people as sports spiraled into the sixties. And some of the angels, as well as the bankrolls, started to come from corporations whose primary business was selling something besides reserved seats to ball games.

CBS was preceded in this gathering sweepstakes by a radio-television man from Michigan named John E. Fetzer, who combined some of the flair of the old-style owners with enough of the capital of the new-style owners. During the thirties, when sports teams were scrounging along with everybody else, Fetzer had staked himself into the broadcasting business by simply building his own equipment. Once he and his wife operated a radio station in Kalamazoo in a way that probably stamped

Fetzer forever as an entertainment impresario — she played the studio piano and he operated the control room.

A generation later, they were no longer turning the crank themselves. Fetzer bought six radio and six television stations in Michigan, Iowa, and Nebraska, and in 1955 he joined ten other businessmen in a syndicate that bought the Detroit Tigers for $5,500,000. A decade later, he bought out his colleagues, and now he was at the controls of the baseball team as well as of the dozen stations.

Fetzer's stations, moreover, were outlets of the Columbia Broadcasting System, which meanwhile was relieving Dan Top-

---

See how they grow: This table shows some of the signs that reflect the growth of professional sports since World War II. The years chosen are 1939, just before the war, and 1969, just before the seventies arrived.

	Number of major league teams	Number of major league games per season	Estimated average payroll per club
BASEBALL			
1939	16	1232	$250,000
1969	24	1944	$800,000
FOOTBALL			
1939	10	55	$150,000
1969	26	182	$1,000,000
BASKETBALL			
1939	none	none	*
1969	25	1003	$500,000
HOCKEY			
1939	7	168	$75,000
1969	12	420	$500,000

* As the seventies began, basketball went to twenty-eight teams in two leagues and hockey to fourteen.

---

ping and Del Webb of the Yankees while Fetzer was relieving Walter O. Briggs's heirs of the Tigers. In Briggs's case, his son Spike had tried to buy the team from his father's estate but was blocked by his two sisters, who felt it wasn't entirely proper to be in the baseball business. In Topping's case, the old Yankee owners felt it wasn't entirely proper to be in any business anymore that required lawyers to negotiate with shortstops and computers to negotiate with tax officials.

Fetzer soon became chairman of baseball's joint committee on TV, meaning that he became quarterback of the owners' group that hassled out the game's contracts with the broadcasters, meaning the National Broadcasting Company. But the baseball club did not represent a major part of his business holdings, any more than the Yankees did for Columbia. It was an investment in the "entertainment business," a slice of the "recreation industry," a piece of the action.

In New York, as the Yankees dropped from the top to the bottom of the American League, the telephone rang in Burke's apartment one Saturday morning. He was about to relinquish his portfolio at CBS to take over full workaday control of the team as chairman of the board and president. The Yankees, after twenty-nine pennants and twenty world championships in forty-five years, had dived into the cellar and attendance had dived with the team to 1,124,648, the lowest in twenty years. The phone call was a warning that "a piece of the action" could be an expensive thing.

"It was from Bill Paley," Burke recalled. "He wanted to ask me if I was really sure I knew what I was getting into, if I realized that I was leaving the security of CBS to run a subsidiary where I'd be on public view like a target, if I appreciated the likelihood that I'd be vilified in the press when things didn't work. I told him I was sure, and he said okay."

• • •

"I've devoted myself to a lot of meaningful things," Michael Burke observed after he had switched his base of operations from a midtown skyscraper to an uptown baseball park. "I fought a war when it was my generation's turn to fight a war. I gave more than three years to the government's high commissioner's office in Germany, and my work enlarging the CBS structure could be described as meaningful if communications are at all meaningful.

"Now, in my view, the goal of giving New York the finest in baseball has sociological ramifications at a time when people are increasingly surrounded by steel and pavements, and are in need of the relaxation baseball brings."

In pursuit of the sociological ramifications of his new job, Burke set about reviving the public image of the Yankees and simultaneously resisting the notion that baseball had suffered a lingering death, prompted by the pressures of "violent" sports like football and hockey in a day and age of violence.

He kept reminding people that baseball was basically a one-on-one contest between a man pitching a missile and a man trying to hit it. He repainted the forty-five-year-old stadium gleaming white on the outside and gleaming blue on the inside. He made a point of sitting just off the Yankee dugout in a box seat, where he often signed more autographs than his ballplayers. He was frequently the host at breakfast in the Edwardian Room of the genteel Plaza Hotel on Central Park South, where he cut a tall and fetchingly modern figure in a rich old setting.

In all respects, he brought a sophisticated and rather cultured tone to baseball, a Renaissance man in a muscle factory, one of the beautiful people in the eddies of New York society. He used four-syllable words like "pejorative" and asked whether baseball could be made "viable" in the hurly-burly of twentieth-century life. He brought friends like Robert Merrill of the Metropolitan Opera to Yankee Stadium to sing the national anthem, and he ordered the ticket-takers to speak politely to the customers.

He also reduced the front-office staff of eighty persons by about a dozen and trimmed administrative costs 25 per cent. But his chief innovations at the start tended to be more qualitative than quantitative, and his greatest coup probably was to induce Marianne Moore to throw out the first ball on opening day.

It did not take too much inducing, since Miss Moore had once played left field for the girls' team in Carlisle, Pennsylvania, and had grown into a spectacularly articulate fan even as she grew into one of the foremost poets of her time. When the Dodgers left Brooklyn in 1958 for Los Angeles she felt forsaken, and it required no great ruse to nudge her allegiance toward the Yankees.

Burke, who had once played football against Ernest Hemingway outside a saloon in wartime Paris, got the idea one day in February of 1968 while flying south to spring training. He already had established himself as one of the Young Turk executives of the major leagues and as the presiding officer of the Yankees' reconstruction era, and he yearned to open the season with "something new."

"I just got personally bored with political figures on opening day," he remembered. So he decided to ask Marianne Moore to heave out the first ball.

His choice was sensationally unorthodox because Miss Moore was not only a poet but was an eighty-one-year-old poet at that. But she had been born in St. Louis three years before Casey Stengel was born in Kansas City and, like Stengel, her credentials were flawless. She had seen it all, from John McGraw to Yogi Berra; she had sculpted Mickey Mantle and Whitey Ford in verse and imagery; she once even kept a pet alligator named Elston Howard.

She was a tiny beauty with braided white hair who lived in a storybook apartment off lower Fifth Avenue, surrounded by clay and glass animals and hundreds of books, and she confessed a strong favoritism toward the "precision" positions in baseball like first base, pitcher, and third base — to say nothing of catcher. She once wrote:

> It's a pitcher's battle all the way — a duel —
> a catcher's, as, with cruel
>   puma paw, Elston Howard lumbers lightly back
>   to plate.

Once she portrayed the youthful Mickey Mantle in these words:

> "Mickey, leaping like the devil" — why
>   gild it, although deer sound better —
> snares what was speeding towards its treetop nest,
>   one-handing the souvenir-to-be
>   meant to be caught by you or me.

And, as for Whitey Ford:

> like Whitey's three kinds of pitch and prediagnosis
>   with pick-off psychosis.

Realizing the precise fantasies of this mind, Burke immediately dashed off a telegram to Miss Moore, inviting her to throw out the first ball of the season. He was not left waiting long. Flashing to her desk like a shortstop starting a double play ("a cruel thing, but necessary"), she whipped back a letter that said:

"I am impetuous. Can you imagine my delaying a moment upon receiving your telegram before writing you that I shall excitedly appear at Yankee Stadium on April 9th, even if I have not the best arm in baseball."

A couple of weeks later, while the Yankees were still in Florida trying to improve their own arms, she completed the double play. She startled the office staff by showing up at the side door of Yankee Stadium with her brother, half a dozen years younger than she.

"I wanted to see how far I had to throw it," she recalled later.

"I thought I'd have to pitch it from the mound. I was frightened by that. But they showed me the box seats where I was to sit, and gave me a ball and glove to take home."

She took the ball and glove home — "to practice," she said — and kept them in her bedroom as a reminder of the day she pitched a right-handed strike to Frank Fernandez, the young catcher, who not only caught it but also returned it to her with a gallant kiss on the cheek and later hit a home run that won the game.

Still, behind these soft moments the hard facts remained: Getting Marianne Moore into the ball park was a lot less challenging than getting a million and a half other fans into the ball park. All that Burke had to do to appreciate the problem was to scan page one of the *Wall Street Journal* later the next summer and read:

"Owning a sports team looks like fun, but it isn't always a gold mine. Contrary to public belief, many professional sports teams have proved to be less than a Bonanza for their owners, even in these days of juicy television contracts and widespread interest in sports. Owners are quick to blame their problems on fast-rising costs — especially players' salaries — but that's not the whole story."

"The fact is that some — maybe most — sports franchises aren't especially well managed," agreed Bill Veeck, who had owned the Chicago White Sox, Cleveland Indians, and St. Louis Browns before switching his flair to the Suffolk Downs Race Track near Boston. "Sensible, successful businessmen have been known to change once they become club owners. They do things they wouldn't dream of doing with the businesses that made them successful."

At that moment, nine of the twenty-four big-league baseball teams were in the red, seven of the fourteen clubs in the National Basketball Association were losing money, four of the ten teams in the American Football League were facing deficits, and several members of the National Football League were thrashing about despite the fact that their stadiums were 90 per cent filled.

"Some pro teams are quite well run, of course," conceded the *Wall Street Journal,* as though ranking conglomerates or petroleum companies. "The baseball Los Angeles Dodgers, Houston Astros and New York Yankees get generally high marks, as do the football Dallas Cowboys and Cleveland Browns, and the N.B.A. Milwaukee Bucks and Philadelphia 76ers, among others.

"No one is shedding too many tears for the rest because pro team ownership contains fringe benefits that make it tough for even the least efficient owners to lose money in the long run. New owners can benefit from substantial depreciation write-offs, and owners of existing teams stand to split handsome bounties when their leagues admit new members, as they've done frequently of late. Enough rich sportsmen are interested in having a pro team of their own to keep pushing up the resale value of franchises."

Another reason was laid on the line by Robert E. Short, the Minneapolis trucking-company owner who paid almost $10,000,000 to buy the comatose Washington Senators. They didn't stay comatose long though. Short immediately enticed Ted Williams back into uniform as the manager, and Williams immediately began raising everybody's batting average and raising as much interest in the Senators as Vince Lombardi was raising in the Redskins in the fall.

"Sports-page identification helps my trucking business so much," Short conceded, "that the Senators will be worth the price if they just manage to break even." (They increased attendance 75 per cent — then Short signed Denny McLain and told Congress he might go bankrupt.)

Some owners thought "identification" did not have to come wrapped in dollar signs — like Veeck, who said the reason people bought sports teams was "ego satisfaction, the prestige of associating with athletes and being on the inside of all the strategy talk before the big game." Or, suggested Gerald and Allan Phipps after shelling out $2,000,000 to keep the Denver Broncos in the football business: "It's our contribution to making Denver a complete city. The football team is as necessary to a community as libraries, museums, and a symphony orchestra."

Still, even museums and symphony orchestras were running out of cash in the great, inflated days of big recreation. And even baseball teams like the Oakland Athletics turned threadbare in a hurry despite the assets of a new franchise, a 50,000-seat stadium, a twenty-three-year-old slugger named Reggie Jackson who hit home runs much of the summer of 1969 at a faster rate than Babe Ruth — and in 1971, a winning team led by pitching discovery Vida Blue.

Oakland, in fact, symbolized both the opportunities and the extravagances of sports in the nineteen sixties, and it soon played a leading role in a series of misadventures that sent baseball into the seventies surrounded by problems.

In the first place, Oakland had a reputation as a "tough" box-office town since vaudeville days. In the second place, it was situated across the bay from San Francisco, which had money as well as charm. And in the third place, the Athletics' baseball team was masterminded by Charles O. Finley, which some people felt would doom it in the first place. Even the *Wall Street Journal* ranked Finley "pro sports' most persistent owner-meddler," noting that he had fired seven managers in seven years at Kansas City and — which was perhaps his capital crime in Wall Street — had lost $3,000,000 in the process.

From his Chicago insurance office or his summer home in La Porte, Indiana, he ran the team in a stupendously detailed way, ordaining that the players should wear green-and-white uniforms on some days and golden uniforms on other days, or personally approving the advertisements for the daily scorecard, or charting the itinerary for the club's pet traveling mule. He once even ordered the players to ride out to their defensive positions on the backs of burros, judging that this would stir hilarious interest in the fans but misjudging the eventuality that it also would stir resentment in the players.

But Finley's number one misadventure arose in 1967, when he decided to move the Athletics from Kansas City, a strong baseball town, to Oakland, the "tough" box-office town. And he did it despite the fact that Kansas City's voters had recently approved a $100,000,000 bond issue that would include twin stadiums for baseball and football. He didn't know it at the time — and the other owners in the American League didn't know it, as they reluctantly went along with him — but he was invoking a "domino theory" that would shortly tumble things in the far corners of baseball.

The first reaction in the chain developed when Kansas City recoiled at his plan. The eleven other owners of teams in the league stood fast. But then they began to disperse when Senator Stuart Symington of Missouri threatened to strip baseball of its traditional immunity under the trust laws if the game abandoned Kansas City. That was a mule of a different color, especially since baseball had grown steadily sensitive during the sixties about its privileged status, an "umbrella" raised overhead in 1922 by Justice Oliver Wendell Holmes in a Supreme Court decision that placed the game outside the regulations on interstate commerce.

The owners in both leagues, in fact, had grown so sensitive on this issue that they had elected General Eckert as commissioner three years earlier. Eckert was a remote, sincere man who had little to recommend him for such a job except the fact that his rank, his position, his home, and his contacts all were rooted in Washington, which also was where the antitrust laws were rooted. By 1967, though, Eckert's days as the commissioner were numbered, just as the Athletics' days in Kansas City were numbered. And the owners were soon to replace him with Bowie Kuhn, the Wall Street lawyer who had even more training and more contacts for the legal pitfalls ahead. But right now, running scared, they decided to delay any showdown on the antitrust issue, and things rapidly twirled from bad to worse.

They decided to have their cake and let Finley eat it too. They voted to allow him to move west, placating Finley, but also voted to expand the league several years ahead of schedule, admitting a new team in Seattle and a new one in Kansas City, thereby placating Symington.

Everybody was placated now, except the National League, which had not intended to expand for several years either. But this was no time for interleague courtesy; the American League clambered ahead, Finley went west, two new clubs were added, and the National League bitterly followed suit, expanding to San Diego and Montreal in order to keep pace. But everybody soon found that dominoes can be a losing proposition.

Attendance at Oakland slipped from 837,466 (which wasn't enough) to 778,232 (which wasn't even respectable). Across the bay, the San Francisco Giants, who had opened the decade with 1,795,356 customers in 1960, closed it with 873,603. Down the coast, San Diego drew a disappearing 512,970. Up the coast, Seattle counted 677,944 heads. Back in Kansas City, the new team in town, the Royals, made it to 902,414. And in Montreal, where bonds for the new domed stadium became a political issue, the crowds reached 1,212,608, which was fewer than they drew in Houston or Minneapolis.

The people of Montreal got out their slide rules and calipers to measure the public's passion for baseball, which made its debut in Canada with international huzzahs before international distress began to creep into the picture. They found that 264,-000 different persons in Montreal had paid to see the Expos play that first season (while 270,000 came from out of town); the average local fan saw three games during the year, traveled eight miles to see them, and bought up 95 per cent of the available bleacher space and 59 per cent of the reserved space in Jarry

The Changing Landscape: New Baseball Stadiums in the Nineteen Sixties

Year Built	City and Stadium	Seats	Cost	Who paid
	NATIONAL LEAGUE			
1960	San Francisco Candlestick Park	42,500	$15,000,000	city
1962	Los Angeles Dodger Stadium	56,000	$15,000,000	private
1964	New York Shea Stadium	55,300	$25,000,000	city
1965	Houston Astrodome	44,500	$27,000,000	county
1966	Atlanta Atlanta Stadium	50,893	$18,000,000	city
1966	St. Louis Busch Memorial	49,500	$25,000,000	private
1969	San Diego San Diego Stadium	50,000	$27,000,000	city
1970	Cincinnati Riverfront Stadium	51,000	$45,000,000	city-county
1970	Pittsburgh Three Rivers Stadium	50,230	$28,000,000	city
1971	Philadelphia Veterans Stadium	50,000	$38,000,000	city
	AMERICAN LEAGUE			
1961	Minneapolis-St. Paul Metropolitan Stadium	45,914	$10,000,000	Twin Cities
1962	Washington R. F. Kennedy Stadium	45,016	$19,800,000	D.C.
1966	Anaheim Anaheim Stadium	43,200	$24,000,000	city
1968	Oakland Oak.–Alameda County Stadium	49,694	$30,000,000	county
1971	Kansas City —football stadium	75,000	$51,220,000	county
(1972)	—baseball stadium	42,000	(joint)	

Park, a onetime playground that had been hastily converted for the advent of the big leagues.

They even found out that fan mail had arrived from as far away as Prague and Japan. But since very few Czechoslovakians or Japanese paid taxes in Quebec, the jubilation was softened when a task force suggested to Prime Minister Pierre Trudeau that "full consideration be given to every means of financing sport, including a sports tax and a sports lottery."

That is to say, the great leisure-time activity of baseball had begun to creep into the halls of Parliament and Congress, while franchises sprang up and withered and while the new owners tried to steer a course between economic straits on one side and legal rocks on the other side. Bill Paley had warned Michael Burke wisely: He was getting into a maelstrom. And so was Bowie Kuhn, who took over as commissioner in February, 1969, just as the players threatened to strike and the senators threatened to rock the antitrust boat.

But, despite their best efforts and corporate brains, the trouble came pouring in anyway. The 600 players in the major leagues began to negotiate through Marvin Miller, the onetime economist for the United Steelworkers of America. The umpires won a collective-bargaining appeal to the National Labor Relations Board and formed a union. And in 1970, an oil-portrait painter named Curtis Charles Flood, who played center field for the St. Louis Cardinals, was traded to Philadelphia and replied by suing baseball for his "freedom."

• • •

Curt Flood was born in Houston on January 18, 1938, but was raised in Oakland, where he was the runt of the litter whenever he played sports. But he was an uncommon runt who overcame, or overlooked, the fact that he was short and skinny. And when he turned eighteen, he signed his first professional baseball contract not long after he had signed for his senior class ring at Oakland Technical High School.

He was in the minor leagues only two seasons, played three

games with the Cincinnati Reds, then was traded to the St. Louis Cardinals in 1958, five years after they had been bought by August Anheuser Busch Jr., in a kind of crusade to restore a piece of the city's social fabric. After that, Flood played twelve consecutive years, never played in fewer than 121 games a season, and became the most uncommon runt of the litter who ever played center field against the big boys.

He won the Golden Glove Award as the best defensive center fielder in the National League seven years in a row. He once played 226 games in a row without committing an error. And in 1966, he went the entire season — 160 games and 391 putouts — without dropping a ball.

It became one of the ironies of modern baseball that the 1968 World Series was decided when Jim Northrup of Detroit hit a long drive to center field in Busch Memorial Stadium and, while Gussie Busch and everybody else in St. Louis watched in disbelief, the little man with the golden glove misjudged the ball, slipped, fell down, and finally scrambled back while Northrup raced to third base, two Detroit runs scored, and an apocalyptic pall lowered over the Mississippi riverfront.

And yet, in the loser's locker room after the game, Tim McCarver stood in the midst of the emotional rubble and called out, with feeling: "Curt Flood, you're beautiful."

Curt Flood not only was beautiful, he was talented, and he had long since caught Busch's eye by the quality of his drawings, cartoons, and paintings. He even did one of Busch in his yachting regalia, and then the proud paterfamilias of the St. Louis Cardinals commissioned his own center fielder to portray the Busch children in oils. By then, Curt Flood was making $90,000 a year for catching the ball in center field, and not many artists had an ace in the hole like that one.

At the height of this renaissance, unfortunately, the Cardinals fell apart at the seams. They had won the pennant and World Series in 1964 after Busch had written off the season as a loss.

Then they plunged into sixth place after their manager, Johnny Keane, had switched to the Yankees. Then they revived, won two more pennants, let the 1968 World Series slip from their grasp at the last moment, and fell into fourth place in 1969 while the New York Mets climbed over the debris to the top.

Busch, bereaved and outraged, especially since his baseball payroll had gone past the million-dollar mark, responded by trading away the rascals. Within weeks, Vada Pinson went to Cleveland while Flood, McCarver, and Joe Hoerner went to Philadelphia. But, more important, Flood went to his lawyer. He owned a photo gallery and painting studio in St. Louis and wasn't about to be "sold" anywhere else. Not without a quid pro quo. The owners might have Oliver Wendell Holmes and his "umbrella" decision; Curt Flood had Arthur J. Goldberg, onetime Associate Justice of the Supreme Court, onetime Ambassador to the United Nations. The boat was being royally rocked.

The "reserve clause" actually wasn't a clause at all; it wasn't even a paragraph. It was a series of interlocking agreements and understandings that "kept order" among the teams in organized baseball — meaning the major and minor leagues and their allied leagues in Mexico, South America, and Japan. When a player signed a contract, he was agreeing to terms for one year, but beyond that he was agreeing to abide by the "reserve clause" in all its meandering meanings. Chiefly, he was agreeing that his services were "reserved" for the following year as well. He could quit baseball or he could be traded to another club (along with his reserve clause), but he could not simply sell his services to the highest bidder.

The idea was not peculiar to baseball, but the small print was. In football, a player signed a contract for one year normally, then he could "play out" his option during the following year. After that, he was a free agent. True, if he pulled up stakes and switched teams, his new employer owed his old employer some compensation; and, if they disagreed about precisely how much compensation, the issue was placed before the commissioner of pro football. In basketball, a player in the National Basketball Association might be "reserved" to one club, but he had an alternative — the American Basketball Association, which was happy during the late sixties to finance any NBA man's trip out of town.

But in baseball, the reserve clause was endowed with tradition, a fear of disarray, and half a century of favorable legal skirmishes.

In 1922, the Supreme Court ruled that baseball was neither interstate nor commerce and that it did not belong under the restraints of the antitrust laws. The score was 8 to 0, a shutout.

In 1949, the Second Circuit Court of Appeals (one step below the Supreme Court) ruled that baseball seemed more interstate and more commerce — but the case was settled out of court and never was passed up to the Supreme Court for review. This case involved a New York Giant outfielder named Danny Gardella who in 1946 skipped to the Mexican League, which was bent on raiding forays across the border. Gardella had not signed his contract with the Giants that year, but was punished anyway because he had "jumped" outside organized baseball. He was blacklisted, later sued for the right to recross the baseball border, asked $300,000 in damages — and settled for something like $65,000.

In 1953, a case did reach the Supreme Court and this time the "umbrella" of 1922 survived, but without a direct confrontation. The prime mover was a New York Yankee farmhand named George Toolson, a pitcher who had been declared "ineligible" after refusing to report to Binghamton in 1950. The nine justices — exactly enough for a baseball team — ruled that the 1922 decision should not be overturned because "this business has been left for thirty years to develop, on the understanding that it was not subject to existing antitrust legislation."

The court commented, though, that it was not reconsidering the basic issues and lobbed the ball to Congress, saying: "If there are evils in this field which now warrant application to it of the antitrust laws, it should be by legislation." The score was 7 to 2, no longer a shutout.

In 1955, the Supreme Court ruled that boxing did come under the antitrust laws and rejected any motion that the Toolson case should imply exemption for all sports. And in 1957, it ruled that professional football was subject to the antitrust laws and again noted that the 1922 "umbrella" protected only baseball. If that seemed unfair, the court suggested, let Congress get into the act.

Since World War II, in fact, Congress had tried to get into the act but had never quite made it. Numerous bills were introduced — some giving all sports the protection that baseball enjoyed, some putting baseball under the same laws as everybody else, some applying the antitrust laws to the building of ball parks but not the "reserving" of ballplayers. Some got past the House, some got past the Senate. None ever got into the White House.

However, as the seventies began — and as the money in sports began to resemble the money in some fairly big businesses — new threats were made to apply the trust laws to all sports, whether played with laced footballs, red-white-and-blue basketballs, or stitched baseballs. And the threat usually sent the new money men of sports rushing to their lawyers.

This was the situation when Curt Flood put down his fielder's mitt and his paintbrushes and wheeled in Arthur Goldberg. As he did, baseball happened to be fending off several other threats to its serenity — umpires going before the NLRB, players negotiating for better working conditions, cities suing to keep franchises. And there in the middle of the muddle stood the runt of the litter, beautiful Curt Flood.

The little center fielder received some flank support from several directions as he brought suit. Unusual support — from

Richie Allen's mother and from a seventy-three-year-old one-time pitcher named Milton Gaston.

Mrs. Allen supplied a footnote to the Great Case when her son was traded to St. Louis in exchange for Flood. It wasn't that Richie wouldn't go along with the trade; he just wouldn't go along at the price posted. And for weeks, he exchanged volleys with the Cardinals through a lawyer, while Flood submitted briefs and Gussie Busch writhed through a difficult spring training, muttering: "I don't understand what's happening in this great country of ours anymore."

What was happening was that Richie didn't want to cut his mother off the payroll just because of the trade. She had ranked as one of his "fringe benefits" in his Philadelphia contract and — while the Cardinals were willing to argue with him over the relative merits of $90,000 a year versus $150,000 a season — they didn't know quite what to do about his fringe benefits.

The stalemate was intensified early in March when the Cardinals decided to invoke the "reserve clause" against Allen, who sometimes had been A.W.O.L. from games with the Phillies but who had not even appeared yet with the Cardinals. It was as though the Redbirds had tossed a final salute to Curt Flood: invoking the very thing that Flood was challenging at that precise moment in the courts. In Allen's case, the appropriate clause was 10–A, giving the team the right to order a player to spring training by March 11 whether he had signed his contract or not. He could not be paid less than 80 per cent of his previous contract, but otherwise he was considered a card-carrying employee. He didn't even have to sign anything; he already had done that the year before.

When the Cardinals sent Richie Allen his summons to the "command performance," there was no immediate response. But shortly thereafter, the lawyers smoothed things over and Richie packed his bags and headed for St. Petersburg, where the Cardinals had conducted spring training for two generations. He was met at the Tampa Airport by a small delegation of deputies, who drove him to St. Petersburg. And there, pacing a bit nervously outside the red door marked "Cardinals" at Al Lang Field, waited Bing Devine.

The station wagon pulled up, the delegation uncoiled, and Richie strolled up the sidewalk in glory: a cocoa-brown Edwardian suit, orange shirt, two-tone brown cowboy boots, magnificently furry lamb-chop sideburns. This was the new generation confronting the old, the "mod" generation and the establishment, employee sizing up employer. Richie Allen, two weeks late for meeting the new boss, shrugged off the ceremonial aspects of the occasion, to say nothing of the financial aspects after long weeks of haggling through lawyers over $100,000 plus fringe benefits. He marched up the sidewalk, thrust out his hand to Devine and said smartly: "Richie Allen."

A few moments later, while television cameras whirred and Bing Devine squirmed a trifle, the new boy on the block got down to brass tacks. As for himself, he said, he didn't need seven weeks of spring training anyway — three was plenty — and the only argument over money had involved security for his mother. As for Curt Flood, he said: "My hat's off to him. There's one hundred sixty pounds of all man. Maybe what he's doing will help one of my kids someday."

A few miles north across Tampa Bay, Flood was picking up some flank support from Milton Gaston, deputy sheriff of Hillsborough County. He was a former pitcher for the St. Louis Browns and Boston Red Sox, who had thrown four of the sixty home-run pitches whacked by Babe Ruth in 1927, and he once was a teammate of a young shortstop named Joe Cronin. On this sunny day, though, Milton Gaston waited in the entrance of the International Inn. The twelve owners of the American League teams were arriving to decide what in the world to do about the collapsing Seattle franchise, a victim of the chain reaction touched off three years earlier by Charles Finley's switch from Kansas City to Oakland.

The National League had its Curt Flood; the American

League had its Seattle. And every time the owners got together
to vote on moving the team to Milwaukee (which had been
abandoned four years before by the National League), somebody would threaten an antitrust suit and suddenly Seattle
sounded like Waterloo. Just the day before, Senator Warren G.
Magnuson of Washington had warned that if Seattle were vacated, he would ask Congress to end baseball's protection under
the trust laws. So the old bugaboo was very much in the owners'
minds as they approached the hotel and as Milton Gaston
stepped forward, greeted his old teammate Joe Cronin, now the
president of the American League, and pressed a subpoena into
his extended right hand.

The subpoena had been obtained by a Seattle lawyer and
baseball fan, who paid $775 for box seats for the 1970 season. It
had been signed at eight o'clock that morning in the 13th Circuit
Court of Florida by State Judge James D. Bruton, who re-
marked: "If I paid seven hundred seventy-five dollars for tickets,
I know I wouldn't want them to be running off somewhere
else."

The judge thereupon ordered the owners not to make any
decision on transferring the Seattle team until arguments had
been heard on his temporary injunction. But even while the
owners were trying to dodge Joe Cronin's old teammate in the
lobby, more legal trouble lurked outside their meeting room.
There they were confronted by Jerry R. McNaul, an assistant
attorney general of the state of Washington, who also handed
out show-cause orders. Those were in connection with an $82,-
000,000 suit filed by the city of Seattle and the state, both trying
to prevent any transfer of the club and both aiming where it
would hurt the most.

Once past the process servers, the owners and Cronin huddled
with Bowie Kuhn and a contingent of lawyers. The commissioner, who had been a high-priced lawyer himself, left the
meeting a short time later, saying cautiously: "I am a friend of

The Circus Maximus: Sports in the twentieth century commanded more and more of the public's mind and heart, and arms and legs, and pocketbooks. The place is Lawrence, Kansas, and the occasion is the Kansas-Syracuse football game. But it could have been any other teams in any other sport in any other stadium on any other afternoon in the nineteen sixties.

Red Grange turned professional hours after his final college game for the University of Illinois in 1924 and during the next two weeks put the National Football League on the map — and, what was more important at the time, put it in business.

Two generations, one depression, and one world war later, another running back named O. J. Simpson of the University of Southern California led the new wave of athletes into the business that Grange had helped to establish. Simpson, an instant millionaire, came with cheering mobs and cheering lawyers.

George Halas, who was Red Grange's first employer, did it all for the Chicago Bears in the pioneer days when "professional football" did not necessarily mean you got paid. He sold tickets, wrote publicity releases, answered the telephone, and also coached the team for half a century.

The Green Bay Packers, who used to pass the hat behind Hagemeister's Brewery on Sunday afternoon, grew in wisdom and wealth under Vince Lombardi. He was a severe man whose life built to moments like these: Don Chandler's field goal beats the Baltimore Colts in the 1965 play-off game.

Truce: Pete Rozelle is flanked by Tex Schramm of the Dallas Cowboys and Lamar Hunt of the Kansas City Chiefs as he announces the merger of the warring football leagues in 1970. Not shown are the bankrolls that the merger saved. Anyway, nobody bothered to pass the hat on Sunday afternoon anymore.

In the age of electronics, Frankie Albert gets wired for sound as coach of the San Francisco Forty-niners. He is making a long-distance call to an assistant coach spying from the press box. Next came closed-circuit TV, game films, and computerized tickets.

You would have to get up early in the morning to beat either Johnny Longden or Willie Shoemaker, both of whom rode more than 6000 winners. The Shoe's mounts won $40,000,000 in purses, making the little man a big capitalist, maybe the biggest in sports.

Everybody is looking up the track for Sir Barton as Man o' War crosses the line in 1920 en route to a legend. Styles were different then, but a $2 ticket still cost $2.

Fifty years later, the great colt Nijinsky is led into the winner's circle after the 191st Epsom Derby by his owner, Charles Engelhard, a man who made a fortune in minerals and who cheerfully spent part of it on horses.

The sun never sets on the sport of kings, not as long as the betting public can find its way to the pari-mutuel window, off-track counter, or old-fashioned bookie. At Aqueduct in New York, a thoroughbred and his shadow . . . and, in another season, his stablemates drive for home through the snowflakes.

But the days of aristocrats in sports seem numbered as taxes, write-offs, depreciation allowances, and inflation bring corporations onto the scene. Dan Topping, the Old Guard, and Michael Burke, the New Guard, both look uneasy as CBS buys the New York Yankees and hastens the changing of the guard.

Joan Whitney Payson, one of the last true aristocrats of professional sports, links two worlds as the mistress of the Greentree Stable and the New York Mets. At Belmont Park, she keeps one eye on her colts and one ear on her baseball team.

. . and domed stadiums put a roof, but not a lid, on major-league sports.
Rusty Staub tests Houston's Astrodome before its official opening in 1965,
and this is how history looks to the catcher.

In the good old days, the faithful would line up outside Ebbets Field in Brooklyn for a wooden seat in the sun . . .

. . . and in the newer days, they still would line up outside the Robert F. Kennedy Stadium in Washington for a cushioned seat in the shade . . .

. . . but either way, once inside, they focused their attention and their money on the same old ball game.

He had help too. His chief counsel was Arthur J. Goldberg, former Justice of the Supreme Court and former Ambassador to the United Nations, who checks signals with his client on a park bench in New York.

Curt Flood, who made baseball history playing center field with the St. Louis Cardinals, made legal history by *not* playing center field with the Philadelphia Phillies. Instead, he sued for $1,000,000, sat out one season, then returned briefly with the Washington Senators — his eye firmly on the small print in the disputed contract.

Millionaires at work: Arnold Palmer and Jack
Nicklaus leave the eighteenth green at Ligonier,
Pennsylvania, where they finished the National
Four-Ball Tournament at ten under par. They
dealt in low scores and high purses.

Arnie and his army follow the pied piper of professional golf, Joe Dey, the sportswriter who became the commissioner of the touring pros after their "revolt" over control of the circuit and its $7,000,000 in prizes.

Laver's fellow Australian, Margaret Smith Court, receives *her* silverware from Princess Margaret after defeating Billie Jean King in a 14-12, 11-9 marathon.

The Queen of England and the king of the tennis court: Elizabeth II presents the silverware to Rod Laver at Wimbledon.

But when tennis players began collecting checks as well as trophies, the old pro Pancho Gonzales was first in line. The check reads $10,000, but his real reward comes from the rapturous look on his wife's face after he upset Laver in Madison Square Garden in five sets. And Pancho was 41 years old.

He bats left-handed, he sticks out his tongue, he lunges with hair flying, but Laver continues as the best tennis player around as the game grows into big business.

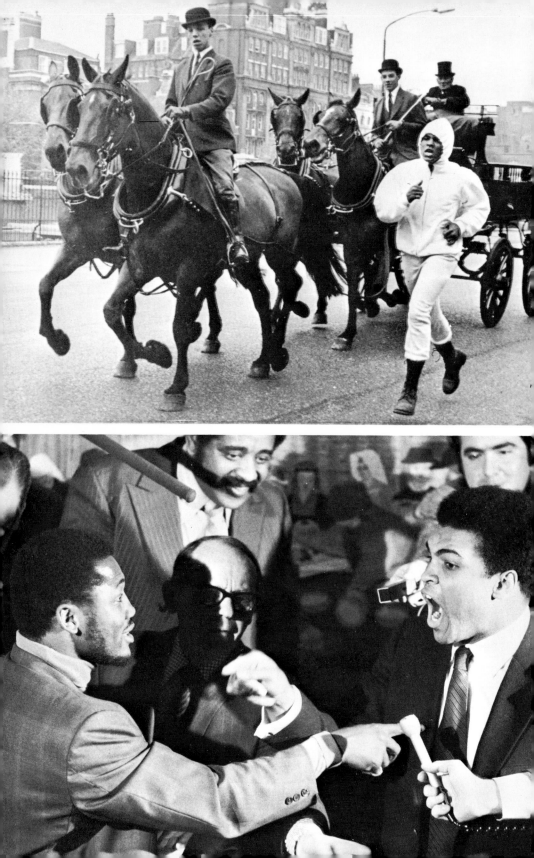

Man with a check for $2,500,000.

Once the fog lifted, there was Cassius Clay jogging through London town training to defend his heavyweight title against Henry Cooper while the four-horse carriage rolls past with bowlers, top hats, and memories.

Back home now as Muhammad Ali, back to work now after a three-year layoff, the former champion is still a man of many words. And he imparts a few to Joe Frazier as they lay the verbal groundwork for their "fight of the century" in 1971.

The student most likely to succeed in the graduating
class at UCLA in 1969: Lew Alcindor . . .

. . . the only undergraduate in the world that spring who became a millionaire with one stroke of the pen. The Milwaukee Bucks picked up the tab, and Alcindor thereupon picked up the Milwaukee Bucks and *his* million bucks on the basketball court.

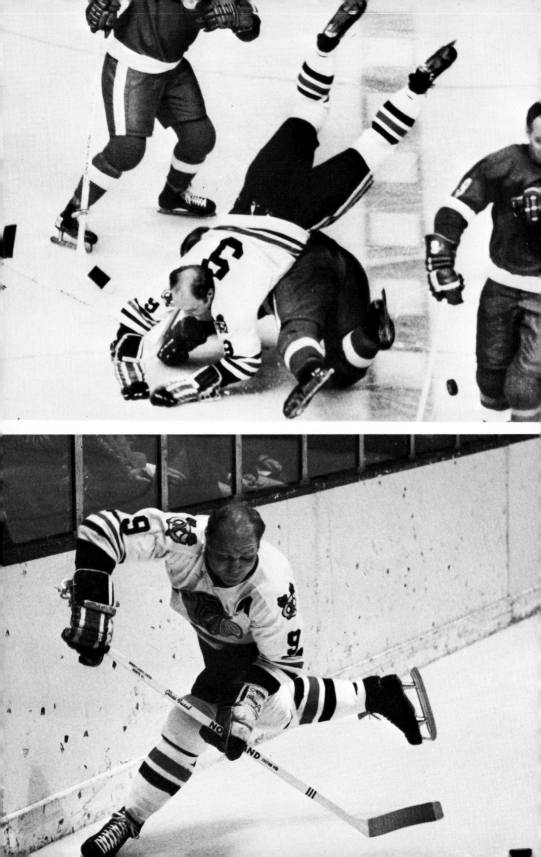

The spoils of victory go to Phil Esposito and Bobby Orr of the Boston Bruins, who follow Hull into the countinghouses of hockey. Clarence Campbell, President of the National Hockey League, bestows the blessing and the treasure.

Man at work: That's Bobby Hull, hockey's first capitalist, flying over Ron Harris of Detroit while Gordie Howe skates clear.

Grace under pressure in a Chicago Black Hawks uniform: number nine, Hull.

Sammy Davis Jr. knee-high to a fortune. The fortune belongs to Wilt Chamberlain, who will laugh all the way to the bank as soon as they finish this bit of slapstick for the "Laugh-In" television show.

Football players, too, found gold in them thar hills of the entertainment business. Joe Namath rehearsing for the big scene: quickest release in pro football, slowest draw in Hollywood.

A happier Joe Willie and a radiant Mickey Mantle at a party celebrating the anniversary of the opening of their employment agency.

Frank Beard, who won this tournament, and Arnold Palmer, who blazed the way for all golfers by winning many more, beam in the presence of the All-American dollar.

both locales. In the long run, Seattle is a fine locale, but it has critical problems right now."

Then out of the meeting came Roy Hamey, the Yankee official who had been appointed temporary overseer of the Seattle franchise by the league, and he said simply: "Money is the whole problem. Somebody's got to take the loss — the six hundred fifty thousand dollars the clubs are chipping in now could grow to two million dollars in a year."

They were engulfed by dollar signs all right. Seattle had lost something like $850,000 that first season and stood to triple the red ink in 1970. The club even was in danger of being evicted from its training headquarters in Arizona, where the neighboring Chicago Cubs laid the facts right on the line:

In 1969 the Cubs had played before 1,674,993 fans in Wrigley Field. Receipts totaled $3,338,715. Concessions brought $858,-770. Revenue from radio, television, and renting the stadium to the Chicago Bears for football amounted to $1,076,553. Expenses — salaries, the farm system, free-agent bonuses, traveling, maintenance of the ball park, and so on — totaled $4,364,939. Overall, the Cubs showed a profit of $909,099.

"If it hadn't been for television," a club official reported, "if we had counted baseball operations strictly, we'd have had a loss of $167,454."

"We play baseball," said another baseball man, generalizing the problem, "just to sell peanuts, beer, and pop."

Not everybody would have agreed with that economic analysis probably. Not Milton Gaston, the pitcher-turned-process-server; not Michael Burke, who had parachuted behind enemy lines as a spy in World War II and who now accepted one of Milton Gaston's subpoenas without a struggle. Maybe Bill Paley had been right; it was one unholy mound of aggravation.

Two weeks later, five days before the start of the season, the Seattle franchise was declared bankrupt and the long-suffering people of Milwaukee pounced back into baseball. Nobody was quite sure why *they* would want to go through all that aggravation again either. But there they were, four years after they had been abandoned for Atlanta, with new uniforms, new ticket plans, new TV sponsors, new parking lots — and a new league.

It was enough to make Burke go off quoting Kipling, or maybe even Marianne Moore. He had enough trouble in his own back yard, though, without getting enmeshed in the Seattle-to-Milwaukee switch. Despite a "five-year plan" of rebuilding, his Yankees were still drawing only 50 per cent of the customers to their stadium in the Bronx that the Mets were drawing to their stadium in Queens. The Yankees could count on $1,500,-000 in broadcast rights, which was the most in the American League; but the Mets could count on $1,250,000 in the National League, and the Los Angeles Dodgers — enjoying the best of both possible worlds — were making $1,800,000 on *their* rights and were a runaway success at the gate besides.

The whole thing was a little incongruous. The Yankees, who once owned New York, now owned a fifty-year-old stadium that would cost a fortune to replace; the Mets, new and successful, rented a gleaming modern stadium from the city. The Yankees, owned by CBS, depended for part of their TV income on NBC, which in 1971 was finishing a three-year, $52,000,000 contract to carry baseball games, and which was starting a four-year contract in 1972. The Yankees, apparently blocked out of Shea Stadium because the Mets held a veto, then wheedled Mayor Lindsay into a $24,000,000 package of municipal improvements — just as Lindsay was crying "crisis" on things like schools and welfare.

On the sidelines, the philosophy was supplied by Ron Taylor, who had outpitched the Yankees that October afternoon when Burke saw his first World Series as an investor. Taylor had problems of his own, like keeping his job at the age of thirty-two and building up his pension potential at the age of fifty, and while the baseball lawyers bore down on the big problems, he bore down on his own problems. After all, it was Kipling's flip of the coin that had put him there.

"If you can keep your head when all about you are losing theirs and blaming it on you . . ." he said, applying the poet to the baseball business in the nineteen seventies.

"Emerson said," he added, wheeling a howitzer into line, "that on the debris of our despair, we build character."

7

Curtis C. Flood vs.
Bowie K. Kuhn et al.

JUDGE IRVING BEN COOPER called the case to trial at ten o'clock in the morning on May 19, 1970, in the United States Courthouse on Foley Square in lower Manhattan. On the docket it was listed as "70 Civil 202: Curtis C. Flood, plaintiff, vs. Bowie K. Kuhn, individually and as Commissioner of Baseball, *et al.*, defendants."

The *et al.*, it developed, included all the high brass and all the corporations at the top of the superstructure known as the major leagues. Specifically, in the nonsporting words of the trial record: Charles S. Feeney, individually and as President of the National League of Professional Baseball Clubs; Joseph E. Cronin, individually and as President of the American League of Professional Baseball Clubs; Atlanta Braves, Inc.; Chicago National League Ball Club; the Cincinnati Reds, Inc.; The Houston Sports Association; Los Angeles Dodgers, Inc.; Montreal Baseball Club, Ltd.; Metropolitan Baseball Club, Inc.; Philadelphia National League Club; Pittsburgh Athletic Co., Inc.; St. Louis National Baseball Club, Inc.; San Diego Padres; San Francisco Giants' Baseball Club; Baltimore Baseball Club, Inc.; Boston Red Sox; Cleveland Indians, Inc.; Detroit Baseball Club; New York Yankees, Inc.; the Washington Senators, Inc.; Golden West Baseball Co.; Chicago White Sox; Kansas City Royals Baseball Club; Minnesota Twins, Inc.; Oakland Athletics; and Pacific Northwest Sports, Inc.

The legal minds going to bat for such a lineup seemed just as imposing and just as numerous.

For Curt Flood, the thirty-two-year-old outfielder who was merely challenging the entire modus operandi of the national pastime on that morning in May: the firm of Paul, Weiss, Goldberg, Rifkind, Wharton & Garrison, Esqs., of 345 Park Avenue, plus Allan H. Zerman, Esq., of 225 South Meremac Avenue, Clayton, Missouri. The team was headed by Arthur J. Goldberg, former Secretary of Labor, former Ambassador to the United Nations, former Justice of the United States Supreme Court.

For Bowie Kuhn, himself a Wall Street lawyer, the defense team was built around Donovan Leisure Newton & Irvine, Esqs., of 2 Wall Street, plus Arnold & Porter, Esqs., of Washington, D.C.

For Joe Cronin, the old shortstop: Baker, Hostetler & Patterson, Esqs., of Cleveland. And "for all defendants except Bowie K. Kuhn," the pitching was supplied by Willkie Farr & Gallagher, Esqs., of 1 Chase Manhattan Plaza, New York, which took care of the defense of *et al.*

In the face of this staggering array of talent, Judge Cooper lost none of his own style or flair as he took the bench that spring morning to umpire the long-awaited challenge to the business of baseball and, by extension, of most professional sports. The defendant New York Yankees were preparing to play the defendant Baltimore Orioles uptown that day and the defendant St. Louis Cardinals, who had touched off the whole thing by trading Flood to the defendant Philadelphia Phillies, were due in the Astrodome to play the defendant Houston Astros.

But for everybody in the business, this was the whole ball game right here in Irving Ben Cooper's courtroom.

• • •

The Court: I take it that Justice Goldberg will be the spokesman for the plaintiff upon this trial.

Mr. Goldberg: Yes, Your Honor, I will be.

The Court: And Mr. [Mark F.] Hughes will be the spokesman for all the defendants except the defendant Kuhn.

Mr. Hughes: Your Honor, before I respond to that, may I also introduce to the Court and move his admission for the purposes of this trial, Mr. Alexander H. Hadden of the Ohio Bar and the Federal District Court Bar in Ohio, Mr. Hadden.

The Court: What can you say about him? We just don't admit anybody here, Mr. Hughes.

Mr. Hughes: Your Honor, that gives me the opportunity to —

The Court: The very fact that you sponsor him is a weighty credential in and of itself.

Mr. Hughes: Your Honor, he has been practicing law for as many years, I think, as I have. He has represented the American League for many, many years. He is a member of the firm of Baker, Hostetler & Patterson, a firm of some eminence in the City of Cleveland.

The Court: And as for his character, you vouch for him?

Mr. Hughes: I do.

The Court: Does he know anything about baseball?

Mr. Hughes: He knows a great deal more about baseball than I do.

The Court: Application granted. I am very glad to have him.

• • •

Judge Cooper: Call the first witness.

Mr. Goldberg: Mr. Curtis Flood, Your Honor. What is your occupation, Mr. Flood?

Mr. Flood: I am a professional baseball player. I play center field.

Q. — And when did you begin to play baseball?

A. — I started at age 9, of course, and I played Little League ball, sandlot ball, American Legion ball right into high school.

Q. — When did you graduate from high school?

A. — In 1968 — 1958, excuse me.

Q. — When did you first begin to play professional baseball?

A. — That was in 1958.

Q. — And how old were you when you signed your professional baseball contract, the first that you signed?

A. — I was 18.

Q. — When you mentioned '58 — and you relax on the stand — do you not really mean '56?

A. — Yes, sir. I am sorry.

Q. — And with whom did you sign your first contract in 1956?

A. — I signed with the Cincinnati Reds.

Q. — Now, you were presented with a contract at that time for signature? Did you read it?

A. — Well, not really. I knew very little about contracts and the provisions of them.

Q. — What salary did you sign for?

A. — It was $4,000.

Q. — Did that result from a negotiation with the Cincinnati Redlegs?

A. — Well, not really. There was a bonus rule at the time where if you received more than $4,000 there was sort of a penalty involved. You would have to stay on the roster of the parent club for at least one year. I forget the exact years. And $4,000 was the limit that I could sign for.

Q. — Now will you tell His Honor, Judge Cooper, your experience in your first year of professional baseball?

A. — Well, of course, I was with the Reds at the time, and they sent my contract on an option to High Point, North Carolina, where I played a full season — this was Class B — with the High Point ball club — in the Carolina League.

Q. — And when you were sent down to the High Point team, were you consulted about that transfer to this Class B team?

A. — No, sir, I was not.

Q. — Will you tell his Honor and others, the counsel, what type of year did you have in baseball terms?

A. — Well, I think I had a very good year. I hit .340, I led the league in everything except home runs that year. I think I hit 30 home runs that year as well.

Q. — That isn't bad, is it?

A. — That is a very good year.

Q. — Now, would you explain your living accommodations in High Point. How did you live, where did you live, how did you conduct your business activity in baseball during that year?

A. — Well, this is very difficult. Back in those days, they were just integrating all the high schools in Carolina, and it was particularly bad being a black ballplayer in Carolina. Of course, we lived separately. We were housed and we ate separately. We would go on a road trip and there would be times when we would stop, oh halfway, for dinner, we would get off the bus and, of course, the white fellows would get off the bus and go into a restaurant and eat a nice meal, and we would have to go around to the back and get our meals there.

• • •

Mr. Flood: [at the end of the 1957 season] I talked to the general manager of the Reds and he asked me if I would go to South America and learn to play the infield, and of course when they ask you to do something like that you are inclined to do it; and I did exactly that. I went to Venezuela to learn how to play the infield and, of course, this is where I learned my trade.

Mr. Goldberg: What kind of infielder were you?

A. — Terrible.

Q. — That is what you learned from your experience in playing in Venezuela?

A. — That I was an outfielder, yes.

Q. — Now, what happened to you then after you had the Venezuelan experience with respect to the future of your professional baseball career? Did you get notice as to what your future career and disposition would be?

A. — Well, of course, I was down there learning how to play the infield for the Reds and I received a telegram stating that I had been traded to the St. Louis Cardinals, and this was rather a surprising thing; after all, I had gone all the way to South America to learn how to play the infield for them, and to find out you are traded is rather shocking.

Q. — Were you consulted?

A. — No, sir.

. . .

Q. — And how much were you paid in 1958 [with the Cardinals]?

A. — I undoubtedly made the minimum salary then, which was approximately seven thousand.

Q. — [in 1959, 1960 and 1961] you made between seven and fifteen thousand during those early years? Do you recall the circumstances under which your salary was fixed?

A. — I would go into the general manager's office knowing full well I couldn't play any place else in the world and "negotiate for a better contract." *** Well, we would negotiate across his desk. I would state my statistics — that I hit a certain amount and I had so many RBI's, I had "X" amount of home runs, and I thought this merited a raise in salary.

Mr. Hughes: The record indicates that in 1961 Mr. Flood's salary was $12,500 with a bonus of $1,000 for signing his contract; in 1962 his salary was $16,000; in 1963 his salary was $17,500; in 1964, $23,000; 1965, $35,000; 1966, $45,000; 1967, $50,000; 1968, $72,000; 1969, $90,000.

Q. — Have you ever been fined by the Cardinals?

A. — Well, I was fined $250 by the general manager for missing a banquet last summer.

Q. — And why did you not appear at that promotional banquet? Those are customary in baseball to help the team?

A. — Well, I suffered an injury the day prior to the banquet — a spike wound five or six inches across my foot.

The Court: I am somewhat disappointed with that answer. I thought it was because he wanted to avoid the typical banquet food.

•   •   •

Q. — [cross-examination by Mr. Hughes] Are you prepared to sign a contract with Philadelphia for $90,000 to play?

A. — No, I'm not.

Q. — Are you ready and eager to play baseball now?

A. — Yes.

Q. — With whom do you want to play?

A. — The team that makes me the best offer.

•   •   •

[Marvin Miller, the Executive Director of the Major League Baseball Players Association, testifying]:

Paragraph 10 (a) of the Uniform Player's Contract is the one commonly referred to as the reserve clause. It actually is an option clause rather than a reserve clause. It provides that the club may tender a contract to a player on or before January 15th. For purposes of this discussion, it is the rest of that paragraph that is important.

It provides that if there is no agreement between the player and his club by March first next succeeding that January 15th, then the club may unilaterally renew last year's contract simply by advising the player with a notice in writing within ten days of March first. The club may place any salary figure it pleases in that contract renewal, except that it may not cut the player's salary by more than 20 per cent below the prior year.

Now, there is another rule which states that a player will not be allowed to play in a regular championship season unless he has signed a contract for the current year. This means literally that a player not in agreement with the terms offered him receives a notice within ten days of March first advising him that he is again under contract under a one-year renewal and if he wants to play he must put his signature to that document, which in effect gives another renewal right for the following year to the club to do the same thing.

So that into perpetuity, as long as the club is interested in exercising this option, the player has no say whatsoever in terms of what conditions he plays under, always bearing in mind he has the one alternative: He may decide to find a different way to make a living.

• • •

[On May 22, the economist Robert R. Nathan was called to the witness stand by the plaintiff and was examined by Jay Topkis.]

Mr. Nathan: From the economic point of view, the lack of an alternative set of opportunities for a ballplayer would tend to depress the wage level of the ballplayer in view of the fact that he has no opportunity to negotiate and bargain away alternative uses of the talents and services.

Mr. Topkis: Does the set of circumstances which we label with that term "reserve system" correspond or not to the conditions and circumstances which prevail in any other area of the American economy, as you have studied it?

Mr. Nathan: To my knowledge — and I have worked in a great many industries — I know first-hand of no parallel in any other general field or any other sector of activity where the economic relationships between employer and employees have anything like similar characteristics to what this reserve system provides.

Q. — Now, were there less full restraint on a player's mobility than exists under the reserve system, would you expect that the best players would tend to gravitate to the teams in a position to offer the highest wages by reason of their gate receipts or whatever other phenomena?

A. — I would not expect this without limitation. I don't

think that — and I think I know considerable about many industries in this country, and we find that in industries where there is freedom between employer and employee we do not find that all the top designers go to General Motors and nobody to Ford or Chrysler, or all the top men designers go to Hart, Schaffner & Marx or Botany 500 and nobody goes to the others.

There is an old saying in economics that we move from shirtsleeve to shirtsleeve in three generations, and what that means is that success tends to come to a firm or a family, but it doesn't last very long because others come in and pretty much displace them, and in a free system one finds that not many groups stay on top of the heap for very long.

• • •

[On May 27, Bowie Kuhn testified and was examined by Victor H. Kramer of the defense.]

Mr. Kuhn: Organized Baseball consists principally of the following: the office of the Commissioner of Baseball; the National League and the American League, the two major leagues; the National Association of Professional Baseball Leagues, commonly known as the minor leagues, which is run by an office in Columbus headed by President Phil Piton. These are essentially the basic structures within Organized Baseball as it exists in North America.

Mr. Kramer: About how many leagues are there that are members of the National Association of Professional Baseball Leagues?

A. — Today the National Association has 21 leagues in the United States, Mexico and Canada. There are four classifications. The first which I will give is the highest and going on down in terms of skill: the triple–A, four leagues; the double–A, eleven leagues — pardon me, three leagues; the A, eleven leagues; the Rookie League, three.

Q. — Mr. Kuhn, suppose that a major league club feels that it has no place for a particular player on its roster. Can it assign the player outright, or can it put him in the minor leagues without further ado?

A. — Yes — yes and no. There are — between 40 and 25 there is a difference of 15, and these players may not be carried during the season in excess of 25. Therefore, they are normally optioned out to the minor leagues.

Essentially, after three years of major league service, no player can be optioned out without the club going through the process of the so-called waiver rule, which is contained in Rule 10 of the Major League Rules, a rather complex rule essentially to guarantee that no player will be sent to the minor leagues who is desired at the waiver price, which is $20,000, by another major league club.***

Your Honor, throughout the history of baseball, one of the most important things we have tried and not always achieved, but tried to achieve, is the equality of team strength, so that within a league we would have good and exciting races. This is very important to baseball. It flourishes when you have it. It tends to pine when you don't. And anything that inhibits trades, again, *pro tanto,* has some effect on the ability of the assignment system to tend to equalize out team strength.

Mr. Kramer: Do not the antitrust laws require businessmen to compete as hard as they can and take as much business away from their rivals as they can short of monopolization?

Mr. Topkis: Objection, Your Honor, on the ground that this witness is being asked for a conclusion of law and while of course he is an attorney, and indeed a distinguished one, I don't think Your Honor needs advice from him on what the antitrust laws require.

The Court: You would be surprised. I learn all the time and I will take his answer.

Mr. Kuhn: The answer to that question is yes.

Mr. Kramer: With what other activities or types of business enterprises if any does Organized Baseball compete today?

A. — Baseball competes with a host of activities in the entertainment field. To enumerate some of these, it competes to a degree with other professional sports, notably professional hockey, professional basketball, professional football and to some extent professional soccer.

It competes, however, outside of the sports field with a great many other types of activity, such as horseracing, both flat and harness; the movie industry; all forms of outdoor recreation, which of course are at their peak during the warm months when baseball is played. This would be golf and tennis and camping and fishing, and the use of automobiles. The vast expansion of our highway systems and our automobile supply has put America on the roads, and not necessarily to ball parks.

• • •

[On June 4, the trial heard Ewing M. Kauffman, President of the Marion Laboratories and Pharmaceutical Company of Kansas City and recently the owner of the Kansas City Royals, making him the newest adventurer in the economics of professional baseball and the proprietor of a new institution: the baseball academy.]

Mr. Kauffman: I have always been interested in baseball, but as a child, due to economic circumstances, I only attended when the Knothole Gang was allowed in for 10 cents. But in 1965, when Marion Laboratories went public with our stock and I came into several millions of dollars, why I subsequently became interested when Kansas City was going to lose its major league franchise in the American League.

Mr. Topkis: Are you able to give the Court an estimate of what your aggregate investment in the baseball club is at this time?

Mr. Kauffman: Approximately nine and a half million dollars.*** I hired a doctor of research psychology from a technology research institute in Washington to analyze the physical attributes necessary to play baseball. He came up with the following qualifications:

First, speed of foot; second, fast reaction time — the nerve impulses from the eye to the brain and down to the hand; third, tremendous eyesight; and fourth, lateral movement of the body.

By this time the research grant was running so much that I hired this man full time to work for the Kansas City Royals, figuring it would be cheaper in the long run. He then developed tests to measure these attributes among players. He developed special machines to do it, and we have now tested 160-some players, minor and major leaguers, who are in the Kansas City organization.

We have definitely proved there is a clear line of demarcation between the minor leaguers and these attributes and the major leaguers. So it is my conclusion that a boy doesn't have to play baseball all his life to learn to be a tremendous major-league ballplayer. ***

As I got into baseball, I was amazed that so many of the ballplayers had so little financial knowledge. You may be familiar with some of the players who take bankruptcy making 40 thousand a year. I saw many of our major leaguers never handling their finances properly. So I wanted to teach them financial management.

This led to the next step, that a major-league ballplayer should be able to make public speeches and use English correctly. So we have tried this with a junior college and they receive ten or eleven credits per semester and take baseball in the afternoon and study at night.

We will finish in a matter of four months a million-and-a-half-dollar complex at Sarasota, Florida, where this [baseball] academy will be held. We can't test the high school graduates until they have graduated because of baseball laws, so we have tested a very limited number of players. But we have tested them and we have probably now our first two candidates, one being a track star who isn't quite fast enough to run track for college and get a scholarship; another being a basketball star who is too short to make the college basketball team.

Mr. Topkis: In your effort to build a pennant-winning club, have you ever made any cash offers to any other clubs to obtain player contracts?

A. — Yes, sir. Prior to the baseball season of 1969, I offered one club one million dollars for the contract of one player. Prior to this year, I offered one club owner three million dollars for any four players we might choose from his team.

Q. — Have either of those offers been accepted?

A. — No, sir.

•   •   •

[Ten weeks later, on August 12, Judge Cooper threw his judicial wisdom and his judicious language against the issues argued by these witnesses and these lawyers, and produced a 47-page document titled: "70 Civil 202: OPINION."

[In it, he related professional baseball to the economy — and to the world — surrounding it, in this way]:

On October 8, 1969, Curtis C. Flood, then a major league professional baseball player for the St. Louis Cardinals, was "traded," his contract transferred and assigned to another National League baseball club, the Philadelphia Phillies, as part of a multi-player transaction between the two clubs. At the time of the trade he was 32 years old, a veteran of twelve years' service with the Cardinals, co-captain of the team, and acknowledged to be a player of exceptional and proven baseball ability. Unhappy and disappointed, Flood was unwilling to play for Philadelphia, but forbidden by his contract and the rules of organized professional baseball from negotiating with any other ball club.

He initiated this action on January 16, 1970, against the twenty-four major league clubs comprising the American and National Leagues of organized baseball, their respective presidents, and against the Commissioner of Baseball asserting in four separate causes of action that baseball's "reserve system" is unlawful. Briefly stated, the reserve system, commonly referred to as the "reserve clause," consists of a number of baseball rules, regulations and uniform contract terms which together operate to bind a player to a ball club and restrict him to negotiating with that club only.

The first of plaintiff's four causes of action alleges that the reserve system constitutes a conspiracy among the defendants to boycott the plaintiff and to prevent him from playing baseball other than for the Philadelphia club in violation of the Sherman and Clayton Antitrust Acts.

His second and third causes of action are state law claims against eleven of the twenty-four defendants with jurisdiction based on diversity of citizenship. The second contends that the reserve system and defendants' practices thereunder constitute violations of the antitrust laws of New York, California and the other states where major league baseball is played and also violate state civil rights statutes, while the third contends that by the reserve system the defendants have restrained the plaintiff's "free exercise of playing professional baseball in New York, California and the several states in which defendants stage baseball games, in violation of the common law."

His fourth cause of action, directed against thirteen club defendants and alleging federal question and civil rights jurisdiction under 28 U.S.C. 1331 and 1343, asserts that the reserve system is a form of peonage and involuntary servitude in violation of the anti-peonage statutes, 42 U.S.C. 1994 and 18 U.S.C. 1581, and the Thirteenth Amendment and that it deprives him of "freedom of labor" in violation of the Norris LaGuardia Act, 29 U.S.C. 102–103.***

The trial record consists of some 2,000 pages of transcript and 56 exhibits. At the close of trial we reserved decision and fixed July 13, 1970, as the date for all posttrial memoranda.

We resolved to allow great liberality in the making of the total trial record to the end that each theory or contention advanced by the litigants would be amply covered and dealt with when all the proof was in.

•   •   •

Baseball and the Reserve System

Baseball is our national pastime and has been so for well over a century. Most of our interest in the sport as fans and spectators centers around professional or organized baseball. Organized baseball consists of the twenty-four major league teams which comprise the American and National Leagues and the various tiers of minor leagues which serve principally as training grounds for aspiring players. There exist no competitive professional teams in North America outside this structure. ***

At the center of this single, unified but stratified organization of baseball leagues is the reserve system, the essence of which has been in force for nearly one hundred years, almost the entire history of organized professional baseball. All teams in organized baseball agree to be bound by and enforce its strictures. It is perhaps the cornerstone of the present structure in that it insures team continuity and control of a supply of ballplayers. It is the heart of plaintiff's complaint.

From the standpoint of the professional baseball player, its effect is to deny him throughout his career freedom to choose his employer. Since 1965 each new player seeking to enter baseball has been exposed to a draft by the major and minor league clubs. If selected by a club in this semi-annual draft, he may bargain only with that club; should he wish not to play for that club, he must wait until the next draft is held.***

Plaintiff's witnesses in the main concede that some form of reserve on players is a necessary element of the organization of baseball as a league sport, but contend that the present all-embracing system is needlessly restrictive and offer various alternatives which in their view might loosen the bonds without sacrifice to the game. Plaintiff points to the present experience of other professional sports such as football, basketball and hockey, each of which survives relatively comfortably with a reserve system or organizational structure whose elements to a varying extent offer more freedom of choice and flexibility to its players.

The defendant clubs and Commissioner of Baseball, on the other hand, contend that the restrictions of the present system are reasonable and necessary to preserve the integrity of the game, maintain balanced competition and fan interest, and encourage continued investment in player development; that none of the alternatives suggested by plaintiff would be workable and still satisfy all three of these criteria; and that, upon comparison, baseball with its player safeguards is hardly more restrictive in its reserve system than are the other professional sports.

Defendants point to the instability in the early history of baseball and before the institution of the reserve system as evidence of the danger to be anticipated from any modification of its substance.

The Reserve System — a Necessity?

Prior to trial we gained the impression that there was a view, held by many, that baseball's reserve system had occasioned rampant abuse and that it should be abolished. We were struck by the fact, however, that the testimony at trial failed to support that criticism; we find no general or widespread disregard of the extremely important position the player occupies.

Clearly the preponderance of credible proof does not favor elimination of the reserve clause. With the sole exception of plaintiff himself, it shows that even plaintiff's witnesses do not contend that it is wholly undesirable; in fact, they regard substantial portions meretorious. It lends support to our view, expressed at another point in this opinion, that arbitration or negotiation would extract such troublesome fault as may exist in the present system and, preserving its necessary features, fashion the reserve clause so as to satisfy all parties.

Thus, former baseball star Jack (Jackie) Robinson responded to questioning in this regard as follows:

"Q. — Do I understand, however you interpret the expression 'reserve clause' or 'reserve system,' that your testimony is that you favor modification of that system? Is that right?

"A. (Robinson) — That is correct, I do.
"Q. — You don't favor destruction of the system, do you?
"A. — No, sir."

Witness Henry (Hank) Greenberg, also a former star player, was of the opinion:

"I think the players themselves, having functioned under the reserve system all these years, recognize the fact that the club has some equity in the players' services . . ."

And former club owner William Veeck declared:

"Well, the complete elimination of the reserve system or the reserve clause in contracts I think would not be helpful to baseball. I am afraid that if you suddenly terminated and there was no control of contracts by any club, that it could — and I say only could — result in some rather chaotic conditions. I feel, however, that this would not be the case if it were done in an orderly manner. *** I feel that there should be some kind of contractual relationship extending over a period of years . . . I don't mean it should stop and there should be nothing in its place."

The Federal Antitrust Claim

The Supreme Court held in 1922 that professional baseball was not within the scope of the federal antitrust laws because the exhibitions were purely state affairs to which the interstate transportation of players was merely incidental and were not trade or commerce in the ordinarily accepted use of the words.

When this question again reached the Supreme Court in 1953, intervening decisions appeared to have vitiated any holding that baseball was not subject to the antitrust laws because its activities either did not sufficiently affect or were not interstate commerce. See *Gardella* v. *Chandler* (1949). Without re-examining this underlying issue of interstate commerce, however, the Supreme Court reaffirmed its prior decision in *Federal Baseball* "so far as that decision determines that Congress had no intention of including the business of baseball within the scope of the federal antitrust laws." *Toolson* v. *New York Yankees*,

Inc. (1953).*** Subsequent decisions established that *Toolson* "was a narrow application of the rule of *stare decisis*" applicable only to baseball and to no other industry or professional sport.***

Subsequent to our determination of the motion for a preliminary injunction and to the trial of the issue herein, we were supported in these same views by the recent decision of our Circuit in *Salerno and Valentine* v. *American League of Professional Baseball Clubs et al.* (July 13, 1970). *Salerno* is unquestionably conclusive, at least at this level, of the Federal antitrust issues herein. The panel in an opinion by Judge Friendly unanimously held:

> "We freely acknowledge our belief that *Federal Baseball* was not one of Mr. Justice Holmes's happiest days, that the rationale of *Toolson* is extremely dubious and that, to use the Supreme Court's own adjectives, the distinction between baseball and other professional sports is 'unrealistic,' 'inconsistent' and 'illogical.' ***
>
> "However, putting aside instances where factual premises have all but vanished and a different principle might thus obtain, we continue to believe that the Supreme Court should retain the exclusive privilege of overruling its own decisions, save perhaps when opinions already delivered have created a near certainty that only the occasion is needed for pronouncement of the doom. While we would not fall out of our chairs with surprise at the news that *Federal Baseball* and *Toolson* had been overruled, we are not at all certain the Court is ready to give them a happy despatch."

Salerno mandates that plaintiff's Federal antitrust claim be denied. Since baseball remains exempt from the antitrust laws unless and until the Supreme Court or Congress holds to the contrary, we have no basis for proceeding to the underlying question of whether baseball's reserve system would or would not be deemed reasonable if it were in fact subject to antitrust regulation.

• • •

Involuntary Servitude Claim

Plaintiff's fourth cause of action asserts that the reserve system violates the Thirteenth Amendment and its enforcing legislation which similarly prohibits holding any person to "involuntary servitude."

A showing of compulsion is *** prerequisite to proof of involuntary servitude. Concededly, plaintiff is not compelled by law or statute to play baseball for Philadelphia. We recognize that, under the existing rules of baseball, by refusing to report to Philadelphia plaintiff is by his own act foreclosing himself from continuing a professional baseball career, a consequence to be deplored.

Nevertheless, he has the right to retire and to embark upon a different enterprise outside organized baseball. The financial loss he might thus sustain may affect his choice, but does not leave him with "no way to avoid continued service."

The Conflicts Are Reconcilable

Before concluding this opinion, we wish to unburden ourselves of two strong and related convictions which we took away from this trial.

First, despite the opposing positions of plaintiff and the Major League Baseball Players' Association on the one hand, the present management and club owners of organized baseball on the other, we found the witnesses appearing on behalf of both sides in the main credible and of high order; they have a genuine enthusiasm for baseball and with constancy have the best interests of the game at heart.

Second, we are convinced that the conflicts between the parties are not irreconcilable and that negotiations could produce an accommodation on the reserve system which would be eminently fair and equitable to all concerned — in essence, what is called for here is continuity without change.***

The Major League Baseball Players' Association, organized in 1954, has proved a particularly effective bargaining representative, obtaining since 1966 highly significant benefits for the players in such areas as pensions, life and disability insurance, health care, minimum salary, arbitration of grievances, expense allowances, maximum permissible salary cut, termination pay, representation at individual salary negotiations, negotiation of rule changes affecting player benefits or obligations, due process in player discipline.*** The National Labor Relations Board asserted jurisdiction over organized baseball in December, 1969.***

From the trial record and the sense of fair play demonstrated in the main by the witnesses on both sides, we are convinced that the reserve clause can be fashioned so as to find acceptance by player and club.

Far more complicated matters, accompanied by an exclusive self-centered concern and by seemingly hostile and irreconcilable attitudes, frequently find their way to amicable adjustment and the abandonment of court claims. Why not here — with the parties positive and reasonable men who are equally watchful over a common objective, the best interests of baseball?

Conclusion

For the first time in almost fifty years, opponents and proponents of the baseball reserve system have had to make their case on the merits and support it with proof in a court of law. As a long line of litigation and congressional inquiry attests, this system has often been a center of controversy and a source of friction between player and club. Existing and, as we see it, controlling law renders unnecessary any determination as to the fairness or reasonableness of this reserve system.

We are bound by the law as we find it and by our obligation to "call it as we see it."

[Flood, asserting his own obligation to call it as we see it, announced that he was appealing the decision to higher courts. Without him, St. Louis finished fourth in the National League's

Eastern Division and Philadelphia finished fifth. Then, shortly after the World Series, he was traded by Philadelphia to Washington and later signed a contract like the one he was challenging in court — only bigger. It guaranteed him $110,000. But within two months of the 1971 season, he suddenly quit the club and flew to Europe. Meanwhile, Richie Allen — the *casus belli* between St. Louis and Philadelphia in the historic trade — in turn was traded by St. Louis to Los Angeles, which seemed the final irony of all to Curtis C. Flood, to say nothing of Bowie K. Kuhn *et al.*]

8

Outdoors: The Greenbacking of America

"I'M NOT AN AGENT," Mark McCormack has said. "An agent is someone who books bands. I'm a manager. I'm a manager not only of people but of things, of concepts, ideas."

McCormack, the nonagent, is six-foot-two with eyes of blue, a fair complexion, a bachelor's degree in French from William and Mary College, a degree in law from Yale, a name on the door of the Cleveland law firm of Arter, Hadden, Wykoff & Van Duzer, a staff of twenty-seven in an office that also contains a blue-and-white eighteenth-century sofa, and a wife named Nancy, a graduate of Smith, who once observed: "He's either going seventy miles an hour or he's sound asleep."

McCormack has not booked a band since his days at Yale, Princeton, and William and Mary, and in fact there is no record that he ever booked one there either. But every spring he is booked himself as a guest lecturer at the Harvard Graduate School of Business, where he explains some of the "things, concepts and ideas" that have carried him from a $100-a-week insurance man to a millionaire in his first dozen years past college.

"Every time I pick up a magazine or Sunday newspaper," he wrote in 1969, surveying the recent years of change, "I am confronted with a review of the decade. It is probably a necessary business, this dragging us back to reflect upon what we have wrought, but it is not the most pleasant way to spend the expiring hours of the sixties. One cannot be much pleased with our achievements or avoid awareness of the erosion of our grand designs.

"I do not foresee, a decade or two from now, Americans looking back upon the sixties and shouting, 'Those were the days.' Wait one moment, though. There is one aspect of our human interests that must be ranked as a flaming success. Sport. And especially sport in the United States, where from a meager financial interest in 1960, television has turned on a golden flow that now exceeds $150,000,000 a year, where there is increasing leisure time and a fever to use it, where the enthusiasm and dedication devoted to play is unprecedented.

"Ask me about the sixties and I must answer that there has never been a time like it: not the era of Mary Queen of Scots or Tom Morris or Walter Hagen or Bobby Jones or Ben Hogan — none of them. This was the decade of Arnold Palmer."

Having expressed the sweep of modern history in terms that might be unmistakable to Arnold Toynbee as well as to Arnold Palmer, the energetic McCormack promptly returned, at about seventy miles an hour, to his more or less full-time job of serving as the agent — forgive us, Mark — as the *manager* of Arnold Palmer, Gary Player, Fran Tarkenton, and Denny McLain, to say nothing of Jeremy Flint, the British bridge genius, and Hank Ketcham, the creator of "Dennis the Menace."

His principal client, though, is Palmer — with Tony Jacklin and Player close behind, giving McCormack a pretty fair grip on talent at the peak of Olympus in golf, a sport he himself plays with eagerness and some skill and a business he manages with eagerness and staggering skill.

There are 10,000 golf courses in the United States, with 300 to 400 new ones being added every year and with 11,000,000 people shuffling or riding over them with woods and irons. Of the 11,000,000, about 25,000 make a living at it and most of those do it as "club pros." They give lessons, run the equipment shops, and lend tone to the fairways at the country clubs of

America, and they have done it during a time when country clubs figured large on the American social landscape.

But about 250 of the pros spend their careers on the road, traveling from course to course, competing for prize money that totaled $7,000,000 a year as the nineteen seventies began. And out of that handful of specialists — the ranking individualists and entrepreneurs of all professional sports — McCormack's clients became the ranking capitalists.

They are members of the Professional Golfers' Association of America, along with the thousands of local club pros. But the traveling prize-seekers, after a "revolt" in 1968, created their own Tournament Players Division of the PGA, with Joseph C. Dey Jr. as their commissioner and with Arnold Palmer as their household god.

"They are like strolling musicians or troubadours," says Dey, a good-looking, cultured, straight arrow of a man who once covered golf as a sportswriter in Philadelphia, sending back flashes from the course by messenger as he followed Bobby Jones at his best, stroke by stroke. "The pros in team sports always perform in much the same places. The pros in golf always perform in various places."

The traveling golfers do this by following the sun from the first week in January in places like Los Angeles, Phoenix, and Pebble Beach, work their way across the Southwest to Florida in other places like Tucson, Fort Worth, and Miami, then head up the East Coast to Greensboro and Augusta in April, on up to New England and the Midwest as the summer lengthens. In the autumn, they are back in California and Nevada, then return to the Southeast by the time the frost creeps into the greens along the Atlantic seaboard. They stick with it week after week, as though riding a carousel that never stops, although the pace slackens in October (because the World Series dominates the public's attention) and again in November (because football dominates the public's attention and the television networks' money).

They drive or fly along this circuit of forty-two major tournaments a year, plus some satellite tournaments that are held at the same time for less money at nearby sites for pros who don't qualify for the big ones. The average pro makes perhaps twenty-five tournaments a year and, if he doesn't survive the "cut" in one of them, he packs his gear and starts "down the road" to get in some early practice at the next week's site.

Some players have been doing this for a long time and making ends meet. As the seventies opened, Sam Snead was still at it after thirty-five years and Johnny Bulla had appeared in the Los Angeles Open *alone* thirty-five times. In the old days, they would make the tour together in Bulla's Ford and, if anybody doubted their resolution, Bulla often played both left-handed and right-handed when the money was on the table.

The gasoline for Bulla's Ford, as well as the jet fuel for Palmer's Lear a generation later, were financed out of pocket by the golfers themselves. The average tab for expenses on the tour comes to about $300 a week. With one tournament a week and maybe 250 pros trying to get into it, that means the boys are spending $75,000 among them for total prize money of $100,-000 to $250,000. Or, if the prize money totals only $50,000, they still invest that $75,000 trying to win it.

Worse, not all the players get into all the tournaments, $300 weekly tabs or not. The typical tournament has room for 144 players, and probably twice as many try to qualify. Then, after the first thirty-six holes, the lucky 144 are reduced to 70 survivors. The others are "cut." They pay their caddies and hotel and laundry bills and head down the road. And as if that weren't tough enough economics, everybody pays to get into the tournament in the first place — $1 for every $1000 of prize money being offered, with a maximum entry fee of $50.

"The emphasis," observed Joe Dey, "is always on first place. To wit: twenty per cent of the purse goes to the winner, eleven per cent to second place and so on. And the last twenty finishers

— meaning number fifty-one in the field through number seventy — share four per cent of the prize money. Under that formula, in a big-payoff tournament like the Dow Jones Open with total prizes of three hundred thousand dollars, the winner gets a check for sixty thousand dollars."

"If a pro wins two or three tournaments," he added, in a nifty little understatement, "it's a good year. Once Frank Beard was right up at the top in total money for one year and he hadn't won a single tournament. In nineteen sixty-eight, on the other hand, Billy Casper took six first places, which was phenomenal, and won two hundred five thousand one hundred sixty-eight dollars, which was phenomenal too. In nineteen sixty, before the purses began to bulge, Arnold Palmer won eight tournaments and took home seventy-five thousand two hundred sixty-two dollars.

"No sport has a bigger field, and you don't have the same seventy golfers surviving the cut each week and getting a piece of

---

The Golf Gold Rush

Leading Money Winners In
The Decade of the Sixties

1.	Arnold Palmer	$1,388,619
2.	Jack Nicklaus	971,816
3.	Billy Casper	915,202
4.	Julius Boros	575,795
5.	Gary Player	569,188
6.	Frank Beard	528,697
7.	Gene Littler	527,795
8.	Doug Sanders	520,137
9.	Dan Sikes	458,833
10.	Don January	397,190

---

the pie. This is a game of repeating, of consistency. A very subjective game, the most subjective except maybe for trapshooting.
Or crapshooting. You're not reacting to what somebody else
has done. You're on your own, and maybe twenty pros survive
most of the cuts each week, and they're the hard core of the
whole sport."

To make certain that the hard core doesn't take the line of
least resistance and set up a profit-sharing pool of prize money,
Rule VI–B of the "Tournament Regulations and Bylaws" puts
it in plain English: "A contestant shall not have any financial
interest, either direct or indirect, in the performance or the
tournament winnings of another contestant." That is, single file
at the pay window, please.

With the tournament fields growing bigger and the odds
growing longer, why do adult athletes spend their productive
years fighting themselves and the mathematical devil known as
"par" — to say nothing of fighting the bustling galleries and the
hordes of sharp new competitors reaching the scene every season? For the same reason Willie Sutton offered when asked why
he robbed banks: Because that's where the money is. And yet,
the rewards of playing professional golf have lagged well behind
the rewards of professional bank-heisting.

In 1934, Paul Runyan made only $6767 for a year on the
links. As late as 1940, Ben Hogan was being acclaimed as the
leading money-winner of the tour, and was being paid only
$10,655. And it wasn't until 1963 that anybody (Arnold Palmer)
won as much as $100,000 playing golf — ten years after Joe Di-
Maggio had retired from baseball at that figure.

"From the start," said Joe Dey, directing the traffic from be-
hind a large flat desk in an office on the thirty-fourth floor of the
Lincoln Building, opposite Grand Central Station in Manhat-
tan, "the amateur was fully as prominent as the professional in
United States golf. And he stayed thus until the era of Bobby
Jones had passed."

Bobby Jones, who was no Willie Sutton, played for the national amateur championship at fourteen, won it at twenty-one, retired at twenty-eight after taking thirteen amateur and open titles in America and Britain, and never won one dollar. He was an amateur born and bred, and an uncommon figure in the ancient and honourable game before it became big business. In eight of the nine times he played for the U.S. Open title, playing against the pros, at that, he finished first or second. First four times and second four times, and he went to play-offs two of the four times he came in second. And in 1930, when Arnold Palmer was a year-old toddler in Latrobe, Pennsylvania, he put together his "grand slam" and then went home and practiced law.

If Jones had been a pro, and if he had been born thirty years later, and if Mark McCormack had chanced along as his manager, there is no telling how great a fortune he might have reaped. Nor, for that matter, is there any telling how great a fortune Babe Ruth might have reaped in baseball if he had lived and performed in the television gold-rush era. Nor Red Grange in football. Nor Bill Tilden in tennis. Nor Jack Dempsey or Joe Louis in the ring, though they flourished at a time of high gate receipts and low income taxes. Translated into the dollars of the sixties, and into the tax structure of the seventies, their purses were huge, all right. Somebody figured out once that Ruth's peak salary of $80,000 in one season would have been worth a quarter of a million dollars to Willie Mays. But *no* athlete probably ever played with the colossal skill of Bobby Jones and, by choice, ever got so little in return.

"I don't think Jones's temperament would have permitted him to be a pro even today," reflected Dey. "He was what you might call a sporting intellectual. A man with a brilliant mind and a legal discipline, and great charm.

"I saw every shot he made in nineteen thirty in the U.S. Amateur at Merion in Philadelphia. He was fantastic. I'd write about every shot he took and give my copy to relays of messengers who would run it back to the press room, where Morse operators would wire it downtown to my paper, the *Philadelphia Bulletin.*"

Dey also wrote about subplots involving amateurs like Maurice McCarthy Jr., who might have made a small fortune on sheer dramatic quality alone in the latter days of exploitation. In the same tournament, McCarthy needed a hole in one to qualify for a tie for last place or be cut, and made it; the next day, he had to survive a play-off for last place, and made it; and after that, he had to go nineteen holes in an overtime round, followed by twenty-eight holes in an even longer overtime round, and he made both of those too — all in the same day.

But his theatrical shooting didn't even make a footnote to the Frank Merriwell record of Robert T. Jones Jr. of Atlanta, as he completed this summer's work as an amateur in 1930:

> May 15–16: He played with the Walker Cup team, which beat the British team, 10 to 2, and Jones won both his matches.
> May 26–31: Won the British Amateur championship.
> June 18–20: Won the British Open championship.
> July 10–12: Won the United States Open championship.
> Sept. 22–27: Won the United States Amateur title.
> Nov. 17: Retired.

In retiring from the game he dominated at the age of twenty-eight, Jones showed that he was human after all, no matter what his competitors might have thought. He received an offer of $250,000 from Warner Brothers to make a series of films on golf, and he took it. Three years later, Johnny Goodman won the U.S. Open as an amateur; he was the last amateur to do it, and the era of Bobby Jones was over.

Then the pros reasserted themselves and, ten years later, golf was spiraling upward along with baseball, football, housing, nylon stockings, white shirts, prices, and everything else. In

1941, just before Pearl Harbor, the touring pros were led by Ben Hogan with $18,358; in 1946, the first year after the battle-ship *Missouri* anchored in Tokyo Bay, they were led by Hogan with $42,556. By the same token, the United States Golf Association had been thinking of buying a headquarters house off Park Avenue in 1941, when the price was $25,000; five years later, the price was $75,000. Inflation had come to golf, and TV was not far behind.

The Golf Prize: See How It Grows

Year	Total Purse	Average Purse
1940	$169,200	$5,307
1950	459,950	13,938
1960	1,187,340	28,959
1961	1,461,830	32,485
1962	1,790,320	36,537
1963	2,044,900	47,497
1964	2,301,063	56,123
1965	2,848,515	79,403
1966	3,074,445	85,401
1967	3,972,362	108,356
1968	5,077,600	112,835
1969*	5,465,875	116,295
1970**	6,259,501	133,181

* With unofficial tour earnings added: $6,041,697
** With unofficial earnings added: $6,906,223

Television, in fact, was crowding into the picture in baseball, basketball, and other sports in a tentative way, as though nobody was quite bold enough to rock the radio boat. Golf had entered broadcasting in 1936, when the USGA's first contract for any sort of broadcasting brought the National Biscuit Company and the Columbia Broadcasting System together at the U.S. Amateur tournament in Garden City, Long Island. Ted Husing cut a dashing figure careening around the course in a cart to do his play-by-play, and so did Bill Stern, putting the broadcasting booth on wheels in deference to those 400-yard fairways.

So even when TV joined the scene in 1947, with local coverage of the U.S. Open in St. Louis, a large dose of radio was laced into the package. "In the first TV contract," recalled Joe Dey, "the rights fee for radio was rated ten to one over TV. Now we practically give radio away."

Besides, golf tournaments were often sponsored by business corporations for advertising and public relations, or by charities, and the whole financial picture seemed like a lamb stew. In 1956, soon after NBC began to focus its cameras on the courses, only five and a half hours of network television time was devoted to golf. What golf needed, besides some new camera angles and some new glamour, was a folk-hero — which is what the National Football League needed in 1924 when Red Grange was a senior at Illinois and Cash-and-Carry Pyle was standing alongside with a proposition. And sure enough, out there in the fairways in 1956 was a second-year professional named Palmer, and before the next decade was out, network golf was being seen for 100½ hours a year and Palmer was the game's first millionaire.

"What Arnold Palmer contributed," said Joe Dey, "was an appeal that went far beyond golf and that triggered the breakthrough. Then in 1966 the United States Golf Association made a deal with a network that obligated them to carry four events in one package for the year: the Amateur, the Women's Open, the U.S. Open, and a fourth tournament. They wanted the Open, but we used it as a carrot."

The carrot had help too. In 1964, it picked up a lawyer named Michael Carmichael, who had been with CBS, and he pieced together a package of tournaments from the entire year's tour. The American Broadcasting Company and Sports Network carried it, and it marked the end of the day when the TV people negotiated separately for tournaments, one by one or even in clusters of one carrot and three assorted vegetables.

Once TV got into the act, money began to flow into the game, the prizes began to spiral, and even Bobby Jones might have had a few moments of agonizing reappraisal if he had still been working with wood and wedge. In fact, it took only three years for the money to exert its customary influence: In 1967, the touring pros staged their "revolt" from the rest of the PGA, the issue being money and who got which bundle. It took a season of tugging and trouble before they returned to the fold, but they did it as the Tournament Players Division of the PGA and with the smooth, straight, civilized figure of Dey as the Daddy Warbucks of the tribe.

Dey was the ideal choice because he had played golf since turning sixteen, had served as executive director of the U.S. Golf Association for thirty-four years, and had won everybody's respect with a judicial composure and personal touch that made him a sort of combination of Kenesaw Mountain Landis and Bert Bell, whom he had known at the University of Pennsylvania. Like an Eagle Scout, he was too good to be true. But he was flanked in his robes of office by a three-way board of overseers that included golf administrators, touring pros, and outside businessmen — the three elements that kept the game straight, narrow, and rich.

They were a strange new breed, these entrepreneurs in sweaters and slacks who began to rival jockeys and college quarterbacks in earnings potential in the sixties and seventies.

Some came from the universities, like Palmer from Wake Forest and Nicklaus from Ohio State. Or like John Baldwin, with a master's degree in business administration, who made up his mind that he wanted to become a pro. Or like Deane Beman, a graduate of the University of Maryland who was a good amateur and a good insurance man, and who walked up to Dey at the Masters one day and announced that he was turning pro.

Some were black, like Charles Owens, who broke his knee as a paratrooper, underwent several fusions in his left knee, emerged stiff-legged, and played cross-handed, but who still went through the PGA qualifying school and made the touring caravan. A generation ago, Owens might not have made it because the PGA had "a Caucasian rule" until World War II, though way back in the second year of the U.S. Open, in 1896, a sixteen-year-old Negro caddie named John Shippen had become a pro and had competed as a teen-ager for the Open title over the Shinnecock Hills Course in Southampton, Long Island.

Some came from the ranks of the country-club pros — the people who rented the golfing carts, gave lessons at $10 for a half-hour or so, and sold equipment and apparel at a markup: a sweater for $40, shoes for $45, a shirt for $10, and clubs at $150 for irons and $150 for woods. They made as little as $2500 a year and as much as $25,000 a year, and maybe a few got up to $50,000 a year working from sunup to sundown, all the while aiming to qualify for The Tour, where the really big paychecks were to be found.

Wherever they came from, they were a far cry from the old breed like Joe Kirkwood, the trick-shot artist of the twenties and thirties, and Walter Hagen, his companion in exhibition matches as well as after-hours social bouts who often was late for his tee-time, and with glorious reason.

"They have a discipline now," Joe Dey said, separating the men from the boys. "They have a business discipline that the players up from the caddie ranks just didn't have. It's a business to them. That's it: They're businessmen today. They even watch their diets, and some of them even have become almost introspective about themselves, almost metaphysical. Some of them get together for Tuesday night prayer meetings, or for prayer breakfasts during the tournaments, and one hundred twenty-five of them once had a meeting with Billy Graham in Atlanta, with Gary Player acting as the leader.

"The tour has become a way of life for them, and they are deadly serious about it."

They are deadly serious, all right. In their frenzy to join the tour, 250 aspiring pros apply each year to the PGA qualifying school and, in district eliminations, sixty make it for two days of schooling in places like Tucson or Palm Beach Gardens — schooling in everything from how to dress to how to play golf. They are mostly college graduates who, like their fraternity brothers pursuing careers in engineering and medicine, are aiming for the big leagues of their profession. *Eighteen* of the original 250 might be admitted to the tour. They become card-carrying members for one year — on probation — and one year later are put under review, along with everybody else on the tour.

Each year, a dozen or two pros retire or lose their privileges, maybe a dozen and a half graduate from the finishing school, and these new men go searching for a piece of that $7,000,000 in those forty-two tournaments.

Not only deadly serious, but deadly skillful in most cases. In 1970, there were thirteen new winners of tournaments — men who had never won anything before. Men who had sat in the classroom a year or two before and had heard visiting lecturers like Dave Stockton, the PGA champion who arrived with seven loose-leaf notebooks under his arm: one for each of his seven years on the tour, seven statistical diaries in which he had recorded comment and analysis on every stroke he had taken in every tournament since golfing had become his business.

"You won't find one or two men dominating the game as in the past," observed Jack Nicklaus, who had been one of the one or two men dominating it in the past. "We will develop twenty or thirty stars on the tour instead of four or five, for as you know, new players are winning tournaments week after week."

"There is no place for fun on the tour now," said Frank

Beard. "It's a serious business. Too much money is at stake. Sometimes I think it would be nice to be like Hagen — live it up all night and come to the first tee in your dinner jacket. But with seven million dollars on the line, you can't afford to do it."

After the 1968 Open, it appeared that the shade of Hagen had returned in the blithe spirit of Lee Trevino, a Texan of Mexican parentage who kidded with the galleries all the way around the course and who even wisecracked with his fellow-capitalists.

"He'd do better if he'd cut out that funny stuff," said Beard, despite the fact that Trevino later won more than $209,000 in half a year. "He's a fine golfer, but you can't win in this business unless you play it seriously."

"I hope to make enough money," replied Trevino, unreconstructed, "to buy the Alamo and give it back to the Mexicans."

In 1971, Trevino made enough money to realize most such ambitions when he won the United States, Canadian, and British Open tournaments within a month's time and became the hottest man on the pro circuit.

Not only that, but he did it with the same insouciant air of a man enjoying himself that he had displayed a few summers earlier as a hustler at a pitch-and-putt course near Dallas. He was as relaxed and flamboyant as they come, too, as befits a sharpshooter who could amaze the visitors by using a quart-sized bottle of Dr. Pepper as a golf club.

"My goal," he quipped, "is to make a million bucks. The way I'm spending money, I have to win a million.

"In the old days, I had trouble finding people who could afford to pay me for golf lessons. Now everybody wants to take lessons from me. Five years ago, I didn't own a car. Now I got five cars. I used to live in a trailer. Now I live in a five-bedroom house. I didn't have a phone. Now I got a phone and the number's unlisted. Boy, that's progress."

• • •

A British Open champion was crowned as far back as 1860, when Victoria was Queen; a United States Open champion in 1895, when Victoria was still Queen and Grover Cleveland was President for the second time; and a PGA champion in 1916, when Woodrow Wilson was in the White House. All three tournaments had one thing in common: Money was no factor.

In fact, it still wasn't much of a factor in 1932, when Gene Sarazen shot his way to the British Open title and pocketed $400 and, a few weeks later, knocked off the American title and pocketed $500. Like Bobby Jones two years earlier, he made some history but no money.

Even some of the more carnival tournaments had a way of keeping people out of the higher brackets, including Henry Ciuci, one of eight golfing brothers who won eighteen tournaments between 1927 and 1950 and accumulated all of $8800. Some of it came in heady doses too — like $1250 for the Florida Open and an even $1000 for the Mexican Open at Aguascalientes. If Ciuci had had a couple of good afternoons in the Westchester Classic one generation later, or even a couple of fair afternoons, he might have matched his career earnings in one long weekend.

But money was a long time coming, especially since golf ranked as a sort of gentleman's game of skill, something like whist or chess, with neither mass support, nor rich sponsors, nor million-dollar gates. It also was somehow related to the sun, and resort hotels and resort cities had a knack of staging the early tournaments with drums beating but with few coins dropping.

San Antonio got the ball rolling first in 1922, and then Los Angeles with its Open Tournament in 1926, a chamber of commerce production designed to get people interested in Los Angeles. Before long, Phoenix was joining the march, and then the Florida colonies, with individual hotels there handling the arrangements and getting the publicity.

By the time World War II started, business corporations were getting the idea. First some breweries, and then a rush of companies with golf-minded presidents and image-minded publicity departments. Finally, movie stars began getting into the act and they did it principally for three reasons: They liked to play golf, especially with name professionals; they usually had favorite charities that got most of the receipts; and they all had tax problems that might be eased by combining reasons numbers one and two.

But the chief appeal in running a golf tournament, whether by a local club or chamber of commerce or corporation, lay in the fact that you could support a charity and boost your own public-relations stock in one swirling weekend replete with well-known names and the attention they would draw. The golfers stood to make some money out of it. But the sponsors generally had other goals, and if you scratched the surface of any major tournament you were likely to find some hospital, boys' club, or other charity beneath the surface.

In order to attract enough golfers to make the whole thing worthwhile, naturally, a pretty fair purse had to be anted up, and television helped to take care of that little problem as the nineteen sixties unraveled. But as long as prices were rising in all of the major sports anyway, there was no way that golf would lag behind as a gentleman's pastime in a world gone wild over cash. Particularly when the list of sponsors began to include Dow Jones, the Avco Corporation, Kemper Insurance, Allied Chemical, Eastern Airlines, National Airlines, United Airlines, the Doral Hotel in Miami Beach, the Florida Citrus Foundation, Buick, and even the Industrial Valley Bank of Philadelphia. And closing fast on the outside were one-man conglomerates like Bob Hope, Bing Crosby, Danny Thomas, Glen Campbell, Dean Martin, and Jackie Gleason.

By 1962, all this attention, to say nothing of all this financial strength, had hatched the first $100,000 tournament, the Thunderbird at Upper Montclair, New Jersey. The Masters, at Augusta, never went so far as to announce its purse in advance but it did guarantee the athletes certain rewards, and in April of the same year the guarantees came to $109,100 — not bad for a traditional event that seemed shy on the subject of money. The PGA championship that same year went to $72,500 at Newtown Square, which was a record, and the U.S. Open of sainted memory rose to $73,800 and then tripled in value to $196,900 seven years later. And, if anybody had any doubt that the millennium had arrived, the Dow Jones people put up $300,000 in 1970 at a time when Dow Jones's Wall Street clients were being fed daily doses of gloom and doom from the stock markets.

Any of these sponsors could count on a few economic facts of life before going into the golf-tournament business. The chief one was that they would probably not make any money themselves. The next, or corollary, fact was that their gross cost would amount to two and a half times the total purse being offered the golfing pros who made up the cast.

On the black-ink side of the ledger, though, they had a few plus signs: ticket sales to the public, the parking lots and concession stands, advertisements in the programs, and, last but increasingly not least, television.

Each of these presented variations on themes. All of the major golfing sponsors involved in the PGA tour, for example, shared in the TV revenue. They didn't share equally, but they shared. If a tournament was carried on national TV, then 21 per cent of the purse came out of the television-money pool; if not on national TV, 13½ per cent. At some clubs, the parking lots were run directly by the local junior chamber of commerce or by the hospital or other charity involved. And tickets were sold anywhere from four to seven dollars, depending on the day of the week and depending on what the traffic would bear. On Thursday and Friday, they went for a couple of dollars less than on Saturday and Sunday; a "clubhouse ticket" carried prestige and drinks; a "season ticket" for fifteen or thirty dollars was good for the whole week, including the practice sessions.

You could even line up your tickets for next August's tournament by ordering them ten months early in a kind of Christmas sale. Maybe ten dollars less on a thirty-five dollar package and, when slipped into the right stocking, not a bad gift for the business customer who follows Arnie's Army like a pilgrim pointed toward Mecca.

Arnie had plenty of other people following him around besides the ticket-plan customers and, as the touring pros became more glamorous and their game more universal, the galleries began to crowd the courses. There were no box seats, no fifteen-minute quarters or three-out innings, no neat little locale of action, no 90-foot court or 100-yard gridiron; just wide open spaces and 144 contestants. But the fans started to give up their own golfing weekends in droves and as the purses soared, so did the crush. As many as 20,000 a day flocked to the headline events, and the U.S. Open in fact was limited to 20,000 a day in order to preserve everybody's sanity, including Lee Trevino's.

That added up to 80,000 people spread over four days and, in the Open at Baltusrol in 1967, they somehow crammed 88,414 cash customers behind the ropes. For a three-day tournament at Oakmont, Pennsylvania, in 1962 — including a Saturday double-header — they counted 62,300, and that was a record too.

In addition to customers, the throngs hanging around country clubs on main-event weekends also might number several hundred "marshals" who volunteered to police the crowds in return for the privilege of rubbing elbows with men who shot in the low seventies. The U.S. Open one year accounted for something like 50,000 man-hours of work *donated* by the amateur vigilantes, while volunteer hospital ladies often sold tickets or parked cars. In three years of pitch-in moonlighting of this sort, the stagehands got close to the stars and hospitals got close to $1,000,000 in revenue from the Westchester Classic alone.

For the lucky few, or the affluent few, there was the great American golfing sideshow: the pro-am — the "preliminary" or pre-tournament tournament, conducted the day before the big one got under way. They customarily made room in it for maybe 50 pros and 150 amateurs, who cheerfully coughed over anywhere from $25 to $1500 for the memorable adventure of matching shots in a foursome with Julius Boros or Jack Nicklaus. The money often went to charity so the fee was tax-deductible, but wild horses normally couldn't hold back the resolute amateurs bent on playing in the one-day sideshow whatever the tab.

The name-dropping reaches a crescendo every year at "the Crosby," which is formally known as the Bing Crosby National Pro-Am at Pebble Beach, California. More than 9,000 amateurs stormed the doors trying to get a piece of the action in 1971, while only 168 made it.

This type of gleeful madness is pretty much an American obsession or, at least, an English-speaking obsession. In Europe, golf remains essentially a private-club bash; in Latin America and part of Asia, a class sport; in the English-speaking countries and Japan, a mass mania. In Japan, where baseball went crazy in the touring days of Babe Ruth and Connie Mack, there were only seventeen golf courses in 1946 at the end of the war. By the seventies, there were 500, and Tokyo even had a three-tiered driving range where the populace could sock balls to their heart's content. And this is in a country where only 15 per cent of the land is arable and where a tax is levied on every round of golf.

As if all this weren't enough to keep the wheels spinning, the mob was lured in the sixties by the certainty that the purse-seeking stars on the tour were becoming the fortune-seeking capitalists off the tour. That is, while Billy Casper — subsisting on the most exotic diet known to science in a struggle against allergy and calorie — might take home $200,000 in sheer prize money, the "peripheral income" could be astronomical. It came in four installments: endorsements, public relations, exhibition matches, and combinations of all these ploys under the masterminding of some genius like Mark McCormack.

Endorsements started slowly and logically with golfing equipment, monogrammed by the superstars in precisely the way baseball bats had long since been etched with the names of Lou Gehrig and Willie Mays. Then they expanded into clothes, both country-club combat styles and extracurricular, and it was a dismally backward baseball player in the sixties who did not lounge around hotel lobbies wearing an Arnold Palmer sweater. Then they got into esoteric things like lawn mowers and heavy stuff, with Palmer and Nicklaus going to the head of the class.

The public-relations coin exchange did not particularly flourish in the days when the game was still a private pastime, but it picked up sensationally once corporations got the message that the way to a client's heart or a customer's pocketbook might lead through the clubhouse. Better yet, consider the prestige to be gained and the image polished if Dow Finsterwald or Don January *went to the customers*. Mohammed to the mountain, in slacks and sweater. The corporate sharks began to schedule three-day outings during which big-time pros played golf with the clients or went fishing with them while the chairman of the board addressed the visiting celebrities as "Arnie" and "Bert-baby."

In return, Arnie and Bert-baby floated among the foursomes of businessmen, giving smiles and tips and collecting a few thousand greenbacks for their time rendered. Jack Nicklaus, a heavy-demand man for this sort of thing, doubtless achieved the most symbolic outing of all by appearing in golf-and-fishing expeditions staked by the American Bank Note Company, which is getting as close to the source as is humanly possible.

"I can putt with Nicklaus," said Joe Dey, summarizing the spirit of such occasions, "but I can never throw a football with Joe Namath or a baseball with Tom Seaver."

As for exhibition matches, they still may lead the list for tradition and profit both. They were moneymaking sidelights from the primeval days of the game, but inflation now has put them over the top and members of the golfing elite would not be overly impressed today by fees of $5000 apiece for eighteen holes on an otherwise idle afternoon.

Finally, there is the managed investment, the sort of guided missile of outside income, and now hear McCormack, the Wernher von Braun of the science of multiplying your money:

"Advancing the financial cause of athletes, and especially golfers, is my business. I think that since I began with Arnold Palmer as my first client years ago, I have become a fairly good judge of golf techniques, of who has promise and who has not. But I have become, in my own estimation at least, an even better judge of what might be called the star quality of an athlete. It is a characteristic that transcends athletic performance, and it is what sustains sport.

"I had thought for about two years prior to the British Open [of 1969]," he added, getting down to cases, "that Tony Jacklin had this quality. I agreed to represent Tony. At about the same time, I said publicly that the first Englishman to win the British Open in this era of celebrity golfers would have a fine chance of making a million dollars.

"To date, Jacklin's British Open win has meant well over half a million dollars in contracts for him. The sources of this financial attention are numerous and growing.

"Dunlop will put out a line of autographed Tony Jacklin golf clubs and has signed Jacklin to a long-term contract for the United Kingdom. Jacklin's golf exhibition fees have increased substantially, and foreign tours to Australia, Sweden, and South Africa are being arranged. His publication contracts include a newspaper column, a biography, his story of the British Open, and the biggest golf magazine contract ever signed in Great Britain.

"I arranged for a newspaper series by Jacklin on 'How I Won the British Open' before Tony teed off for his last round. It pays to be prepared. And when somebody handed Jacklin a bot-

tle of champagne after his win, I quickly turned it around so
that the label — Bollinger — wouldn't show in the photograph.
(Sure enough, a champagne company — Bollinger, in fact —
approached us about endorsement possibilities.) Clothing contracts have been arranged, exclusive VIP golf days have been
scheduled, Pan American Airways has signed Jacklin to a large
contract, British Colgate plans to use him for endorsements, and
Sea Island, a United States resort, has him under contract.

"Several Jacklin television projects are being prepared for use
in the United Kingdom. By year's end, Jacklin had received
almost every British award for an athlete, including a commen-
dation from the prime minister. He was even invited to drive a
golf ball across the Thames."

McCormack, who started his life as a money manager by ac-
cepting 10 per cent of his client's loot, wound up collecting up
to 50 per cent. The golfer got sole possession of only his trophy.
But in return, McCormack brought the touch of Midas to just
about everything his hero could reach with a number one wood.
He gave full credit for the premier "star quality" to Arnold
Palmer, with whom he joined forces in 1959, and for whom he
set up fourteen businesses, from insurance to golf-course design
and the Arnold Palmer Golf Company, whose sales of equipment zoomed to $20,000,000 a year. The main thrust of the em-
pire was delivered by Arnold Palmer Enterprises, Inc. The
leading stockholder was Palmer and the second biggest was
Mark McCormack.

"Very often," McCormack observed, depicting himself as an
institution with some historical significance, "an agent, in the
most often used sense of the word, was out to get quick money
and get his per cent off the top. He would not be interested in
longevity, he would not be interested in the tax consequences of
how the money should be paid, where it should be paid, the
quality of the product endorsed, or anything else. When you
look at some of the contracts these athletes signed, it's incred-
ible."

Tracing Palmer's rise to the financial status of something like the Union Pacific Railroad, McCormack recalled that in 1960 — the year after they shook hands — Palmer startled the golfing world by winning eight tournaments. He also finished in the top five in nineteen of the twenty-nine tournaments he played.

"This was the year," McCormack recalled, "he made famous the Palmer 'charge,' a heart-attack approach to golf that demanded the situation look hopeless before one really began to play. His last-round sixty-five which enabled him to come from seven strokes back and win the U.S. Open was the supreme example that the public will never forget, but there were others: He won at Palm Springs with a last-round sixty-five, at Pensacola with a sixty-seven, at Hartford with a sixty-six that got him into a play-off which he won, at Mobile, with a sixty-five.

"Nothing seemed impossible for him, and nothing was. He brought golf to life as a mass spectator sport, and by the year's end he was the world's most famous athlete. Soon he was counting among the people he knew, kings and diplomats, presidents and power merchants."

All of which prompted James Roach, the sports editor of the *New York Times,* to comment in a radio broadcast:

"Once upon a time, I wrote about horse races for the *Times* and when I learned what leading jockeys were paid I decided that if I ever had a male child, I'd start him on big, black cigars at an early age and stunt his growth and make a jockey of him and retire early. Now I'm not so sure. I think maybe I'd give the male offspring plenty of vitamins and fresh vegetables and other nourishing food and buy him a 7-iron at the age of 6 and in time make a professional golfer of him."

Roach's conviction was fortified when he calculated that the second-ranking money-winner in all golf on July 2, 1970, was a twenty-eight-year-old Californian by the unfamiliar name of Dick Lotz. He had earned $107,000 by then and still had twenty-two tournaments to go, seventeen of which listed prize money in excess of $100,000.

The weightiest pot of gold in all that summer's fortune totaled $300,000, courtesy of Dow Jones. But Joe Dey, surveying the rich green scene, wondered if maybe the lid might blow one day, just as it did in Wall Street.

"How far do you allow it to grow?" he asked one day, checking the list of corporate sponsors who were bankrolling many of the weekends. "Do you let corporations take over the tour, or do you try to keep a balance with the old-fashioned chambers of commerce or civic groups? I say you do have to keep a balance. Dow Jones came in to get the rub-off from golf. But after one year and the record purse of three hundred thousand dollars, they were out. They lost money, as they had expected, but meanwhile they found themselves paying out more for newsprint and other regular business equipment. The problem is that companies run into expense considerations and even changes of management. The president may be a golfer this year, but a tennis buff next year. They want to come to sell something."

They wanted to sell something, all right, and they found a way to sell it through the growing lure of golf, just as other people found a way through other professional sports. And they all found that national headlines, national magazines, and national television in the sixties provided a more magnetic way to sell their corporate names and products than the old door-to-door salesmen had provided a generation ago.

"The decade began with Palmer," noted Mark McCormack, translating the lure in the personal terms he liked best, "and it ended with Palmer scoring the only back-to-back win in nineteen sixty-nine, the last one coming in the long-remembered fashion — seven strokes behind with just seventeen holes to play — as if the clock had been turned back, or perhaps had never moved, and the cry of 'charge' was not just a fond memory but a weekly call to arms.

"The clock has moved, though. There is more than one millionaire golfer now, and more than a few who are willing to look at Palmer at forty and figure they can take him head to head. 'Charge' is a battle cry, but also an echo. The seventies are here.''

The seventies were here in tennis too — another sport that long had languished in a kind of Victorian docility, a kind of Henry James civility, a kind of simon-pure nobility. But, as in golf, the people who long had "cherished" tennis were learning that modern athletes and the men who managed their money were beginning to cherish other things.

"The signs of success," observed Neil Amdur in the *New York Times,* "were everywhere: record crowds, national television, sizable prize money, the introduction of a sudden-death scoring system, a grand slam, a public protest by women players, renewed talk of synthetics replacing grass, manufacturers peddling their wares and, of course, politics.

"For better or worse, after years of languishing in a hypocritical amateur state, organized tennis has joined the professional sports revolution, two decades behind pro football, a decade and millions of dollars behind its recreation rival, golf."

But, as in all revolutions, especially those in a gyrating national economy, there came a warning that a grain of salt should be added. The warning was sounded by Eugene L. Scott of the United States Davis Cup team, who welcomed the seventies by cautioning all hands that comparisons between tennis and golf contained "the markings of a self-destruct cartridge in Mission Impossible."

"Golf," he said, "stands alone in that its athletes are not paid a salary or appearance money. Golf tournaments provide such lucrative rewards for leading finishers that wages are eschewed in favor of prize money. The highly paid performers in football, hockey, baseball, and basketball don't get paid by the hour, but are still employees in the strict sense because their income, bonuses notwithstanding, is fixed regardless of whether they win. Even boxers, auto racers, and jockeys receive appearance money without regard for results.

"Now tennis, which Major Wingate conceived as gentle recreation for elderly couples a hundred years ago, and which has progressed little further since its acceptance as a spectator sport, is puckishly proclaiming to offer only prize money for its tournament participants. The concept is superlative. However, the practicality of accelerating tennis to the financial structure of golf is absurdly premature."

The problem, Scott noted, was that without TV interest, there just wasn't enough money to support a full circuit of $100,000 tennis tournaments — not with performers like Rod Laver, Roy Emerson, Pancho Gonzales, and Arthur Ashe. There wasn't even enough money to induce the contract professionals to appear in the new "open" tournaments sponsored by the United States Lawn Tennis Association, which controlled the long-standing amateurs as well as the "independent pros" who had not yet joined the circuit carnival. The issue, if Major Wingate will excuse it, was money: prize money versus appearance money, otherwise known and coveted as "show-dough."

"Tennis administrators," Scott concluded, "have sounded like the mosquito floating down the river requesting the drawbridge be raised. Either players will be patient and compete for prize money alone, in a sense subsidizing the game until purses can be bolstered, or all players must receive guarantees regardless of their affiliation with promoters.

"Until a decision is reached, it provides insight to imagine Fran Tarkenton's reaction to the concept of his salary being contingent upon the number of games his team wins. He would sooner self-destruct."

But despite the obstacles that tortured the pros' path to the nearest bank, the draw of the dollar signs kept the tennis players treading the path pretty much the way their contemporaries in other sports had done during *their* formative years in business.

In September of 1970, all the rival claimants buried the hatchet long enough to stage the United States Open Championship at Forest Hills. They met on ten and a half acres bought in 1913 for $77,000 by the West Side Tennis Club, which had started operating in 1892 at Central Park West and Eighty-eighth Street in Manhattan with a membership of thirteen, four dirt courts, and a shack clubhouse. The switch to Forest Hills, in a high-toned neighborhood of Queens, was enhanced in 1915 when the United States championship was switched there from Newport Casino, and in 1968 the whole shooting match was enhanced — or maybe embroiled — when the tournament became the first United States "open" championship. Amateurs and pros playing side by side, along with the newest arrival in the neighborhood: money.

So now in the fall of 1970, they were all there on the same courts: simon-pures, touring pros, purses that totaled $160,000, a tournament of eleven playing dates, a record total of 122,996 spectators (21,000 more than had paid for twelve dates the year before), and a first-prize purse of $20,000 for Ken Rosewall, who at the age of thirty-five could finally count on the sort of payday that even a respectable golfing pro might envy. Fourteen years earlier, as a boy wonder (but not a rich boy wonder), Rosewall had won the National Amateur title on the same courts and had been rewarded with a gold tennis ball and a handshake.

On the same afternoon that Rosewall drove away from the West Side Club in a new Ford Pinto, which was another bauble of victory, Mrs. Margaret Smith Court completed a sweep of the major women's championships. At 5-foot-9, she was two inches taller than Rosewall, but she still was a mite shorter in the bankroll because women's lib had not yet liberated the ladies from the sizable disparity that existed in payoffs in all sports. She had taken the Australian, French, and Wimbledon titles, and now the U.S. Open, and she got more than a handshake too: $7500 in prize cash; 500 shares of stock from the Chemold Corporation, which made the tennis racquets she used; a new contract for 1971; and countless offers for commercial endorsements.

"There was a lot of tension," Mrs. Court confessed after her match against Rosemary Casals. "I was praying on that last serve that Rosie would hit it into the net."

Margaret wasn't the only person praying at Forest Hills that day. So were the bagmen, front-men, and sponsors who had flocked there hoping to line up the talent that was flourishing despite the growing pains in the professional side of the game. The sponsors were aiming for publicity for their products and for some link to a sport that was played by 11,000,000 Americans, just as the golfing sponsors were aiming at publicity and some link to *their* sport, which was played by 11,000,000 Americans. At Forest Hills, their chief target was Mike Davies, once the ranking player in Britain and now the executive director of World Championship Tennis, the professional group that had signed almost every important player to a contract.

Davies, who had played with Rosewall in the handshake era, reflected on the commercial traffic swarming around the courts and remembered a day ten years earlier when tennis was more subtle.

"I was sick of being paid under the table," he said. "I wanted to declare myself a professional and be paid openly for what I did best. From playing amateur tournaments like Wimbledon, where they have a man in the dressing room to look after you, and a masseur, I went on tour with Tony Trabert. Pro tennis was a little different then.

"Our first match was at a convention hall in Marseilles. We were shown to a room to change clothes. A storeroom. I couldn't believe it. I turned round to Trabe. 'Where's the dressing room? Where are the coat hangers?' He looked at me blankly. He went into his bag, took out a hammer and a nail, smacked it into the wall, and hung his coat on it. He shook his head like I was a dummy. 'You're not an amateur anymore. You're a pro now. You carry your dressing room with you.' "

The pro pioneers in those days included, besides the bewildered Davies, people like Frank Sedgman, Rod Laver, Ken Rosewall, Pancho Gonzales, Andres Gimeno, Butch Buchholz, Barry MacKay, Pancho Segura, Lew Hoad, Kurt Neilsen, and Ashley Cooper. They had turned pro under the musical overtures of Jack Kramer, the former champion, but the lure was vague and the prizes were meager. That is, until they lured a pair of big spenders into the tent: Al G. Hill Jr. and his uncle, Lamar Hunt, the Texas oil baron who loved sports and who proved his love by paying the bills for the Kansas City Chiefs.

Hill and Hunt promptly sank $1,000,000 into the tennis tour, and greater love hath no man that that. Part of it went to stocking the tour with five well-known amateurs: John Newcombe, Tony Roche, Cliff Drysdale, Nikki Pilic, and Roger Taylor. They had competition from other promoters like George McCall, but when they bought him out they acquired the contracts of Laver, Rosewall, Gonzales, Gimeno, Emerson, and Fred Stolle. And when Herman David, the chairman of the All England Lawn Tennis and Croquet Club, announced that the main event held there every year — the Wimbledon championship — would henceforth be open to pros, they had status to go with all that talent and all that money.

There still were a few holdouts, but Hunt solved that particular problem a week after Rosewall and Mrs. Court had scored their sweeps at Forest Hills. He signed three young stars — Arthur Ashe, Bob Lutz, and Charles Pasarell — who had made the tricky transition from amateur standing to "independent pros" under the protective umbrella of the United States Lawn Tennis Association. They had maintained their relationship to the amateur world but had graduated into the professional side of the family while still avoiding the outright entanglement of Hunt's touring empire.

But now the call of the wild had grown too powerful to ignore, and when the call came by telephone at five o'clock in the morning with long-term security, they capitulated. For Ashe, the ranking black tennis player in the world at twenty-seven, the call provided guarantees and deferred payments worth three quarters of a million dollars.

"I appreciate everything the USLTA has done for me," he said. "But they just move too slowly for me. They make bad appointments, their hands are tied by antiquated rules, and they don't want to assume a role of leadership."

The lawn-tennis association replied with a few high cards from its own hand; maybe not trump cards, but high ones. It threatened the pros with a sort of excommunication. It would ban thirty-two contract pros, as well as twelve women who also had answered the call of the cash, from the blessings of the main events like the United States Open and Wimbledon.

The reasons for the war of the tennis worlds, it said, were chiefly these: the twenty-city, million-dollar tour for 1971 created by World Championship Tennis, which would conflict with events sanctioned by the USLTA; the signing of Ashe, Lutz, and Pasarell; the similar defection of the top women players in America, including Billie Jean King, Nancy Richey, and Mary Ann Eisel Curtis; and the continuing battle on all fronts between the contract pros and the various national associations.

As the first year of the seventies came to an end, the World Championship Tennis empire tried to weather the storm, and truce proposals were made on all sides. It was a little like the early struggles and early rivalries in football when the AFL challenged the establishment, in basketball when the ABA challenged the establishment, and in golf when the touring pros revolted from the PGA. The *casus belli* was the same: the division of the spoils. And in the long run, the outcome would probably be the same: bigger pies, bigger splits, enough to go around.

To herald the dawning of the day of such an accommodation, Lamar Hunt's people mailed holiday cards that showed five

Christmas balls, a tennis ball, a holly sprig, and the caption: "Season's greetings." But a footnote was added with a dart directed at the International Lawn Tennis Federation: "I.L.T.F. Sanction Pending."

"We couldn't resist," explained an official of World Championship Tennis. "After all, peace on earth has finally come to tennis. We can all learn to laugh again for a while."

The war and its aftereffects were not really over when he said it. But some of the combatants were already laughing — all the way to the bank:

— like Arthur Ashe, who already was making $50,000 as a freshman in the professional class and figured to make $200,000 overall from his moonlighting for a cigarette company, a racquet manufacturer, insurance agency, and elsewhere.

— like Rod Laver, the Australian corporation who won $123,855 in prizes during 1969, who was good for $300,000 overall in 1970, and who had Mark McCormack lining up endorsements and operating his "business" when McCormack was not busy making Tony Jacklin a millionaire or Arnold Palmer a zillionaire.

— like the six British tennis players who had beaten Brazil in the interzone semifinals of the Davis Cup matches and who immediately were rewarded with bonus checks of $600 apiece. The "checks" were written on tennis balls and, in the spirit of the times, the players bounced into the bank in London and bounced their "checks" on the manager's desk.

The British team, in the spirit of the times, was being sponsored by a cigarette company whose managing director leaned across the desk and across a decade of bouncing values in golf, tennis, and other professional sports.

"What's wrong with tennis balls?" he asked the startled bank manager.

And the bank manager, in the spirit of the times, recovered his poise and replied: "Nothing."

9

Indoors: Madison Square Goldmine

IN THE DAYS when the full life in America revolved around an evening at home — complete with popping corn, listening to the radio, and checking pictures in the family encyclopedia — a man named Jack Kent Cooke traveled door to door trying to earn a piece of the action. He peddled encyclopedias at $39.50 a set. And when that didn't work, which was often, he earned a piece of the full life, to say nothing of his supper, by playing the saxophone in a dance band.

A generation later, America's idea of the full life had changed, and the change did not particularly include popcorn, the radio, *or* the family encyclopedia. So Jack Kent Cooke, laying aside the saxophone and the spiel, nimbly converted his own thinking in order to keep pace with the times.

In the best traditions of the capitalist dream, he climbed the ladder of business success, becoming something rather vaguely known as a "sportsman" and not so vaguely known as a millionaire: a partner with Roy Lord Thomson in newspapers, radio stations, and cable television; part owner of the Washington Redskins football team; full owner of the Los Angeles Lakers basketball team, the Los Angeles Kings hockey team, and the Inglewood Forum, which was one of the things that had replaced the family encyclopedia in the rush of an evening's entertainment; the absolute owner of a $28,000 Bentley and half a dozen other luxury cars; a mansion in Bel Air; and a set of electric-eye gates that sheltered the Bentley from other arriving traffic — including, perhaps, a stray peddler or two of family encyclopedias.

Cooke's grip on the rungs of the ladder of financial success was so secure, in fact, that his bank in California demurely — and probably conservatively — estimated his wealth "in eight figures." And his grip on the modern notion of an evening's entertainment was so secure that when Andrew Jerrold Perenchio came up with the most sensational idea for an evening's entertainment in the nineteen seventies, he turned to Cooke for the alliance and the cash to promote it.

The idea centered on two men, both athletes, both unbeaten, both black, both claimants to the world's heavyweight championship: Muhammad Ali, who won the title as Cassius Clay on February 25, 1964, at the age of twenty-two by knocking out Sonny Liston in seven rounds in Miami Beach and who lost it May 9, 1967, after he had been indicted by a federal grand jury for refusing to be inducted into the army; and Joe Frazier, the sole asset of Cloverlay, Inc., of Philadelphia, who occupied the crown Ali had "vacated" and who cemented his claim by knocking out Jimmy Ellis in five rounds in New York on February 16, 1970.

The idea was not so radical, but the cash required to float it was. Ali's return to the ring after three years had taken on the tinge of a crusade at a time when crusades were widespread, particularly against the United States' military involvement in Vietnam. He had challenged the system, he had paid a substantial price in terms of his career as a professional fighter, he had appealed through the courts, he had resumed his work and his quest for the "vacated" title — by then held, with some distinction, by Frazier. Two careers were on the line, two winning streaks were on the line, two shares of one title were on the line. And somebody would have to post a colossal purse for Ali and Frazier to decide the classic questions on the line.

Enter Andrew Jerrold Perenchio, a forty-year-old Californian who had never peddled encyclopedias but who had literally labored in the vineyard on the way up his own ladder in business. As a boy in Fresno, he grew up working in the family vineyards, which his father lost in 1944 during a price war. The family moved to Los Angeles, where he entered the business school at UCLA and where he did some boxing of his own in the intramural ring. "But I quit," he confessed later, "when the same kid kept beating me up."

He played some golf too, but the closest approach he made to fame on the course came when he worked once as a caddy for Howard Hughes, who got into the big business of sports himself in more direct fashion — by buying a sports television network. Like a man selling encyclopedias, though, Perenchio got in through the back door, first as a theatrical agent and then as the president of Chartwell Artists, an agency that beat the drums for people like Elizabeth Taylor and Richard Burton, Andy Williams, Jane Fonda, Glen Campbell, and Henry Mancini and that developed the practice of concert appearances on college campuses.

Perenchio had engineered a few sizable deals in his time, as befits a man who masterminds the bread-and-butter details for the Burtons and their high-fee film friends, and he even had arranged the sale of Caesar's Palace in Las Vegas for $83,000,000. But even in Las Vegas, where Barbra Streisand reportedly commanded a million dollars for a single engagement and where Howard Hughes holed up like a mystery maharajah, it took some doing to underwrite a single engagement featuring Muhammad Ali and Joe Frazier. And that was in spite of the fact that Vegas had been the site of Ali's assault on Floyd Patterson in 1963, a match that drew all of 7816 customers, a small and almost select gathering that the Boston Red Sox could have attracted almost any night of the week during hard times.

However, it was a fact that the Ali-Patterson fight in turn had generated total receipts of $4,747,690, and two years later they met in a rematch that drew 412 *fewer* persons but that still did $3,570,000 worth of business. The reason, and it was not lost on Jerry Perenchio, was that many more persons had paid to watch the fights over closed-circuit television far from the Strip.

For Ali and Frazier, though, the cost in purses alone would come to $5,000,000 — two and a half million apiece for the gladiators, or about $55,555 a minute apiece if it lasted fifteen rounds — and not even Barbra Streisand could improve on that kind of loot on her best night.

"This fight," reasoned Perenchio, rising to the bait, "is entertainment. It's like *Gone with the Wind;* you could show it on the side of a supermarket and people would come to see it."

But before he could win the enormous right of picking up such an enormous tab, he had to post a guarantee of $5,000,000 just for the two heavyweights' signatures. After that, he could worry about all the other expenses.

"Usually when you need that much money," he said, "you go to ten or twelve people and put together a group, with each person putting up half a million dollars. In this case, there wasn't time."

That is, instead of rounding up ten or twelve well-heeled angels, he needed one exceptionally well-heeled angel, and needed one in a hurry. It took him ten minutes to decide to take the plunge, and it took him a few hours more to convince Jack Kent Cooke, whom he had never met, to take it with him. Cooke put up $4,500,000, got a letter of substantiation from the Chase Manhattan Bank, got the other $500,000 from Madison Square Garden, designated the Garden as the site instead of the Astrodome in Houston, and then left the details of the door-to-door peddling of the package to Jerry Perenchio.

"The fight," announced Cooke modestly, "is the greatest entertainment and sports spectacle of all time."

"For our five million dollars," said Perenchio clinically, "I'd

like the opportunity to explain. We're business people, we intend to make money out of this. We're not in it for the exercise.
It should gross between twenty and thirty million dollars."

"Thirty million dollars!" shrieked Muhammad Ali. "Frazier,
we've been taken. They got us cheap."

The anatomy of the financial monster pieced together by
Cooke and Perenchio looked like this: Madison Square Garden
would sell out, 19,000-strong, with tickets scaled from $20 in the
rafters to $150 at ringside, creating a live gate of $1,250,000.
But that would provide only one quarter of the fighters' purse
and, even by the standards of half a century earlier, would not
overwhelm anybody. However, the "live gate," which half a
century earlier had been the only gate, now was merely the tail
that wagged the dog.

"The live gate," Perenchio explained, making the mathemat-
ics appear elementary indeed, "is not the primary factor. The
closed-circuit TV network is. We expect to have a million and a
half seats in the United States and Canada at a minimum of ten
dollars a seat. That's a potential of fifteen million dollars, and
we're counting on at least seventy per cent capacity. Plus the
foreign sales round the world."

To make certain that nobody would view or even hear the
fight without paying directly into the till, the packagers ruled
out all broadcasting, whether by radio or delayed TV. In that
sense, they were carrying Bert Bell's "blackout" policy into a
new dimension. Not only would "home screens" be blacked
out, but all screens would be blacked out except those hooked
into the pay-network. Football and baseball long had worried
about the doomsday when sponsors could not afford to foot the
advertising bill; now boxing, a sport once killed by overexpo-
sure to television in the postwar years, was being revived with
the help of "closed TV." At least, the definition of the "gate"
was being broadened: People would pay premium prices to
watch the event either on the scene or 3000 miles away on a
large screen.

The history of million-dollar gates, in fact, was written in two distinct phases. Before TV, there had been eight such bonanzas — five involving Jack Dempsey, three involving Joe Louis. After TV, there had been eight in a fifteen-year span, and all had depended on TV. This was phase one:

Year	Match	Site	Attendance	Total Receipts
1921	Dempsey-Carpentier	Jersey City	80,183	$1,789,238
1923	Dempsey-Firpo	New York	82,000	1,188,603
1926	Dempsey-Tunney	Philadelphia	120,757	1,895,733
1927	Dempsey-Sharkey	New York	75,000	1,083,530
1927	Dempsey-Tunney	Chicago	104,943	2,658,660
1935	Louis-Max Baer	New York	88,150	1,000,832
1938	Louis-Schmeling	New York	70,043	1,015,012
1946	Louis-Conn	New York	45,266	1,925,564

After that came inflation, television and phase two:

Year	Match	Site	Attendance	Total Receipts
1955	Marciano-Moore	New York	61,574	$2,248,117
1960	Johansson-Patterson	New York	31,892	2,468,278
1962	Patterson-Liston	Chicago	18,890	4,665,420
1963	Clay (Ali)-Patterson	Las Vegas	7816	4,747,690
1965	Ali-Liston	Lewiston, Me.	2424	1,602,190
1965	Ali-Patterson	Las Vegas	7402	3,570,000
1966	Ali-Cooper	London	42,000	1,200,000
1970	Frazier-Ellis	New York	18,079	1,281,369

So the ringside crowds were growing smaller but the broadcasting revenue was growing larger and, when Ali finally ended his exile in 1970 by knocking out Jerry Quarry in Atlanta, he took home nearly $1,000,000 dollars — despite the fact that the live gate in the Municipal Auditorium reached only a fourth of that total. In Madison Square Garden, by contrast, the crowd watching the fight via pay television kicked in $201,622. Now Cooke and Perenchio were staking out the best of both possible worlds by staging their "fight of the century" in the Garden while piping it to the paying customers outside.

"I'm a traditionalist," Perenchio said, as though apologizing for their choice of the Garden in the new era of the coaxial cable. "I'm a cornball. I believe if you have the biggest fight in history, you should have it in the greatest boxing arena in the world. Ever since I was a kid, I associated boxing with Madison Square Garden, all the way back to the Gillette days.

"The live gate with these numbers is the tail to the dog. Whatever we would have done in Houston, let's say two million dollars, that's not the ball game. What was important was how big a network we could put together."

In so many words, Perenchio was welcoming the new era of TV-studio sports while at the same time shedding a tear for the old era of arena sports. He had taken the gamble because of the former and he had stamped himself "a traditionalist" because of the latter. But regardless of the semantics, he was trumpeting a revolution: Ali, a heavyweight boxer, was fighting Cloverlay, Inc., a Philadelphia corporation; broadcast rights, once considered "residual," now formed 90 per cent of the total gate; and the traditionalist old shrines like Madison Square Garden, on the nights when they were not being used as television studios, would have to venture beyond professional sports into the wider business of professional *entertainment* in order to pay the electric bills.

In the case of the Garden, shrine number one, such a transformation had long been in progress. Then, as the seventies arrived, the trend to broader entertainment took on some of the aspects of a stampede — financed by conglomerates, directed by theater and television people, housed in a modern tower that rose above the railroad tracks of Pennsylvania Station in mid-Manhattan. The whole complex was part of a business empire that included oil wells, shopping centers, and harness tracks. It was not even the anchor of the empire but, like Jack Kent

Cooke's Forum in Inglewood, California, it was a sort of show-place, a sort of billboard, a sort of beachhead in the staging of public spectacles that suddenly were paying athletes two and a half million dollars for one-night stands.

It was a far cry from the first building to carry the name Madison Square Garden, an abandoned rail terminal at Madison Avenue and Twenty-sixth Street farther downtown. And a far cry from the Garden that was remodeled there in 1890 by the celebrated architect Stanford White — who was shot and killed on the site sixteen years later by Pittsburgh millionaire Harry K. Thaw, in a roof-garden drama that centered on Thaw's wife, the noted beauty Evelyn Nesbit.

The second Garden, a windowless barn at Eighth Avenue and Fiftieth Street, farther uptown, became the home of the six-day bicycle race, the New York Rangers, Joe Humphreys, Tex Rickard, Harry Balogh, basketball double-headers, and Joe Louis. The gates may have been smaller in those days, but the tumult was not. When the "new" Garden opened in 1925, Mayor James J. Walker presided at ringside and Humphreys — the voice of old New York, who once had introduced prizefights on river barges — recited an elegiac poem titled "The Temple of Fistiana."

When Humphreys passed from the clamorous scene, his funeral service was conducted in the lobby of the Garden, a tribute also conferred upon Rickard, who had booked Dempsey in his heyday. Then the voice in the center ring became the voice of Balogh, a genius at delivering ad-lib remarks and extemporaneous speeches. Balogh probably reached a peak of achievement in delivering his "thing" one night when he received an urgent appeal from the management to delay the proceedings. So he launched a meandering monologue that covered topics far and wide and that ended brilliantly when he intoned: "And in conclusion, may I extend to you my best wishes for a happy and enjoyable *Memorial Day.*"

Then there was Joe Louis, who once had lugged fenders in a Detroit auto factory for five dollars a day and who wound up making so much money, much of it in the Garden, that he wound up owing the government $1,000,000 in taxes. He was twenty-three when he won the heavyweight title by knocking out James J. Braddock in 1937 after a tune-up career of thirty-six bouts, of which he had won thirty-five and thirty-one of those by knockouts. Then he defended his title twenty-seven times before retiring, only to be drawn into a "comeback" twenty-seven months later when boxing needed his name and the government needed his million.

Louis was so innocent in some respects that he would hand out $100 black chips in Las Vegas when panhandlers applied the bite. Once he was walking along the street with Billy Conn, his friend for thirty years and his heavyweight opponent twice. Conn admonished him for being careless with cash, warning that he'd have to line up John D. Rockefeller or Andrew Mellon to finance Louis's crap games. Joe asked who Andrew Mellon was, and Conn decided to reduce the information to its simplest terms by replying: "Just some guy I know in Pittsburgh."

Later, Louis spent three years in the army, put on ninety-six exhibition bouts before two million soldiers, gave one of his fight purses totaling $47,000 to the Navy Relief Fund, and calculated ruefully that it still would take 200 years for him to square things with the Internal Revenue Service. In 1970, just as Muhammad Ali and Joe Frazier were signing for their coup of the century, he entered a veterans' hospital in Denver suffering from a mental breakdown at the age of fifty-six.

Back at the Garden, meanwhile, the new decade of entertainment was arriving, and none of the swivel chairs was being occupied by old-line promoters like Tex Rickard or Mike Jacobs. In their place came the outside money men like Jerry Perenchio and the inside impresarios like Alvin Cooperman, who had graduated from the Shubert Theaters and the National Broadcasting Company, and, at the top of the superstructure, until his sudden death in August of 1971, Philip J. Levin — lawyer, banker, real-estate man, and theatrical investor.

Levin appeared on the scene after a series of business mergers and acquisitions that placed the Garden into the mammoth corporate family of something called the Transnation Development Corporation. He owned the titles of chairman of the board and president of Transnation and also owned 31 per cent of the stock, while Gulf & Western Industries owned 42 per cent. Through his alliance with the Garden, he also controlled a large chunk of the Roosevelt Raceway harness track on Long Island, as well as the New York Knickerbockers basketball team, the New York Rangers hockey team, the Felt Forum and its rotating entertainment events, the Holiday on Ice show, and the Garden's boxing programs, which had come a long way from Joe Humphreys and the river-barge days.

Levin came to his swivel chair with an impressive background in making money out of sows' ears. He already owned 100 shopping centers around the country plus half of the Paramount Building in Times Square, and had just made two unsuccessful attempts to take over Metro-Goldwyn-Mayer when he took up the challenge of developing the Garden from a money-loser into a moneymaker. He also ran the Arlington and Washington Park racetracks in Chicago and made a personal visit to the winner's circle to present the silverware to Sonny Werblin when Silent Screen won the Futurity and pocketed $206,075 for ninety-three seconds of racing.

Levin's zeal for acquiring real estate once boomeranged, leaving him the proud possessor of a golf club for six years. He actually had wanted to buy the site of the Suburban Country Club in Union, New Jersey, and turn it into a shopping center. But he knew he would never get it unless he could offer the members another club for their golfing weekends, so he bought a semipublic, rundown course at Scotch Plains, poured money into improving it, and then got the revolting news that the members at Suburban had vetoed the switch.

"I'm stuck with a golf club," he said, a little amused at the thought. But, like other people who can laugh all the way to the bank, he plunged into the deal for Madison Square Garden, not too perturbed by the possibility that he also might become stuck with a four-acre gymnasium.

The Garden, meanwhile, was using up a lot of red ink despite its ranking as the indoor sports center of the country. In its first fiscal quarter just as Levin was closing in, it lost $2,000,000, and in the previous year had cleared a trifling $93,000 on revenues of $54,500,000 just after it had lost $2,000,000 more the year before that.

Nevertheless, Levin had enjoyed living dangerously ever since he invested $18,000 into a filling station in 1937. Thirty years later he made $20,000,000 by selling his stock in M-G-M after a bid to control the company had narrowly missed connections. Now he owned 11 per cent of the Garden, which was 3 per cent less than Gulf & Western Industries but 1 per cent more than the Penn Central Railroad. And the board of directors that took over the company was awesomely diversified, considering that its assets included things like basketballs and boxing gloves: ten of the nineteen directors represented the Garden management or the Penn Central, two were nominated by Roosevelt Raceway, four by Gulf & Western and three by Transnation.

"An office building is an office building," Levin said, like any whirling dervish who spins from movie studios to supermarkets to racetracks. "But I think entertainment and leisure are the business of the future. I don't believe in having just real estate. I believe in real estate with a mix — with a certain percentage of it oriented toward entertainment and leisure-time industries. In other words, real estate with sex."

The only problem was that inflation was driving up the price of everything, including real estate and sex, and there were just

so many seats in places like Madison Square Garden for the public to spend those leisure-time hours and dollars.

It was something like the squeeze that success had forced on
pro football, except that football stadiums might hold 60,000
seats while the Garden stopped at 20,234 or fewer. For ice
hockey alone, for example, it held 17,250 seats and sold more
than 13,000 of those on a season basis for forty-one games (including two exhibitions in *September*).

The "price" method of allocation didn't discourage many
people either. Every seat in the house on the loge level was
snapped up *before* the season at $348.50, as was every seat in the
first promenade section at $348.50 and the second promenade at
$287. Beyond that there might be some seats left, but beyond
that it took $225.50 and exceptionally good eyesight to qualify a
fan for the upstairs rows.

Money was no barrier even when the Garden offered seats in
monster packages for several sports. That, in Garden literature,
was known as Plan I: ninety-seven events, including forty-one
Rangers hockey games, forty-three Knicks basketball games, and
thirteen "special sports and entertainment events," all for the
irresistible price of $985 down front, $815 farther back, and $705
farther back than that. And all those seats were still sold out before the season began, leaving the public to grapple for the $560
or $440 bargains in the boondocks.

Worse, the caliber of play was decreasing in sports like hockey
because the number of "major league" teams was increasing,
doubling, to be precise. Even an expansion team like the Oakland Seals, which had an average attendance of 4000 customers a
game during three seasons — the worst in hockey — went to
Charles O. Finley in 1970 for $4,500,000. And in order to spend
his money for such a dubious proposition, Finley had to win out
over a rival bidder, Jerry Seltzer, the "roller-derby king," who
cut his long hair and wore a conservative black suit in an effort
to improve his image before the board of governors of the Na-

tional Hockey League. But Seltzer's barber and tailor were no match for Finley, who came to the meeting armed with $4,500,-000, seventeen letters of recommendation from baseball owners and officials, and a pledge to move his residence from Chicago to Oakland.

But even while Seltzer was consulting his barber, the league was visualizing still wider expansion for the mid-seventies, with Miami, Dallas, Seattle, Atlanta, and other cities already on line. When the time came, though, the new "markets" would be forced to go through the same song-and-dance as Finley and Seltzer had gone through in Oakland, with the sole certainty that the price of membership in the big leagues would go even higher — as it had gone in baseball, football, and basketball.

Any doubts on that score were dispelled when the NHL opened its doors, its arms, and its cash registers to the first two new entrants of the seventies: the Buffalo Sabres and the Vancouver Canucks. They anted up $6,000,000 apiece, and for that tidy sum were permitted to join the league with players drafted from the established clubs. Eighteen skaters and two goaltenders in all — starting sensationally with the sixteenth best skater and the third best goalie on each team. The reason was that the regular owners had already voted to "protect" fifteen players each. As a result, Buffalo and Vancouver put their money into the pot and selected a total of forty hockey players, only thirteen of whom had spent the better part of the previous season in the league and only three of whom might be considered quality players. And *their* average age was thirty-six.

Once past the entry fee, the new clubs immediately were plunged into the economic facts of life that the old-line clubs already had been juggling: too many fans for the number of seats available, too many seats for the number of fans available, the pressure to meet the players' spiraling salary demands, the pressure to make an ally of national television in order to soften the pressure of all the demands.

The trick was to raise more money all the time without pricing yourself out of business, and there were several ways to do that: Charge what the traffic would bear on tickets. Lure more crowds into the place during a 365-day year. Offer a greater variety of events along with the varsity sports — the old side-show trick. Expand the audience and the market beyond the walls of the arena by television, public or pay. And, if all that wasn't enough, invest your money in outside businesses.

In pursuing all these avenues of trade, the Garden had long since divided itself into specialty sections, like the State Department and the Bank of America. There was a basketball department, established in the early nineteen thirties after a sportswriter named Ned Irish had attracted sellout crowds by scheduling college basketball double-headers. There was a hockey department, headed by a lawyer (and golfing enthusiast) named William M. Jennings. There was a boxing department, which dated to the days of Tex Rickard and Mike Jacobs and was now directed by Harry Markson. There even was a television department, headed by Jack Price, which struck in two directions: A network of independent stations anchored by WOR in New York carried basketball and hockey games played on the road, and the Sterling Manhattan cable company carried home games for a price to subscribers in New York.

So much for the apparatus. As for talent, judgment, and skill, the Garden also shared that problem with the State Department. For years, the only certain moneymaker in the house was bowling, which didn't require too much management judgment to promote. Then came ice hockey, because New York always had been "a Ranger town," even in the days when the team shared the home rink with the New York Americans. But basketball, supposedly the country's biggest sport in terms of fans at all levels, had required special attention because money tends to follow winners and the Knickerbockers had spent eight straight years in the Eastern Division cellar of the National Basketball Association.

The drought started in 1959 and continued until the winter

of 1966–1967, and if anybody needed a reason, this one would do for openers: None — that is to say, none — of the Knicks' number one college draft choices between 1960 and 1965 proved to be worth the price of admission. In 1960, the scouts suggested Darrell Imhoff, and he was duly selected and was duly forgotten, as far as number one draft choices go; in 1961, Tom Stith; in 1962, Paul Hogue; in 1963, Art Heyman; and in 1964, Jim Barnes. And this was happening at a time when cellar-dwellers got first shot at the campus talent.

But the spell was broken in 1965, when Eddie Donovan was promoted from coach of the team to vice president of basketball operations. He had been the coach at St. Bonaventure University, switched to the pros in 1961, and remained with the Garden until 1970, when he returned upstate to run Buffalo's new club. But before he did, he put the Knicks back on the map, financially as well as artistically.

The revival actually started in 1964, when the team drafted Barnes in the first round of the college grab bag. More significant was its choice in the second round: Willis Reed. A year later, Bill Bradley and Dave Stallworth. A year after that, Cazzie Russell. A year later, Walt Frazier. And the same year, 1967, Bradley returned from his Rhodes Scholarship at Oxford, signed a half-million-dollar contract for four years' work, and things began to perk up.

Bradley, a 6-foot-5-inch intellectual from Princeton, had scored 2503 points in eighty-three college games, the equivalent of one full season in the NBA. He read Camus, quoted Spinoza, made the 1960 Olympic team, served as the Knicks' player representative, toured the world in 1970, and smiled only faintly when politicians speculated that a White House might be in his future. For the moment, though, his impact on the sports scene was measured in dollar signs as basketball players finally reached the brackets already staked out in football, baseball, and golf.

The first to get there was Russell, a physical-training fanatic and perpetual-motion machine from the University of Michigan, who signed for $250,000 for four seasons. Then came Bradley, who doubled the take, and then Lew Alcindor of UCLA, who doubled *Bradley's* take: $1,000,000, including annuities, deferred payments, and extra added attractions like land and even cows. Alcindor's arrival demonstrated the mixed blessing inherent in the escalating situation: his million put a huge dent into the ledger of the new Milwaukee Bucks team, but his presence guaranteed the survival of the franchise, and also for a time threatened the survival of the American Basketball Association, the "rival" league, which had come calling with a bankroll too.

As high as the bidding had gone, it still had not reached the ceiling. Bob Lanier of St. Bonaventure signed with the Detroit Pistons for $1,200,000 for five years, and then along came Pete Maravich of Louisiana State at $1,500,000, courtesy of the Atlanta Hawks, and Spencer Haywood of the University of Detroit at almost $2,000,000, courtesy of two teams, two leagues, and a brace of lawsuits, as the whole soaring war finally broke into litigation and the old familiar bugaboo of antitrust actions.

Maravich, a gangling twenty-two-year-old with wild hair and a wild style on the court, exceeded even the fondest expectations of his father, Press Maravich, who also was his college coach. He averaged forty-four points a game for three varsity seasons and did it with a runaway temper that cost him a career total of eleven technical fouls. But once he was ready for graduation into the pros, he jubilantly became the centerpiece of a financial tug-of-war between the Carolina Cougars of the ABA, led by thirty-seven-year-old Jim Gardner, the Hardee hamburger heir who also had served in Congress and just missed being elected governor of North Carolina, and the Atlanta Hawks of the NBA, led by thirty-eight-year-old Tom Cousins, whose real-estate development firm listed assets in excess of $2,500,000.

Their frantic wooing made Pete a rich man, with guarantees

of $300,000 a year, including a straight salary of $40,000, a new Plymouth GTX equipped with a telephone, a country-club membership, and an apartment in Atlanta. "I wouldn't need a car telephone in Baton Rouge," Pete explained, "but Atlanta is much larger."

The salary-plus-bonus packages that went to Maravich and his contemporaries were obviously inflated in the public's eye, since they included everything and the kitchen sink that might have been thrown in as an inducement. But they were big enough, and legitimate enough, to create a whole new class of agents and money managers. Typical of these, in a rags-to-riches way, was Chuck Kaufman, who used to run a dry-cleaning store on Eighth Avenue in Manhattan alongside the old Garden and who doubled as an "uncle" to the Knicks' players and as a sort of assistant equipment manager to the team. When the ABA began making its bid in 1966, he decided to do some real cleaning up. Along with a lawyer named Norman Blass, he became a full-time agent and by 1970 was representing gold nuggets like Lanier, Dave Cowens of the Boston Celtics, and Mike Price of the Knicks.

Some agents even acknowledged that they were scouting players in college, signing them to personal-services contracts, nursing them along on monthly payments of maybe $200, and biding their time until the rival professional leagues started waving the big money around. And in a few cases, they even lined up the talent, and tied up the talent, in high school.

To pay for all this, the basketball franchises were forced to go to extreme lengths, as the Garden did in 1968 with its new eight-and-a-half acre entertainment center. It was a $133,000,000 complex that was grouped around the main arena, a circular thirteen-story building that resembled a giant's hat box or snare drum. But while the arena for basketball, hockey, and boxing formed the center ring, so to speak, with seating space for 20,234 persons, the new Garden also included auditoriums, nooks, crannies, and rinks. The idea was to build a gigantic play-ground for sports, industry, and entertainment and, with this in mind, the promoters surrounded the arena with these offshoots:

The Felt Forum, an auditorium that seated 5227; a Cinema with 501 seats; forty-eight bowling alleys; a Hall of Fame; a sports art gallery; and an exposition rotunda. In addition, a satellite company called Madison Square Garden Attractions, Inc., took care of "road-company" entertainment around the country and another satellite called MSG-ABC Productions, Inc., handled television. For a time, the Garden even operated the Skyliners soccer team and flirted with the notion of buying the Jets football team. You name it, they had it — or at least they were interested in having it.

"The existing Garden wasn't obsolete in nineteen sixty," noted Irving Mitchell Felt, who had taken charge of the enter-prise that year, "but we believed it would be by nineteen sev-enty. And we figured that by then, good available property in Manhattan would be nonexistent. Madison Square Garden had become a household name over the years, and we intended to keep it that way."

When the curtain was rung up on February 11, 1968, a lot of other household names were gathered on a stage in the center of the arena for the kickoff. Bob Hope, Bing Crosby, Pearl Bailey, the West Point Glee Club, and, to lend a trace of old-fashioned sports, folk-heroes Jack Dempsey and Gene Tunney. It was true, some seats had restricted views in spite of the architectural brains behind the project, and it was true, somehow no press box had been provided in the plans. But there it was — open for business 365 days of the year, restaurants and all, and an office building towered overhead to supply space, rents, and the final commercial flourish.

The man who scheduled the acts, Cooperman, reached to the far corners of his show-biz imagination to keep things jumping. The old standby, the Ringling Brothers–Barnum & Bailey Circus, soon was joined by rock 'n' roll troupes, a Disney carnival that ran most of the summer, the Mrs. Black America pageant, the Moscow Ice Show with Russian bears playing hockey — on skates — and a roller derby. Then, as the supreme test, 400 professional motorcycle racers took over the boards early in 1971 and whipped around the arena for $25,000 in prize money while the customers paid between four dollars and seven dollars to watch them climb the walls.

The need for volume business was as acute on Thirty-third Street as on Wall Street. The cost of payrolls alone was skyrocketing, even though the storybook bonus deals bestowed on the Laniers and Maraviches were by no means universal. At the other end of the scale, the *minimum* pay in the NBA had climbed from $6000 or $7000 in the early sixties to $10,000 in 1967, when the players' association started interceding, then to $13,500. And late in 1970, a three-year contract between the owners and the association increased the ante to $15,500 immediately and $17,500 by the 1972–1973 season. Two generations earlier, in the pioneer days of pro basketball, the original Celtics in one of their plushier seasons had drawn a team total of $14,-376 — including traveling expenses.

On the road to affluence, the NBA players had twice threatened to strike during disputes similar to those in football and baseball — once before the 1963 All-Star game and again before the 1967 play-offs. Both times, they were pacified: first by the establishment of a pension plan, and next by an increase in the pension itself. Now, like the players in the other major sports, they negotiated through a lawyer, Larry Fleisher, who dickered across the table from Walter Kennedy, who had become commissioner of the NBA in 1963.

As a result of the game's surge in popularity, and of their own economic strength, the big men had won not only the highest minimum pay of the major sports but also the highest average pay: $35,000. To feed their seven-foot frames, the daily meal allowance had risen to nineteen dollars besides. Sometimes even the average salary seemed tiny, especially in the big cities, where the average man tended to be a good deal above average. The Philadelphia 76ers, for example, were reported to be paying these salaries, emoluments and considerations as the seventies began:

Billy Cunningham (who jumped the team to join the ABA, then jumped back) — $235,000; Archie Clark — $125,000; Luke Jackson — $100,000; Hal Greer — $100,000; Bailey Howell — $62,500; Wally Jones — $40,000; Jim Washington — $30,000; Matt Goukas (later traded) — $30,000; and four other players, a combined total of $110,000. That added up to a payroll of $832,500, or almost $70,000 a man.

Oscar Robertson, the old smoothie, already had switched from Cincinnati to Milwaukee at $175,000 a year for three years. Rick Barry had played musical and financial chairs from San Francisco to Oakland to Washington to the New York Nets, where, between courtroom briefs, he collected $250,000 in a two-year contract that the Nets hoped would put them into business vis-à-vis the "other" team in town — the Knicks, who were merely the world champions and who probably had the gaudiest payroll around.

The college class of 1970 alone cost the rival leagues something like $10,000,000. One coach, Joe Williams of Jacksonville, even moved up a notch or two by leaving a $12,000 job for a $20,000 one at Furman that included fringe benefits like a rent-free home, television set, medical expenses for the family, country-club membership, a new car, radio and TV shows, and a summer basketball camp. Not exactly Pete Maravich, but not bad for a mere coach. And Rick Barry, before joining the Nets, was heard to lament the previous hop in his table-hopping career between San Francisco and Washington: "It would be ridiculous to complain about making only seventy-five thousand dollars with the Caps, but if I had played with the Warriors this season I would have made one hundred sixty-seven thousand five hundred dollars."

Barry, who also had owned 15 per cent of the Oakland franchise when he played there, meanwhile had seen the club move (with him as the star attraction) to Washington at a price of $2,600,000 to the new owner. The Boston Celtics, though, changed hands the same season for $6,000,000. But the rising tide of money caused the Houston team to collapse on the threshold of joining the NBA. It couldn't come up with the $750,000 down payment on the $3,700,000 entrance fee and folded while it was still on paper.

The three clubs that survived the initiation into the fraternity were Cleveland, Portland, and Buffalo, and they went into business in the 1970–1971 season with pot-luck draft picks and bills. Cleveland tried to foot the bill by "going public," a novelty in basketball but an old technique in business. It offered 400,000 shares of common stock to residents of Ohio at five dollars a share, then treated the new "owners" to forty-four defeats in the team's first fifty games. The Milwaukee Bucks had raised about $2,000,000 that way by selling 400,000 shares to residents of Wisconsin at five dollars a share, but the man in the street and his investment were spared when Lew Alcindor arrived and the stock doubled in price.

At Seattle, though, the SuperSonics did it with flair. They sold 240,000 shares of common stock to the public at seven dollars a share. Half of the $1,700,000 raised that way went back to the Sonics; half went to the nine original owners — whose investment worked out to something like sixty-seven cents a share.

The investors, who did all this with their eyes wide open, and in some cases with their eyes popeyed open, were counting on the lure of superstars like Alcindor and the further lure of outside cash: like television. They got both. Alcindor and most of the other college heroes made it as professionals, and TV was not far behind. In 1970, the NBA signed a three-year agreement with the American Broadcasting Company for $67,000,000, a gain of $4,000,000 over the previous contract, while people around the league tipped their collective hat to the New York Knicks, the chief draw of Madison Square Garden, who had turned on the cash-carrying public with their whirlwind work in the winter of 1969–1970.

"Having a winner in New York is the greatest thing to ever happen to the NBA," said Ben Kerner, who had tried to make a winner with the St. Louis Hawks until he did a little arithmetic and figured that he stood to lose his shirt. "The glory rubs off on the rest of the league. That's what made the American Football League — the Jets, not Denver or San Diego."

"That's how the NFL grew too," said Roone Arledge, the president of ABC Sports, who could remember how Y. A. Tittle and the Giants had turned on the cash-carrying public too. "Three networks were bidding for the NFL television contract, and that started the whole thing."

The "whole thing" in the indoor sports, said basketball commissioner Walter Kennedy, could be pinpointed even more precisely than that: "In the period of one month when the Knicks won eighteen straight games, we got more national coverage than any month in the previous twenty-four years."

More coverage, more money. "The Knicks," Arledge reported, getting down to cases, "made it a lot easier for us to sell advertising during telecasts because a winning team in New York creates more excitement among advertisers. When everyone started talking about the Knicks and how they were winning, advertisers said, 'We've got to get that.' The cost of a minute of advertising during an NBA game in 1970 was about twenty-three thousand dollars and it will go up."

It was headed up, everyone agreed, because basketball had reached the star-quality status that baseball long had enjoyed back to the days when bubblegum cards were being snapped up by small boys in Nebraska, that football had reached in the sixties, and that golf was reaching in the seventies. And basketball was reaching it despite a complex system of rules that awarded one, two, or three foul shots in various situations, that required the use of *two* clocks during games, and that kept separate lists of "team" fouls as well as "personal" fouls. The game might never be decided until the final fifteen seconds, with the teams tied at maybe 119 to 119, but along the way they had treated the viewers to some unthinkable running, passing, and shooting.

When the Knicks won their championship in a seven-game match with the Los Angeles Lakers, the best in the West, they set records for public concentration in Los Angeles even when playing in New York. The TV statisticians somehow figured that one in every three television sets on the Coast was tuned in to the game in Madison Square Garden, nearly 3000 miles away, and more than twice as many people were following the game as were following the top-rated world-news broadcast at the same time.

Newspaper statisticians were kept busy too, measuring the public's response. The Associated Press estimated that basketball had begun the decade of the sixties as the tenth "most popular" sport in reader interest. By 1967, with the ABA making its pitch and the money war heating up, it had risen to eighth place and, by the seventies, to fourth — behind pro football, college football, and baseball.

At the turnstiles too the tempo was quickening. The NBA was playing to 60 per cent of capacity, with five million tickets sold, and the Knicks were arriving at the one-million level, which was almost as high as half the teams in the major leagues of baseball (who played almost twice as many games).

The statistics were read with enthusiasm by everybody who had a finger in the pie — Roone Arledge and his counterparts at NBC and CBS, Carl Lindemann and Bill MacPhail; the old command at places like the Garden, headed by Felt; the new command, headed by Levin; the agents like Kaufman; the lawyers like Fleisher; the commissioners like Kennedy of the NBA and Jack Dolph of the ABA, and last, but by no means least, by the players themselves. They had watched the advent of the millionaire freshmen like Alcindor and Maravich, and they appreciated the fact that even the veterans had benefited. Earl Monroe went from $20,000 a year at Baltimore to $150,000, and John Havlicek at Boston from $50,000 to $100,000.

The chief reasons, they concluded, were television and the war between the leagues. So when the leagues decided in 1970 that it would be wiser and cheaper to merge, the players decided to resist. Their sense of constitutional history told them that a merger would become a monopoly, and their sense of economics told them that a monopoly would end the picnic. So they did the only sensible thing for men about to lose a long-range feast: they hired two law professors from New York University and sued.

They had plenty of company. Connie Hawkins had sued the NBA after he had been barred for "associations" with gamblers in high school and college and won a $1,500,000 settlement. Spencer Haywood sued after he was barred because he had dropped out of college, though he later signed with Denver of the ABA and Seattle of the NBA, thereby embroiling both leagues at the same time. He also created the most serious internal schism in the NBA's twenty-five-year history because Seattle insisted on keeping him despite the league's ban. And in baseball, Curt Flood was carrying the antitrust cudgels, while in football a federal grand jury opened hearings in 1971 on the same issue.

That is, professional sports had three antitrust lawsuits going in its three major sports, something that even the robber barons might have envied in the days of Teddy Roosevelt. Joe Namath probably expressed the general feeling when he testified in the football inquiry, suggesting that a monopoly did exist and that it did work against the player, and then later confessed: "It's all over my head."

The money malaise, moreover, was spreading to hockey, and with good reason. It long had been considered "the most secretive" of all sports, and probably the lowest paying of the major ones. Since the NHL was founded during World War I, few clubs disclosed salary or even cost information. The salaries were embarrassingly low, for one thing, and even when the Boston Bruins were prodded in 1970 to reveal Derek Sanderson's pay, the answer compounded the confusion. They were prodded, actually, by Sanderson himself — the long-haired, swinging, blithe spirit of the game, hockey's answer to Joe Willie.

His income, the team replied, was $39,000. His *salary*, Sanderson shot back, was only $14,000 of that amount, one-third what the neighboring Celtics paid their number six man, Larry Siegfried. The Bruins, replied the front office again, fattened his salary with an $11,000 bonus, while fringe benefits and league bonuses pushed the total to $39,000.

But behind the semantics and digits lay the simple truth of Sanderson's day and age: Hockey players wanted more ice.

Although the league had been in business longer than any of the basketball or football leagues, only one $100,000-a-year man had emerged: Bobby Hull of the Chicago Black Hawks, with the prodigy Bobby Orr of Boston coming up fast on the outside. Willis Reed of the Knicks (at $100,000) earned three times as much as Jean Ratelle, the best player on the Rangers. Nobody on the Rangers earned more than $50,000 as the seventies opened, except for Tim Horton, who had been acquired in a trade from Toronto, where he had been wealthy enough off the rink to hold out for $80,000.

In an effort to break loose, four of the Rangers formed a united bargaining front for the 1970–1971 season and negotiated as a unit through a lawyer. The four were Brad Park, Walt Tkaczuk, Vic Hadfield, and Ratelle, and their statistical argument was imposing: The Rangers had made almost as much money in hockey as the Jets in football, but little had trickled down to the players. Mike Riordan, a reserve player on the Knicks, got $35,000, more than any Ranger except Rod Gilbert and Horton, and any eighth-round draft choice in football got more than any top rookie in hockey.

It was true that the Rangers were paying a quarter of a million dollars a year to support amateur hockey in Canada, where 178 of the league's players lived. It was true that they paid half a million dollars a year to sponsor a development team. It was also true that television returned $100,000 to each hockey club in the United States, while pro football clubs got fifteen times as much. But the players, who apparently spent the off season doing their arithmetic homework, noted that the Rangers had increased ticket prices more than one dollar a seat on the average and would gross $800,000 more from the customers alone.

"I served my apprenticeship," said Tkaczuk, who was earning $14,000 a season, or about $150 a game. "This is my only chance to make it."

"It was bound to come," said Arnie Brown. "There will be more hard talk next season, not only among the Rangers but all over the league."

"It's a matter of pride now," said Brad Park. "Sure, I know what effect this has on a team. But I can't think of that. There's a time when you have to think of yourself. I think we work harder even than football players."

Not everyone could become a Sanderson, with a Lincoln and forty-five suits in the closet, nor a Bobby Orr, with a yellow Firebird *and* Cadillac, plus endorsement arrangements with General Motors of Canada, Yardley, Bic Pens, and a brewery, plus a boys' camp where 1700 Canadians paid $125 a week. Nor could everyone grow into a Bobby Hull, who signed a four-year contract in 1968 at $100,000 a season but who then fell into an argument with the Chicago management over tax benefits. The argument started when nobody could locate a handwritten rider to the contract supposedly composed by William Wirtz, the president of the Black Hawks, and initialed by Hull. It outlined details on how the money would be paid with the least possible tax damage.

Later Wirtz denied he ever had signed such a rider and Hull responded in the accepted manner: He refused to play. Nobody had thought to make a copy and, Hull's lawyer said, Bobby took the original, stuffed it into his pocket, followed a police escort from the office to the Chicago Stadium to play against the Rangers — and somewhere along the line, his tax formula blew away in the Chicago wind.

Which is what everybody caught up in the inflationary spiral feared: that it was all written on the wind.

It was the same fear that the promoters had when they invested $133,000,000 into entertainment centers like the new Garden — real estate with sex, and with problems. The same for the fan who paid $700 for a pair of season hockey tickets in the gleaming new arena, then found them partly obstructed, and then became upset when he got a look at the ice and saw expansion teams flubbing around it like the junior varsity. One of them grew so vexed that he complained in a letter to the *New York Times:*

"What hockey has done aside from doubling the admission is indeed an insult to the hockey fan. In the old Garden we were usually treated to good entertainment and competition by the best six hockey teams that money and talent could build. In exchange for a tidy sum given to the old teams, eight new ones have been created, none of which has a chance of beating the Rangers except possibly after the Rangers spend a long night at Mr. Laff's or Maxwell's Plum. They are in reality of minor league caliber. If this were a Broadway show, it would have closed the following night."

It was the same fear that even Muhammad Ali could express in a half-joke at the moment he signed to fight Joe Frazier for two and a half million apiece, and then learned the fight might gross between twenty and thirty million.

"Thirty million dollars!" he shrieked, sounding the battle cry for all the Bobby Hulls, Pete Maraviches, and their lawyers. "Frazier, we've been taken. They got us cheap."

10

The Members of the Cast

IN THE GOOD OLD DAYS, at least in the particular Good Old Days before World War II, a nickel would buy a subway ride, a cigar, or an Eskimo Pie. Not only that, but people seemed interested in all three options — some because they could be bought for a nickel, some because they were remnants of a way of life that was coming under increasing pressure, from Manchuria to Czechoslovakia to Spain and wherever else the armies were rolling.

In view of the ominous future that was gathering, nobody could be blamed for clinging either to the nickel or to the way of life. Even Hollywood saluted the past, bestowing its Academy Awards in 1939 on Vivien Leigh for *Gone with the Wind* and on Robert Donat for *Goodbye, Mr. Chips*. The Pulitzer Prizes the same year went to recorders of Americana like Marjorie Kinnan Rawlings for *The Yearling,* Robert E. Sherwood for *Abe Lincoln in Illinois,* and Carl Van Doren for *Benjamin Franklin.* And, in case the point needed emphasis, to Frank Luther Mott for *A History of American Magazines.*

In sports too, the old favorites were still surfacing. The New York Yankees won 106 games, the American League pennant, and the World Series. Joe Louis fought four opponents and only one went past the fourth round. Joe DiMaggio hit .381, Jimmy Foxx whacked thirty-five home runs, Lefty Grove pitched fifteen victories in nineteen decisions, Paul Derringer pitched twenty-two in twenty-nine decisions, Byron Nelson won the United States Open, Bobby Riggs dislodged Don Budge as the national tennis champion, and Wilbur Shaw got his racing car up to 115 miles an hour and took the Indianapolis 500.

So the nickel cigar and the nickel beer were still in the picture, though people could not feel too blessed by such bargains because the Great Depression was still in the picture too. Farmers were selling hogs for five dollars or so a hundred pounds, the United States Army was living on half a billion dollars a year (including its Air Corps), and the federal debt was still somewhere around the forty-billion mark, which caused Franklin Roosevelt some problems with the thrifty but which soon came to be regarded as a drop in the bucket.

It was, in short, a time when Eskimo Pies were not to be sneezed at in the marketplace.

Consequently, a few eyebrows were raised when the Treasury Department reported some economic facts of life to Congress, notably the peaks of income on the American sporting landscape, and the Associated Press duly passed the word that "athletes and sportsmen took good-sized parts of the nation's payroll last year."

The list of bonanzas was headed by James J. Braddock, the former heavyweight champion, who drew $51,000 in salary from the Braddock-Gould enterprises — a holdover from the days when Braddock collected purses instead of weekly paychecks. Then, the report noted, Lou Gehrig "got $36,000 for playing first base for the New York Yankees." After that, these were some of the revelations:

Carl Hubbell, the pitching hero of the New York Giants — $22,500.

Hank Greenberg, first baseman and premier home-run hitter for the Detroit Tigers — $25,000.

Bill Terry, the manager of the Giants — $30,000.

Joe McCarthy, the manager of the world champion Yankees — $27,500.

Connie Mack, the long-time manager of the Philadelphia Athletics — $20,000 (which may have made McCarthy feel better about Terry).

Gabby Hartnett, who did the catching, managing, and several other things for the Chicago Cubs — $17,835 (which may have made Mack feel better about McCarthy *and* Terry).

Bill Dickey, who was considered by McCarthy, Terry, and probably most baseball fans as the best catcher around, as well as a fixture on the Yankees — $18,000.

Paul Derringer, the number one pitcher in the National League — $18,000.

Billy Herman, the second baseman for the Cubs — $17,000 (which may not have made Hartnett feel better about anything).

Dick Bartell, shortstop for the Giants and later for the Cubs — $17,000.

Mel Ott, the home-run king of the Giants and later their manager — $17,500.

Charley Gehringer, second baseman for the Detroit Tigers, probably the best in the business — $18,500.

Eddie Collins, Vice President of the Boston Red Sox and the Hall of Fame second baseman — $24,000.

John Reed Kilpatrick, president of Madison Square Garden — $30,000.

George M. Weiss, Vice President of the Newark Bears and empire builder in-training for the Yankees — $21,500 (which may have explained McCarthy and Dickey).

By the pinchpenny standards of the nineteen thirties, all this represented a pretty good haul. At least, it bought a lot of Eskimo Pies. But the war economy was about to revolutionize people's values, including the value of the dollar, and the trend was intensified during the booming television economy after the war.

So, by the time the sixties arrived, most athletes had begun to

suspect that they really were the *underpaid* members of the cast
— usually without agents, lawyers, or labor unions. And the
pressure began to mount for them to acquire all three. The situation was probably personified by Ken McKenzie, a Yale alum-
nus trying to make a living as a baseball pitcher. During a hold-
out for more money one day, he went to George Weiss, by then
the general manager of the Mets.

"Mr. Weiss," said McKenzie, introducing a poignant note
into the negotiations, "I have conducted a survey, and I find
that I am the lowest-paid member of my graduating class."

• • •

"I could have sat around bars all day, telling stories of my days
at Notre Dame and having people think I'm a colorful character," said Dick Lynch, reflecting on the American athlete's determination to force a change of fortune in the sixties and seventies. "But then what would I do? I didn't want to finish my
career and then walk into a company and tell them I played
eight years as a defensive back for the Giants.

"They might look at me and say, 'We don't need any defensive backs right now.' "

"The players' big concern is after they finish playing," said Al
Kaline of the Detroit Tigers. "Baseball players may be different
because so many come up for only three or four years and they
must worry about a business afterward."

"Leaving baseball can be a big shock to a player," said Jim
Lonborg of the Boston Red Sox, who was twenty-six years old at
the time, "because he may never really have prepared himself
for a different kind of life. It has motivated players to think of
the future and in many cases has led them to secure advisers who
tell them they can help secure that future."

"Too many ballplayers wear everything they own," observed
Sid Gillman, the professional football coach. "Suddenly they get
some money and try to make a big impression by wearing a new

suit of clothes every day and driving a fancy car. There's no tomorrow."

"If it weren't for football," said Dick Modzelewski, whose father was a coal loader in a Pennsylvania mine, "I might have been in the mines or a steel mill for the past twenty years."

"It's all a dream world," warned Bart Starr, the quarterback of the Green Bay Packers, "and we must remember that. As long as our names are in front of the public, the speaking engagements and the tie-ins are there. When we drop out of sight, they all end."

In an effort to feather their nests both on and off the playing fields, the athletes of the sixties made economic history of sorts. Along with the rest of the population, more and more of them went to college; and, as television and other pastimes began to disperse the minor leagues and expand the major leagues, more and more professional sports went to the colleges for their talent. In the scramble for that talent, salaries and bonuses were forced up, lawyers and agents were forced in, weak franchises and poor TV markets were forced out. The average salary in baseball spiraled up to $17,000 (ah, there, Dick Bartell), in hockey to $21,000, in football to $22,000, and in basketball to $25,000.

But, as heady as such figures seemed in contrast to the Eskimo Pie days, it was *off* the field where the professional athletes made their greatest yardage as capitalists — from Yogi Berra, the impresario of the Yoo-Hoo beverage, to Merlin Olsen, the Phi Beta Kappa monster of the Los Angeles Rams.

Food, always dear to an athlete's heart, still seemed dear to his pocketbook, and hordes of the modern pros followed the old-time boxers like Jack Dempsey, Mickey Walker, and Lew Tendler straight to the kitchen. It was a lonely town, after a while, that didn't have a drive-in, hamburger stand, bar, restaurant, or fried-chicken haven marked by neon lights flashing names like Gino Marchetti, Joe Namath, Mickey Mantle, Brady Keys, John

Unitas, Willis Reed, Ron Swoboda, Ed Kranepool, Jerry Koosman, Willie Stargell, or Fran Tarkenton. And, during the salad days for such investments, one or two of the flashier spots even might have featured Denny McLain at the electric organ.

Some of the more enterprising players touched off chain reactions that went far beyond simple moonlighting — like Keys, who retired after nine years as a defensive back for the Minnesota Vikings, St. Louis Cardinals, and Pittsburgh Steelers to devote full time to business. His organization was called All-Pro Enterprises, and it included a network of fried-chicken franchises manned by other athletes as well as by just plain businessmen in cities from coast to coast.

His franchise operators were baseball players like Lou Brock of St. Louis and Stargell of Pittsburgh, as well as football players like Lonnie Sanders of St. Louis and Bob Vogel of Baltimore. And, in one stunning example of mass ownership, four members of the Kansas City Chiefs — Ernie Ladd, Buck Buchanan, Otis Taylor, and Jan Stenerud — cornered the chicken market in their area under the symbolic aegis of the "Front Four."

Keys, moreover, gave his business the added dimension of minority investment, with an emphasis on Negro proprietors in what he termed "an experiment in black capitalism that will work." He later proved to be as articulate as he was resolute, and when a food critic undertook a magazine roundup of athletes' dining establishments, he wrote a rebuttal that said in part:

"Never in my experience have I seen this acutely significant subject treated in such a blasé and flippant manner. I would like to point out that the emphasis of our All-Pro Enterprises is not on sports but on providing jobs and business opportunities for blacks all over the country, which we have been doing by the hundreds. The All-Pro Group also includes All-Pro Equities, Young Professionals, and Inter City Development, as well as Brady Keys' Kentucky Fried Chicken.

"Before nineteen seventy-one is over, the number of people who have been helped will be in the thousands."

Other athletes took up the cudgels too, in impressing their seriousness as businessmen on a public that remembered them chiefly as ballplayers. No less an entrepreneur than Yogi Berra went before a Big Business Men's Seminar in New York in 1970 to answer executives' questions about the production, sales, exploitation, and other technical aspects of his Yoo-Hoo soft drink. And, just in case the going got rough, he was flanked by Tucker Frederickson of the football Giants and Wall Street's Allen & Company, Mike Ditka of the Dallas Cowboys and Wall Street's Shearson Hammill & Company, and Bill Swain of the Detroit Lions, who also was his own investment counselor.

The musclemen didn't flinch either on occasions when the questions were pegged by legal pros of the Association of the Bar of the City of New York. At a panel discussion in 1970 that might have made economists wary, the guest experts were Marvin Miller, the baseball players' chef d'opérations; John Gaherin, the baseball owners' negotiator; Jack Kemp, then the quarterback of the Buffalo Bills and president of the American Football League Players Association; and John Gordy, the former Detroit Lion who served as executive director of the National Football League Players Association. The topic — and a far cry it was from the old-fashioned locker-room dice game — was: "Home Run or End-Around at the Bargaining Table: The Professional Athlete and Collective Bargaining."

A few months later, Kemp executed a sort of quarterback sneak by winning election to the House of Representatives from the Buffalo area, switching his game to political footballs. When he arrived in the halls of Congress, though, he found that a beachhead already had been established by Wilmer "Vinegar Bend" Mizell, the ex-Met, ex-Cardinal, ex-Pirate, who had been elected in 1968 from North Carolina.

By then, Bob Friend, the onetime pitcher and graduate economist, already had been elected controller of the city of Pittsburgh; Al Rosen, once a third baseman with a home-run bat, was a flourishing securities man and a member of the board of directors of the Cleveland Indians, his old team; and Jean-Claude Killy, the skiing hero of the 1968 Olympics, was threatening to become an international financier through an avalanche of endorsements and equipment deals on two continents.

But the coup probably was achieved by Dick Hall, a forty-year-old relief pitcher for the Baltimore Orioles, whose stiff-legged, stiff-armed style once was compared somewhat unfavorably with that of "Molly Klutz." When he was done pitching for the Orioles in the World Series, Hall would hurry to his business office, hang out his shingle as a certified public accountant, and pitch in with his colleagues in auditing company books — including those of a client named the Baltimore Orioles.

Sometimes they worked in groups, like the "Front Four" of the Chiefs. As early as 1960, George Strugar, Will Sherman, and Don Burroughs of the Los Angeles Rams pooled their resources and established a small truck company: four trucks, four drivers, and they sometimes included Strugar himself.

"I'll always be grateful to football," said Strugar, once a good defensive tackle before he slipped behind the wheel. "It's amazing how many persons still recognize us."

He wasn't exaggerating. Within seven years, they owned 100 trucks and were grossing $1,250,000.

Sometimes they worked in pairs, and unrelated pairs, at that — like Mickey Mantle and Joe Namath, two "loners" in sports who were brought together in a job agency under the banner of Mantle Men and Namath Girls. It was set up by an advertising agency, Lois Holland Callaway, which was headed by George Lois and which built up $31,000,000 in billings in two years with clients like Braniff International, Edwards & Hanly, and Restaurant Associates Industries.

"We wanted to get the two most popular athletes in New

York, maybe the world, as the spearheads of the business," said Lois. "So we asked Mantle and Namath. They'll be writing letters, cracking hard accounts, having lunch, or playing golf with the president and chairman of the board."

Sometimes the teams ran their own job agencies — for their own athletes. The Washington Redskins started a placement bureau in 1965 to help their people continue college and launch their long-range careers while still playing football. Elijah Pitts, when he was doing his thing for the Green Bay Packers, set up the Pitts Personnel Consultants in Milwaukee. The Minnesota Vikings once sent letters to every major employer in the Minneapolis–St. Paul metropolitan area, putting the message in these words:

"It is easy for us to recommend to prospective employers that they consider our players. If you look at the typical Viking, he is a young man in his early twenties, keen and alert, with a college education and with the will and determination to succeed. He works well with others, or he would not be with our football team. We are not disclosing player names because we feel that consideration given the men should be on the basis of aptitude and ability rather than on a popularity basis."

The same pitch was made by Scientific Research Associates in a four-page prospectus to employers that furnished the background of an athlete, his problems, the "pros and cons" of his sports career, and the economic highlights of his life. And the office of the commissioner of professional football turned over *its* extracurricular careers to Buddy Young, once a running back with the University of Illinois and three pro teams.

"The time is long past," Young observed, "when a player wants to sit around doing nothing between seasons. He looks ahead to the future, to when he is finished with football. Every player should start preparing for his post-football career immediately, so that when he leaves the game, he has someplace to go. He should step across to equal footing, not down."

Some of the boys exceeded Young's fondest expectations, and they did it while they were still big box-office. They streamed into radio and television behind Dizzy Dean, Phil Rizzuto, Jerry Coleman, Ralph Kiner, Lou Boudreau, Pee Wee Reese, Eddie Arcarco, Cary Middlecoff, Frank Gifford, Pat Summerall, Don Meredith, Tony Kubek, Don Drysdale, and Sandy Koufax and Mickey Mantle, both of whom stepped from the diamond into the booth at guarantees of $100,000 a year.

Others took the bull market by the horns and made straight for Wall Street as brokers, customers' men, and salesmen — Jim Bunning, Carl Yastrzemski, Gale Sayers, Dave Herman, Moe Drabowsky, Billy Ray Smith, Ed Kranepool, and platoons of others, not all of whom survived the economic slump that devastated the securities business in the late sixties.

Then there were the glamour pusses who hied off to Hollywood for a whirl at films, led by Jim Brown, Joe Namath, and Chuck Connors. Or to the television studios as song-and-dance men or dramatic actors, like O. J. Simpson ("Medical Center"), Drysdale ("The Donna Reed Show" and others), Bob Gibson ("Gentle Ben" and "The Ed Sullivan Show"), Aaron Rosenberg (producer of numerous movies and the "Daniel Boone" series on TV), Roosevelt Grier (on his *own* TV show), and Maury Wills, strumming his banjo and singing solos on "Hollywood Palace" and elsewhere. And in the nightclubs, Mudcat Grant, Tony Conigliaro, and Dennis Dale McLain, boy wonder of the keyboard.

Not many football players — in fact, not many actors — got the ink that Namath did in 1970 when he went to Italy to make a film, went to Hollywood to make another, rode a motorcycle on the giant screen, cooed at Ann-Margret, missed most of the New York Jets' exhibition season while all this was going on, then broke his right (or throwing) wrist and was unable to play football *or* ride a motorcycle. Not many football players or actors got his full range of critical reviews either, to wit:

Wanda Hale in the *New York Daily News* — "Joe Namath projects the same image on screen as he does on the football field [in *C.C. and Company*]. In his first starring role, Joe projects his cool and calm, his easy, innate charm at the DeMille and Showcase Theatres around town."

Vincent Canby in the *New York Times* — "Here, at last, is the picture to name when someone asks you to recommend 'a good bad movie.' Even if that weren't enough (and it almost is), the movie stars Joe Namath and Ann-Margret, probably the only two people in the United States who have no identity problems, as, respectively, a nice, clean-cut, long-haired Hell's Angel sort, and a high-fashion writer for — if I remember correctly — *Harper's Bazaar* . . . Mr. Namath has almost as many changes of wardrobe as his co-star, an easy wit, and the unruffled manner of a guy who'll try anything twice, which means that he's a perfect match for Ann-Margret, who already had, in all sorts of pop movies."

And Judith Crist, in *New York* magazine, giving Joe a tougher time than old Ben Davidson of the Oakland Raiders ever did — "Anything is endurable after *C.C. and Company*, wherein Joe Namath is a clean-cut member of a filthy-cut motorcycle gang that he quits when his teeth fall in love with Ann-Margret's. When cheaper, cruder, fouler-mouthed trash is made, let's hope Namath will be concentrating on football."

Oh well, you can't win 'em all. But Joe Willie and his nouveau riche playmates from all sports plunged ahead, aching knees and bulging pocketbooks and all. By the nineteen seventies, they were striking gold in so many places that even golf tournaments like the American Airlines Astrojet Classic were resembling *Cimarron*, with a cast of thousands. The tournament started as a sort of promotional sideshow, and in its first year "name" athletes had to be begged to compete. They were paired with one another for fifty-four holes and were locked up with business executives for four days, and it all sounded pretty

humdrum to them until the last part of the commercial began to
sink in — *locked up with business executives for four days.*

After that, they started to besiege the invitation committee
with so many requests to appear that the committee had to restrict the entries: 600 athletes, managers, and coaches offered to
play in 1970 at Phoenix, and the harried committee admitted
only sixty-eight — thirty-four from baseball, thirty-four from
football.

"The athletes pay their own way," a tournament official explained, "but they're glad to do it for the chance to rub elbows
with top executives. A lot of good business deals are made in
this tournament."

So out they flocked to the golf course, egged on by the certainty that there was gold in them thar hills and aroused by the
report that Lance Alworth of the San Diego Chargers had
started one round with a business foursome and finished it with
a valuable food franchise. They weren't deterred by public
exposure of their tournament handicaps either, ranging all the
way from a three for John Brodie, a six for Joel Horlen, a sixteen for Joe DiMaggio, right on up to a thirty-six for Don Maynard, and a sensationally distant forty for Reggie Jackson.

They weren't deterred either by warnings that they would
forfeit their amateur golfing standings if they took home any of
the loot, which totaled $5000 apiece for the winning pair. Ama-
teur standing was the last thing they were worried about. When
Paul Krause of the Minnesota Vikings finished on top, he was
asked — as he pocketed his five big ones — if he was sure he
wanted to become a professional golfer.

"No, I don't want to be a pro," he replied.

"Then what charity do you want the money to go to?" the
tournament official asked.

"Have it go to my wife," replied the star cornerback, cheerfully surrendering his amateur standing and adding a notch to
his moneybelt.

The only drawback in all this new-found gilt was that hunger tends to diminish with affluence, and spirit on the sporting fields frequently springs from hunger. Either hunger to win games or hunger to win affluence. The New York Mets learned that stern lesson of life in 1969, when they swept from the old neighborhood in the boondocks of baseball to fame and fortune.

They traveled that spectacular journey with their college degrees, their briefcases, their mod clothes, and their subscription copies of the *Wall Street Journal.* Off the field as well as on, they were successful and stylish beyond the wildest dreams and fantasies of Roadblock Jones, Marv Throneberry, or Casey Stengel, tastefully bundled in striped double-breasted suits, Nehru jackets, and Edwardian coats. They visited art galleries, bought oil paintings, left game tickets for business counselors, dined in French restaurants. And on one of their trips to the top, Tom Seaver buried himself in John Steinbeck's *East of Eden,* Kevin Collins read through Alistair MacLean's *Ice Station Zebra,* Gus Mauch studied Louis Watson's bridge tome *The Play of the Hand,* and even Yogi Berra peered through new spectacles at *A Small Town in Germany* by John Le Carré.

When somebody asked Ed Charles why he was reading Philip Roth's *Portnoy's Complaint,* he answered in the idiom of the splendid new time: "It's like going from Manhattan to New Jersey by way of the Verrazano Bridge. It's part of your education."

In 1970, though, the Mets dropped from first place to third, and somebody suggested that they no longer had last year's magic up their sleeves. But a front-office man who had observed players in good times and bad shrugged and said:

"The trouble is that they still have last year's money in their pockets."

And *that* was part of their education too.

• • •

Two things accompanied the money athletes on their road to the banks of America, in addition to hoopla and cash: agents and confrontations with the sports establishment.

It was inevitable, since the agents confronted the establishment with well-calculated demands for bigger portions of the purse for the players, who previously had negotiated man-to-man, face-to-face, across the boss's desk. It was inevitable and also natural, as inevitable as the fact that haggling and strife often accompanied similar dealings between labor-union officials and management, and as natural as the fact that pain accompanies any knocking of heads.

Both the hoopla and the money, of course, were greater wherever competition existed for talent — when two mutually antagonistic leagues, for example, were tossing money around to outbid each other for college players. Once the leagues merged, though, the auction-sale aspects of signing kids faded, and the prices began coming back down to earth. It happened to the American Football League and the National Football League, to the American Basketball Association and the National, and it had happened in baseball a century earlier. It even had happened in baseball as recently as a few years earlier, until the big leagues created a common drafting system to distribute the talent and to save everybody's sanity and bankroll.

In football during the jungle days before such a draft was installed, players often were chased in dormitories, dining rooms, and motels by scouts with open checkbooks. Fred Biletnikoff, a wide receiver at Florida State, even was chased down on the playing field. He was an All-American in his senior year, 1964, and State responded with an 8–1–1 record that brought the bird-dogs streaming to the campus. It also brought Florida State to the Gator Bowl against Oklahoma, and the day before the game the Jets had signed Namath in the granddaddy of all the early body-snatching operations.

Biletnikoff was drafted by the Detroit Lions of the NFL and by the Oakland Raiders of the rival AFL, and, the day before the Gator Bowl game, Sonny Werblin telephoned Al Davis of Oakland and chirped: "We've got ours. Now you get yours."

In those days, he meant, every body snatched by the new league represented a triumph over the old league. Biletnikoff, meanwhile, had given his agent the power of attorney to bestow first signing rights on Oakland. But after he had caught four touchdown passes in the game, helping State to a 36–19 victory, he found himself surrounded by more people than just fans.

"It was vicious on the field after the game," Davis said. "The Lions tried to grab him. But he signed his contract with us in front of a national television audience."

The TV spectacular cost the Raiders a two-year contract and a bonus of $140,000, payable over three years. Biletnikoff did not even give them the satisfaction of proclaiming love at first sight. His reasons for signing with Oakland, he said, were pragmatic in the best traditions of a pragmatic era. He noted that Detroit already owned two distinguished pass receivers in Gail Cogdill and Terry Barr and concluded that "it would take two or three years to play with the Lions." Besides, he said, adding a geographic consideration, "I didn't want to play in all that snow."

Biletnikoff, who had not been particularly flamboyant before the rival leagues started pursuing him, promptly followed his economic victory with a personal one. A few days later, he was married under the goal posts in the Florida State stadium.

Five years later, the two leagues had ironed out their differences and agreed on a common draft as the keystone of their future life under one corporate roof. One of the first financial victims of their unity was O. J. Simpson, the running back from Southern California who became the number one draft choice in the country. He became a "victim" because the new system outlawed competitive bidding, leaving O.J. to dicker with the team that selected him first, the Buffalo Bills.

But O.J., dealing through Chuck Barnes of Sports Headliners, was still capable of firing a few economic weapons. He let it be known that he would prefer to be traded to Oakland, because his home was in San Francisco across the bay. Or, if that didn't work, he would prefer to be traded to the New York Jets, presumably because they played 3000 miles away from his home in San Francisco across the bay. In any event, his price was $650,-000 — five seasons at $100,000 a season, plus a bonus of $150,-000.

In Buffalo, the owner of the Bills, Ralph Wilson, put two and two together and concluded there was "a good chance Simpson doesn't care for Buffalo and is trying to force a trade by asking a totally unreasonable amount." To Simpson, though, the amount was "unreasonable" only because the new draft system made it unlikely that any football player could bid his price up to the $800,000 level reached earlier by Donny Anderson of the Green Bay Packers before the football merger had put a lid on such things.

He finally signed for $350,000, flew east to join his new employer, received a kiss from Miss Buffalo as he stepped from the airliner, and was greeted by a cheering, shoving crowd of 2000 fans — before he ever had put on a jersey in the National Football League.

Wilson's suspicions about O.J.'s efforts to "force" a trade were probably true, though Simpson did not have too many choices open to him in conducting his economic warfare in the context of a closed, unified league. At least, very few twenty-two-year-old athletes were likely to invoke their ultimate weapon: retirement. Plenty of other established players *did* threaten to quit, though, and *did* force trades on managements that thereby were faced with two choices: let them quit and lose your investment altogether, or trade them while the trading is good.

A variation of this technique was used effectively in baseball by Ken Harrelson, who threatened to retire when the Boston Red Sox traded him to the Cleveland Indians; Donn Clendenon, who threatened to retire when the Montreal Expos traded him to the Houston Astros; and Maury Wills, who threatened the same when the Montreal Expos threatened to trade him to nobody. All three were monumentally successful. Harrelson, after the personal intervention of the commissioner of baseball, consented to work in Cleveland for more money; Clendenon, after the same sort of intervention, was allowed to stay with Montreal until traded to the New York Mets; and Wills, after intervention by the Los Angeles Dodgers, was allowed to un-retire and play for the Dodgers, which he had wanted to do in the first place.

Sometimes the contract system, which came under legal attack in the sixties, boomeranged on the ball clubs, leaving *them* with only expensive options. When George Mira was released after nine years as a roving quarterback, his lawyer won a court judgment ruling that *somebody* had to pay him $50,000 a year because his original contract guaranteed him that much for an extended period, and if nobody else did, then the tab would have to be picked up by the San Francisco 49ers. When Ed Kranepool was sent to the minor leagues in 1969 by the Mets, half a season after they had won the world championship, his $40,000 salary went with him. And when Billy Cannon was placed on waivers by the Oakland Raiders in 1970, the Buffalo Bills immediately claimed him — but then immediately disclaimed him upon learning that he had a two-year, no-cut contract at more than $50,000 a season. So he was returned to the Raiders, who then assigned him to their taxi squad — at more than $50,000 a season.

The day of the no-cut, $50,000 contract was hastened by a number of things — bidding between rival leagues for the rights to sign and hold players, the increase in the total of "big league" jobs available because of the explosive increase in franchises, the general inflation in the economy with levels of all pay going up, and the big exposure and big money poured into sports by television.

In the case of TV, with its pre-game shows, post-game shows, and between-games shows, any athlete worth his salt soon was making frequent appearances on camera as the day's hero or assistant hero, and he soon was no longer making such appearances for free. He received either outright cash or such gifts as a good portable radio or a good TV set or fishing equipment, and he quickly came to appreciate the fact that television exalteth the spirit and the ego of man at the same time the sponsor enricheth his bank account or trophy room.

Once these ideas were established and confirmed, it took no mental giant to figure out that television rights went into the team's coffers just like hot-dog revenue and tickets. And just as promptly, agents and lawyers began to accompany the boys to the bargaining table — and beyond.

The difference between the primeval days and the payola days was convincing too. In 1942, Stan Musial was the star of the St. Louis Cardinals, who won the World Series over the New York Yankees, and he did not pocket so much as a dollar of fringe revenue. But in the nineteen sixties, half a dozen New York Mets were clearing $10,000 a man for two weeks of songs and gags at Caesar's Palace in Las Vegas and Joe Namath was banking $15,000 for shaving off his Fu Manchu beard for a shaving company's television commercial.

"If a man wants to pay Joe Namath a million dollars for something," commented Wilt Chamberlain, "he must expect to get back at least a million. Most likely, he expects ten million."

"I'd just like to have the opportunity to say no for fifteen thousand dollars," said Bill Russell, who had worn a Fu Manchu beard while Namath was still a freshman in high school. "Who knows what I would have said?"

"They are nothing more than business deals," explained Jim Lonborg, the Boston pitcher. "We consider them negotiable items which depend on time spent, standards met, and image represented. If someone wants to use the athlete, there is nothing wrong in paying for the privilege. After all, the athlete is bringing attention to a particular product or function, and he wouldn't be asked if it wasn't for this purpose."

The agents who helped line up these bonanzas were usually a different breed from old Cash-and-Carry Pyle, who had promoted Red Grange with a circus barker's certainty for the buck. They even tended to go beyond latter-day intermediaries like Frank Scott, the New York manager of players' business affairs, author's rights, and endorsements, who for years was a voice crying in the economic wilderness.

Sometimes the new agents were players themselves, like Nick Buoniconti, the roughhouse linebacker for the Boston Patriots and Miami Dolphins, who brought a law degree to the bargaining table. Sometimes they were athletes surrounded and backed by lawyers and businessmen, as in the case of Sports Satellites Corporation — with Willie Mays and Gerry Philbin as vice presidents but with a supporting staff of specialists in endorsements, licensing, marketing, franchising, investment, and taxes.

"I don't think there's a ballplayer alive who doesn't get business offers," Mays said, speaking as both a vice president and a client. "The tough thing is to know good from bad, especially when you're busy playing. And, if it is good, how to keep it going without making expensive mistakes."

Sometimes the agents drew a bead on the professional athlete and his potential and fired away full-time — like Marty Blackman and Steve Arnold, a pair of Columbia Law School graduates who practiced law two years, got bored, and decided to pitch in the big leagues instead.

They got the notion when Arnold served as legal beagle to a major advertising agency represented by his law firm. Part of his job was to sign a football player for a one-minute commercial on television. Arnold's client, the producer of the commercial, had been told by the agency that he could offer up to $5000. The football player came in and asked for $250. Arnold, a fast man with a $4750 gulf, made up his mind to work the *other* side of the street.

The other side of the street was not too green for a while. Blackman and Arnold anted up $2000 apiece for starters, drew no salary for nine months, then gave themselves raises to fifty dollars a week for the next nine months. They handled anything from a $150 speaking engagement to a player's contract in six figures, taking between 10 and 15 per cent as their fee and visiting the spring-training camps and football camps personally to line up business. After three years, they were grossing $1,000,000 a year.

On the other side of the coin, though, they were building plenty of resentment, especially when they began to operate a kind of black market for players during the war between the basketball leagues. When Connie Hawkins, Rick Barry, and Billy Cunningham announced plans to switch leagues, other stars began to put out feelers too, and the firm of Blackman and Arnold found things booming.

"We just let the word out in the business about our services," Arnold recalled. "We were willing to support either league as far as stocking teams. We're very discreet, and we don't try to create dissatisfaction. The owners resent us because we stand in the way of them getting a guy cheap. I know they make us sound like leeches and bloodsuckers, but there's a need for us. Just ask the players, not the owners."

In pursuit of their talent-stocking program, Blackman and Arnold roamed 100,000 miles a year from home base, a renovated brownstone on Manhattan's East Side. Their early prizes included Jim Maloney, Charley Johnson, John Unitas, and Jim Brown. And when a halfback needed some leverage while trying to work a contract out of the San Francisco 49ers, they even used Canada as a ploy.

"The first thing we did," Blackman said, "was find out what Montreal would offer. Then, we approached the player and checked to determine whether he'd be interested in going to Canada. We told him that Montreal was a good town, a sophisticated city. When he told us he wouldn't mind playing there, we then were in a position to lay it on the line with San Francisco.

"We're fortunate," he went on, "that today's athletes — more often than those of a generation ago — are well-educated, well-spoken, and photogenic. They are a combination of brains and brawn that cannot be found in other fields. We're not loved, but we are respected."

To put a few teeth into the "respect," Blackman also doubled as chairman of a series of seminars held by the Practicing Law Institute in New York under the working title of "Counseling Professional Athletes and Entertainers." These were some of the courses offered:

Tuesday A.M.

The Impact of the Tax Reform Act of 1969. New tax problems in advising professional athletes and entertainers.

Tuesday P.M.

The Anti-trust Threat in Professional Sports. An incisive discussion of the vulnerability of major sports to anti-trust proceedings by the Federal government.

Wednesday

Team Sports and Non-League Sports. The role of the agent and manager, the place of the coach, the relationship of the player to the team owner, and to the players' associations; a consideration of specific sports situations in football, basketball, baseball, tennis, golf and racing.

Thursday

The Professional Athlete Engaged in Business. The athlete in endorsements and advertising, in commercials, in the entertainment business, and as an executive.

The seminars, predictably, were not heavily supported by the owners of teams, who already had their hands full with the representatives of organized player groups like the baseball and football associations. Agents and lawyers for individual athletes, they felt, were likely to become an irritation on top of a headache.

"I will not deal with agents," announced Sid Gillman, as the coach and general manager of the San Diego Chargers. "I tell that to all the players we draft, and they had better believe it."

"No agents," said Red Auerbach, the major-domo of the Boston Celtics. "What the player gets is between me and him, no one else. He'll be paid what we feel is fair, and he'll get more if he is worth it, less if he isn't. I refuse to talk about a man's contract with anyone but him."

"If a man gets a lawyer to do his bidding," said Dick O'Connell, the general manager of the Boston Red Sox, "then I'll get one to do mine. I'll not be put at any disadvantage by an outside force."

"I'm not in favor of an agent doing my salary negotiating," said Carl Yastrzemski, one of O'Connell's well-paid and satisfied employees, who occasionally was criticized by some other baseball players as a fat cat or a sort of house man. "They look out only for their fifteen per cent and think only of themselves. As soon as you go, he'll pick up someone else. I don't want to spoil the relationship I have with the Red Sox. I guess it's hard for a lot of people to understand the relationship between the players and the owner, but to me it is something very strong, very personal."

The key to the tug of war, as well as one of the chief causes of it, was the great gleaming eye of TV. As the seventies began, about fifty pros in all the major sports were earning more than $100,000 a year. And there was more where that came from, suggested Arthur Morse, who had negotiated some of football's big contracts and who also worked as legal counsel for the Chicago Black Hawks.

"I think the area of profit will be even greater," he said, "provided professional sports can handle its use of television. I have studied the law in relation to pro sports and I feel that all the salaries, bonuses, and deferred payments are a sign of our times, not a freakish thing."

"I'm going to try to capitalize as much as I can," said Tom Seaver, modeling a $2500 golden mountain-lion coat between commercial coups after the Mets had won the 1969 World Series, "until it affects my wife or affects baseball. I really am turning down a lot more offers than I am accepting. To me, money is not the most important thing. But you get a funny feeling when you realize how much there is to be made."

Seaver, who contributed twenty-five victories to the "impossible dream" that year, got an even funnier feeling the next season when he stopped winning after eighteen victories. He analyzed the situation and decided that he was suffering from "a tired arm."

• • •

"Once upon a time, football was fun," observed Alex Hawkins as he ended his career with the Baltimore Colts. "The feeling that the fun was ebbing began to creep up on me in nineteen sixty-five, when John Unitas and I fell to reflecting on our training camp that year. We agreed that for the first time the place had no zest. You had to search high and low for a poker game. Players sat around checking their investment portfolios.

"In the past, if the coach gave the team the weekend off, thirty players would get together for a party. But now, with a free weekend starting, you would see them scattering like quail. The briefcase carriers had taken over. We were now a team during working hours only.

"With the coming of bonuses and high salaries and pensions and opportunities for investment, a great many players have achieved security and are bent on looking and acting not a whit different from the average guy who walks into the Harvard Club. It's comforting for the players but terrible for the sport. The surest way to destroy pro football is to give the players a sense of security, yet that is what we have come to. Where the number of available jobs in the game during my first year was four hundred eighty, it's now one thousand forty. When a few players occasionally get together, they talk about their Dairy Queens."

Hawkins' nostalgia for the carefree old days, and his misgiv-

ings about the future, were intensified by the series of mass
holdouts, boycotts, strikes, and lawsuits that began to accompany the change of sports seasons as the otherwise rich decade of
the sixties turned the corner into the seventies. The baseball
players stayed away from spring training over pensions; the football players stayed away from summer training over television
money; the baseball umpires boycotted the play-offs over their
fees; other umpires sued over union recognition.

In July, 1970, the owners of the twenty-six teams in the National Football League offered to increase their players' pension
fund by $18,000,000 over the following four years; the players,
with an eye on the $140,000,000 in television revenue expected
to flow into the game during that time, held out for $26,000,000.
The opening of training was delayed, except for rookies — who
were not yet members of the players' association — and then
federal mediators tried to break the impasse. But when the
owners finally decided to "open" their camps to any players who
would show up, a task force of eighty-seven player "representatives" met in Chicago and composed a telegram to Pete Rozelle,
the commissioner, that read:

"This is to inform you that the National Football League
Players Association is now officially on strike, and we believe it
would be in the best interests of the fans and pro football to
quickly conclude this dispute."

The word was simultaneously spread to the individual players
in their home cities by a telephone network known as "the four-
eight system" — each of four players telephoned eight others
with the message, and so on. In six hours, the association believed, it could reach all 1200 players. It was a labor dispute in
the grand manner, perhaps novel in football but old stuff in industry. Even the emotions, reactions, and divisions conjured up
scenes of strained relations that had long since been common
in coal, automobiles, steel, shipping, and all the other major
leagues of business.

"I'm not pro-owner," complained Craig Morton, the quarter-back for the Dallas Cowboys, "I'm pro-me and pro-team. We can't wait any longer, we have to get started."

"As much as I want to go to camp, I won't," said Dick Schaf-rath, the tackle for the Cleveland Browns. "I think the owners did this to find out if we'll stick together. It could destroy some teams if some players go back. A team's success is based on morale, and something like that could kill it."

"I'm not making any threats," said Ben Davidson, the 6-foot-7-inch defensive end for the Oakland Raiders, "but you know how bitter some of these labor disputes get. There are bombings and everything. Football is a rough game, and it's conceivable that a team that went against us and all the other teams in the dispute might find itself suffering an unusual number of injuries."

In Washington, the Redskins' player representative, Pat Richter, referred to Vince Lombardi, who was in the hospital after two operations and who died a few days later, and said:

"That's one thing Coach Lombardi preached — singleness of purpose. He wants to keep this team together. If a couple go to camp, it would destroy the whole thing."

"I played for Coach Lombardi at Green Bay," said Bob Long of the Redskins. "We were forty players together. We went to church together, partied together, worked together."

"It's a sad day," said Paul Brown, coach of the Cincinnati Bengals. "But we have no choice but to send the rookies home and abandon camp. I will be in favor of canceling the season."

"One day," warned Melvin Durslag, the Los Angeles columnist, "pro football is going to blow the whole damn thing because of greed. Crowds will be back to 29,000. And if Helmet Day is successful, the clubs will try Ball Day, Shoulder Pad Day and Mouthpiece Night."

In the midst of all the gloom and doom, individual hardship cases sprouted on the sidelines — even after the pension dispute was settled and the season got under way. John Carlos, the 215-pound Olympic sprinter, tried his hand at football and signed with Philadelphia for $30,000, accepting a "cut" from his asking price of one million. Don Meredith, who had thrown 135 touchdown passes in nine seasons, retired as the quarterback for the Dallas Cowboys at thirty-one and at $100,000 a year. He preferred to spend more time with his family and his business interests. And Lance Alworth, the $70,000-a-year pass-catcher for the San Diego Chargers, found his dry-cleaning and real-estate investments collapsing and complained that the team had not fulfilled a long-term loan for his outside activities and threatened to quit if he wasn't traded. He wasn't, and he didn't — though a year later he *was* traded.

But the biggest flap was created by Joe Namath, the motor-cycle rider of Hollywood, who a year earlier had "retired" rather than sell his interest in Bachelors III, the East Side restaurant and bar that Rozelle deemed to be a questionable place of business for a quarterback. The place was drawing gamblers, Rozelle said.

"It's a friendly place," Joe Willie acknowledged. "Sometimes strangers use the office phone."

Namath's decision to quit was temporary; he relented, sold his interest, and rejoined the Jets. But it was costly. Another of his restaurant interests, Broadway Joe's, had gone public a few months earlier and Joe and his partners had sold a million and three-quarter dollars worth of stock — which opened at ten dollars a share and quickly zoomed to sixteen dollars. Joe owned 145,000 shares himself. After his "retirement" was announced, though, the stock began to slide, and Joe's loss on paper, at least, reached $181,250 in one day.

The next year, while the players' pension strike was being thrashed out, Joe was spending the summer in Italy making his film. When he got back to New York, he said his knees felt better but he wasn't sure his heart was in football anymore. Other people said he was in money trouble and was really trying to pressure the Jets into extending a large loan — so that, as a businessman, he could afford the luxury of being a quarterback.

It was not too good a time for either businessmen *or* football players. When the strikes and flaps had finally been settled, the Jets played their first exhibition game against the Buffalo Bills. They won the game but lost Gerry Philbin with a shoulder separation, Cliff McLain (broken rib), Mike Stromberg (pulled hamstring muscle), Gordon Wright (broken ankle), Cecil Leonard (cracked jaw), Lee White (bruised knee), and Al Atkinson (temporary retirement caused by violent reaction to Namath's comings and goings). Two months later, Namath fractured his right wrist and was sidelined as a restaurant owner, motorcycle driver, and quarterback.

· · ·

Across town, the New York Giants were streamlining their roster, while Namath and the other capitalists of football were streamlining their portfolios. One of the victims was Steve Wright, an offensive tackle who had been rated ferocious by defensive lines for the previous two seasons. His coach, Alex Webster, said Wright's chances for the job had been hurt by the loss of two weeks of training time during the players' strike. Wright replied that he probably just wasn't "one of the Giant-type people."

Whatever the reason, the Giants were inviting him to end his career as a member of the cast. What were his plans in the face of that threat to his economic security?

"I'm going to sit back and have a Chivas Regal and water," Wright said, surveying the landscape like any red-blooded American businessman. "It only costs a little more to go first-class.

"I've got a good off-season job with Everseal *industrial glue*. If worst comes to worst and I can't play football, I'll just go to work and do what the rest of the people do."

11
Greed

IT WAS ST. GEORGE'S DAY, April 23, the feast day of the patron saint of England, and the most famous Englishman, Sir Winston Churchill, was the speaker when the occasion was celebrated by the Honorable Artillery Company, the oldest serving English regiment. Sir Winston, bridging the generations and even the centuries in the flux of time, tried to picture what would happen if St. George the dragon slayer were alive today.

"St. George would have arrived in Cappadocia," he related, "accompanied not by a horse, but by a secretariat. He would be armed, not by a lance, but by several flexible formulas. He would be welcomed by the local branch of the League of Nations Union. He would propose a conference with the dragon. He would then lend the dragon a lot of money. The maiden's release would be referred to Geneva or New York, the dragon reserving all rights, meanwhile."

Flexible formulas or not, it was doubtful as the nineteen seventies began that changes brought by the rush of time would have been particularly recognizable to St. George *or* the dragon, or even, for that matter, to Sir Winston. In the United States alone, in a decade alone, the population had soared from 179 million to more than 205 million, a steady migration was crowding both the Atlantic and Pacific seaboards, and the country was adding one person every fifteen and a half seconds.

Moreover, the rich seemed to be getting richer and the poor

poorer, though rich and poor alike were scrambling to spend more of their share on the supposedly good things of life. More than 91 per cent of the families owned vacuum cleaners, 92 per cent had washing machines, and 99 per cent refrigerators, radios, ranges, and electric irons.

Twelve years had passed since John Kenneth Galbraith had characterized this as an affluent society and, in that time, 47 million hair dryers had been sold, along with 22 million electric carving knives, and 86 per cent of the families in America had bought electric coffee makers. The cost of a college education might still lie beyond the budget of most families, but five radios per household was reportedly the national average and 80 per cent of the households had one car, 30 per cent had two, and 95 per cent had at least one TV set — which was almost exactly the proportion of families with complete plumbing facilities.

For those who might question the public's scale of values, an answer was provided by a schoolteacher in Seattle, a city hit hard by the recession in 1969 and 1970. His old "second car" broke down and the remedy seemed obvious: a small economy car. But he promptly bought a full-sized $3500 station wagon.

"We needed something," explained his wife, "big enough to tow the boat."

The implications of all this, observed James Reston, were clear: "Sport in America plays a part in our national life that is probably more important than even the social scientists believe. Sports are now more popular than politics in America, increasingly so since the spread of television. The great corporations are now much more interested in paying millions for sports broadcasts than they are for all political events except for the nominations and inaugurations of Presidents, because the general public is watching and listening.

"For sports and games, in a funny way, are not only America's diversion and illusion, but its hope. The world of sports has everything the world of politics lacks and longs for. It will not be like most of the backstage conflicts of politics. Seaver and Koosman will either have speed and control or they won't, and unlike Bill Rogers in the State Department or Henry Kissinger in the basement of the White House, everybody will know whether they are effective or not.

"Will the Mets make it after those nine games with the Pirates? Will Joe Namath repeat in the Super Bowl this year? Will Arnie Palmer come back after 40 or merely make money? Nobody knows, but America will be watching these sporting questions probably more carefully than the larger issues of politics."

America was already watching because sports, since World War II and most especially in the decade of the sixties, did two things for the besieged public mind: They reflected and dramatized the tumultuous days of change, inflation, and revolution in life-styles, and they simultaneously offered some escapes, if not solutions.

Even if people could not identify fully with the athletes and the money men behind them, they could identify with their problems, challenges, dreams, and rewards. They could dig the onetime truck driver who became a supermarket owner financially capable of bidding $405,000 for an untested yearling filly at a Kentucky horse auction, and they could appreciate it as he turned to his trainer and said: "Do you think people will know who Wendell P. Rosso is now?"

They could marvel at a fifty-year-old cardiologist and father of twelve children, Dr. George Sheehan, who joined 1151 other contestants for the seventy-third running of the Boston Marathon — 26 miles 385 yards from the rocky pastures of Hopkinton to downtown Boston. They could even transfer themselves into that mob of jogging masochists, particularly when Dr. Sheehan said with simple conviction: "Where you finish doesn't matter. The tragedy is when you have to walk in."

And they could stand up and cheer at the thought that a black boy named O. J. Simpson was a twelve-year-old throwing stones at buses in San Francisco when the decade of the sixties began, and that he was grossing $1,000,000 from professional football and other business enterprises when it closed.

For those constitutionally or emotionally unable to sit on the sidelines and just marvel, there developed a great tide in the direction of the arena itself. They joined the swim, so to speak, and shared some of the passion if not some of the money with their heroes. They did it in such numbers that more than 9000 amateur golfers applied for the Bing Crosby Pro-Am tourney, which could accommodate only 168. Even when the equipment rose in price from a set of golf clubs to a yacht, they swarmed to the front line, and they did *that* in such numbers that the people who ran the Newport to Bermuda ocean race were forced to limit the fleet to 151 yachts. And even at the pinnacle of the pile, other unpaid yachtsmen found the time and cash in the sixties and early seventies to make three successful defenses of the America's Cup.

"They're really pouring it on," Steve Cady reported in the *New York Times*. "When the little guy suddenly gets a little money, he spends it."

It was, he observed, a time when most ski-country families had two or more snowmobiles in the barn. It was the decade of the Super Star, the Super Salary, the Super Stadium, the Super Horse, the Super Synthetic, the Super Upset, and the Super Controversy. It was a time when the Big O meant Oscar Robertson; the Big A stood for Aqueduct, where the horseplayers bet as much as $6,000,000 in one day; and the Big E meant either Elvin Hayes or the Big Exacta, depending on whether a fan was talking about the basketball star or the strike-it-rich wagering gimmick designed to lure people to racetracks.

It was a time, though, when the biggest initials were NBC, CBS, and ABC — the major television networks, which poured millions of dollars into sports subsidies to improve their ratings, polish their images, and hold their member stations. By the time the seventies had arrived, TV gold had become so important that program directors routinely signaled referees when to call time-out for a commercial; sudden-death golf play-offs began not at the first hole but at whichever hole was most convenient for the TV camera crew; and the President of Mexico could be told politely to cool his heels for half an hour while the closing ceremonies of the Olympic Games in Mexico City were delayed to coincide with prime television viewing time.

It was a time when Bill Hartack kept the stewards at Pimlico waiting while he calmly (and in direct violation of racing rules) told a national television audience he didn't think the foul claimed against his horse in the Preakness was justified.

It was a profitable decade for the bookie, a dangerous one for the compulsive gambler, who bet perhaps $50,000,000,000 a year, 90 per cent of it illegally. And he was betting it on legions of new teams with strange new names and obscure new athletes, teams with nicknames like the Bucks, Caps, Rockets, Flyers, Colonels, Suns, Pacers, Floridians, Seals, North Stars, Angels, Buccaneers, SuperSonics, Cougars, Saints, Bills, and the Mets, the Jets, and the Nets.

Even the beleaguered housewife came to know the difference between a blitz and a blintz, while her husband huddled like Walter Mitty in front of the tube and watched Bob Beamon long-jump 29 feet 2¼ inches at the 1968 Olympics, two feet farther than anybody else in history; Maury Wills steal 104 bases in one baseball season to break Ty Cobb's supposedly unbreakable record; Wilt Chamberlain score 100 points in a professional basketball game; an amateur tennis player named Arthur Ashe beat the pros in the first $100,000 United States Open tennis tournament; Roger Maris pop sixty-one home runs over fences, and may Babe Ruth forgive us all; Sandy Koufax pitch no-hitters in four consecutive seasons before retiring at thirty-one with arthritis in the elbow; Phil Esposito score seventy-six goals in one hockey season; Don Schollander win four gold medals in

Olympic swimming; Jim Ryun race a mile in 3 minutes 51.1 seconds.

He could even watch the Super Animals and wonder at it all. Kelso, winning five straight titles as horse of the year; Dr. Fager, running a mile in 1:32⅕ with 134 pounds on his back; Nevele Pride, trotting a mile in 1:54⅘; Bret Hanover *pacing* a mile in 1:53⅗.

He might be bamboozled by the dizzying growth of everything. By the fact that the old national pastime entered the sixties with sixteen baseball teams in the major leagues, added two in 1961, two in 1962, and four in 1969 for a two-league, four-division total of twenty-four as the seventies arrived. By the fact that football mushroomed to twenty-six teams in six divisions in two leagues, basketball to twenty-eight teams in six divisions in two leagues, and hockey to fourteen teams in two divisions in one league. Or even by the fact that his new weekend (and Monday night) pastime offered 371 pro football games in one season played by 1250 professionals — once their legal problems had been untangled after a pension strike.

Yet, even when Mitty was confounded by the statistical excesses of the day, he somehow could share the general sense that things had grown astronomical. When Reinhold Bachler of Austria flew 505 feet on a pair of skis, that was gigantic, any way you looked at it. When Wilt Chamberlain made fifty-five rebounds in one game, that was a fantasy of jumping, however you measured it. And when Valery Brumel of the Soviet Union leaped off the ground seven and a half feet, he not only cleared a world's record but also would have cleared Chamberlain's head if Wilt had been standing there watching too.

After all, it was a time when 6000 people on skis competed in the Vasa Lopp Nordic race in Sweden and 7000 jumped into the Dead Sea for the annual swimming marathon in Israel. If all that didn't dazzle the imagination, then it was finally a time when men walked on the moon — and again, Walter Mitty gaped on television.

He gaped, in fact, in front of 225 million screens in 100 countries around the world, from Albania to Zambia. As the astronauts and the athletes did their separate things, their performances were beamed to more than 80 million sets in the United States, more than 20 million in Japan and on down the road to Gabon, Mauritius, and Southern Yemen. It was no time for secrets in public life, and in Italy the linguists even began to notice that the regional dialects gradually were being merged into something like a national (network) tongue.

When England played Brazil at Guadalajara in 1970 in the World Cup soccer matches, a roaring crowd of 70,000 packed the modern bowl-shaped stadium while 29 million persons watched on TV back in Britain and, it was estimated, perhaps 700 million watched the world over. The BBC and the competing independent network each scheduled seventy hours of viewing time to the matches, undismayed by the fact that some games lasted until three o'clock in the morning, Greenwich time. In Italy, eleven of the matches were carried late at night, and in France, the state network programmed eighteen matches, eleven of them live.

Norwegian travel agents reported that people were postponing vacations in the mountains and the seaside huts where there were no TV sets. Swedish sociologists feared permanent schisms in families because the existing TV system offered the soccer tournament while a second channel went into business with alternate programs available. And in Brazil, President Emilio Garrastazu Médici ordered that official programs on radio should be rescheduled later so as not to interfere with the soccer reports.

In Moscow, they recorded some of the games for showing the next day, at more favorable times. In Hong Kong, live coverage was found to be too expensive so the TV sytsem recorded the matches and offered them three days late. In Switzerland, the announcers apologized for disrupting regular programs — then rolled the soccer films. And in the United States and Canada, fifteen cities showed the Cup matches on closed-circuit television and set up box offices in auditoriums, which promptly became crowded and even tumultuous.

If anyone doubted that the world of the Super Star was being staged by the Super System and paid for by the Super Sell, the doubts were chased by John E. O'Toole, the president of the advertising agency Foote, Cone & Belding. When the decade of the sixties began, he told the agency's stockholders, there were 6250 commericals on network TV in the United States; when it ended, there were 14,250.

The sports world's share of this money pie put television firmly in the picture, to say nothing of firmly in the saddle, of the sports revolution of the sixties and seventies. The broadcasting of games, which had started innocently enough as "special events" along with parades, ship arrivals, and political speeches a generation earlier, now moved into the frenzied area of commercial programming, with separate departments of the networks handling sports and rushing wildly for headline events and the sponsors to pay for them.

It didn't take the teams long to appreciate the fact that they suddenly were being wooed by three network suitors, all exceptionally well-heeled. It also didn't take them long to appreciate the fact that everybody else was appreciating this fact too: All hands, from the hod carriers who helped build the stadium to the halfbacks who ran across the grass in it, began to demand their piece of the action. As a result, even flourishing clubs like the 1969 New York Jets, the world champions of football, did not play before one unsold seat all season and yet cleared only $135,000 at the gate. Another team reported that between 1953 and 1968 its player salaries had increased 700 per cent, administrative costs 745 per cent, and scouting costs 2700 per cent.

"Costs go up and attendance is at the maximum," noted Sonny Werblin just before he got out from under the Jets, "and there is no longer any maneuverability for management."

"There is no way we could survive," said Bill Ford of the Detroit Lions and the Ford Motor Company, "without television. We couldn't make it without the income and we couldn't make it without the exposure."

"If we dropped pro football," said William C. MacPhail, the vice president of CBS–TV Sports, "our affiliates would crucify us. But this thing has got to level off or our stockholders will start screaming."

"The prices we pay [to get the rights to broadcast sports]," said Roone Arledge, the president of ABC Sports, "are valid only in relation to each other. Since antitrust laws won't let the networks talk with each other about prices for certain events, we have to go in swinging with the biggest dollar we dare to spend so the competition doesn't cream us. It's absurd, but we're trapped."

"It was like a patriotic cause," said Carl Lindemann, the vice president of NBC Sports, remembering the melee for pro football rights in the midsixties. "Betrayal meant death."

None of the networks could particularly afford to pay the escalating prices for sports, but then none of them could particularly afford *not* to pay them either. So they all pursued the commissioners of football, baseball, hockey, basketball, and golf with sealed envelopes containing statistical messages like "$28,000,000" as the top dollar they could bid. If the bid was high enough, they were in business — the business of exclusively broadcasting those games back into Walter Mitty's living room, and the allied business of somehow scrounging the money to support it all.

By 1970, they were committing themselves to tabs like these for football alone:

For college and pro games — $62,500,000.
For local radio rights to NFL games — $2,100,000.
For local pre-season rights for NFL games — $375,000.
For local radio and delayed-TV rights for 125 college games — $1,305,375.

Once   networks' scramble had been sorted out, it developed t   NBC-TV had lined up eighty-two American Conference   nes in the NFL plus the divisional play-offs and the chan ionship game itself (for $15,000,000), the Gator Bowl coll ge game (for $200,000), the Senior Bowl ($50,000), the Orange Bowl ($700,000), the Rose Bowl ($1,400,000), and the Super Bowl ($2,500,000).

Two blocks north in Manhattan, the people at CBS-TV had staked out the National Conference games ($20,000,000), the NFL All-Star Game ($1,000,000), various play-offs and championships as part of the pro package, and the Sun Bowl and Cotton Bowl college games at undisclosed figures.

A few blocks crosstown, ABC-TV was scheduling eleven national telecasts and twenty-four regional games for the National Collegiate Athletic Association ($12,000,000), plus the Coaches All-American Game, the College All-Star Game, the Liberty Bowl, the North-South Shrine Game, the East-West Shrine Game, the Sugar Bowl, and the Hula Bowl, *plus* a new package of fourteen Monday-night professional games ($8,500,000). The radio networks of all three national networks made separate deals for many of the same events.

For the schools involved in the college coverage, the good news to the pocket-weary alumni broke down into these payoffs from radio and local TV alone:

Conference	Members	Radio Stations	TV Stations	Total Rights
Atlantic Coast	8	240	13	$73,500
Big Eight	8	228	20	98,500
Big Ten	10	303	27	156,000
Ivy League	8	59	2	13,475
Mid-America	6	22	3	10,600
Missouri Valley	7	21	4	16,000
Pacific Eight	8	131	14	328,400

Southeastern	10	576	42	$252,000
Southern	7	36	2	7,500
Southwestern	8	200	19	92,500
Western Athletic	8	73	3	39,200
Independents	38	619	83	217,700

In addition, Notre Dame, which could afford to stand alone at the cashier's window as well as on the football field, received $50,000 from the Mutual network for radio rights to its own games.

So the schools and the leagues and the teams got the money from the broadcasting networks and stations, who in turn rushed to their nearest advertising agency for help. The cost, they advised the nearest advertising agency, would break down into something like $65,000 a minute for sponsors' messages on the NCAA games. They could get it for the sponsor wholesale, so to speak, at $53,000 a minute if he bought a package of regular-season games and for the fairly irresistible price of $50,500 a minute if the Liberty, Sugar, and Hula Bowls were thrown in.

For those sponsors intensely interested in package deals, CBS-TV offered a selection. The "white" package contained five Sunday pro games (the second half of a double-header in each case), two Saturday games, and a Thanksgiving Day game, all for $50,000 a minute. The "blue" package included three pre-season packages only, at the bargain-basement price of $40,000 a minute. The "red" package, for the real free-spenders, listed fourteen Sunday games, the Eastern and Western pro championships, and the National Conference championship game — at $70,000 a minute.

At NBC, the packages embraced Sunday single games at $35,000 a minute, pre-season games at $40,000, Saturdays at $35,000, Thanksgiving Day at $65,000, Sunday double-headers at $65,000, the American Conference play-offs at $70,000, and the conference championship at $110,000. If anybody had any money left after that, the Rose Bowl game was available for

$120,000 per sixty seconds of "message" time and the Super Bowl at $200,000, and hold your hat.

In exchange for little considerations like $200,000 a minute, the sponsors and their friendly advertising agencies naturally expected something extra for their money. A ringside seat. A voice in the counsels of the mighty. A camera in the dugout. A microphone on the manager's lapel. An obedient referee with a two-minute whistle. A convenient kickoff time. A network banner on the fifty-yard line. A hand on the throttle. A quid pro quo.

After the Chrysler Corporation had begun to succeed the Gillette Company as the biggest plunger in sports broadcasting, Chrysler's interest in the staging of spectacles increased along with its sports budget, which increased beyond $12,000,000. So naturally, the advertising director of the company began to be flanked at World Series games *on camera* next to people like Commissioner Bowie Kuhn, former Chief Justice Earl Warren, and Julian Goodman, the president of NBC.

Still, there were those maddening little slip-ups, like when "The Game of the Week" director discovered that the Minnesota Twins used a Ford Mustang to drive relief pitchers in from the bullpen — a competitor's Mustang, at that. But on that day, at least, the crisis was resolved by requiring the bullpen pitchers to walk across the field to the mound while the competitor's car stayed out of sight in the back barn.

But if Chrysler was outraged at the prospect of its TV cameras capturing a Ford in the public's future, consider the corporate outrage on that memorable afternoon in 1969 when the New York Jets were leading the Oakland Raiders with less than one minute to go. And, as the old second hand on the control-room clock ticked upward to 7 P.M., which was kickoff time for a network special on the adventures of Heidi, the demigods of NBC made the sort of decision that sends the gods straight up the wall: They clipped the football game and let Heidi roll across

the land. The Raiders, meanwhile, were scoring two touchdowns and winning the game while sane men cringed, the public waited, the network gasped, and the sponsor raged.

For years, Whitey Ford went above and beyond the call of
duty by slipping the pick-off sign in advance to the TV director
so that the cameras would not miss Whitey's slick move to first
base or second. It was one thing for the base runner to be
caught napping, but another for the broadcasting booth. In
fact, sometimes the director knew the pick-off play was "on," but
Joe Pepitone did not, and was he surprised when Ford whipped
one across the bag at the knees.

Hank Bauer, who had been Whitey's old teammate on the
Yankees, later became manager of the Baltimore Orioles and
would tease Ford that he had detected the signs. But Whitey
would just laugh and keep switching them — and keep tipping
off the TV director.

But sometimes Whitey would forget himself and betray his
trust to the cameras. He was a rapid little worker who could
finish a nine-inning game in two hours flat, which was annoying
enough to sponsors. But they really found him lacking in savoir-
faire during the important seventh-inning commercial. He simply warmed up too fast and was ready to pitch to the first batter
before the commercial had run its course, causing teeth to be
gnashed in control rooms downtown.

When the 1967 All-Star Game was played in Anaheim's new
stadium in California, it was the thirty-eighth game in the baseball series but the first with the novel starting time of 4:15 P.M.
That was Pacific Daylight Time, and the reason was to project
the game into those living rooms along the Atlantic Coast at the
prime time of 7:15. Which was okay, except that the stadium
lights had to be switched on at 4:15 when the brilliant afternoon
sunshine and equally sharp shadows already made the ball a blur
as it left the pitcher's hand, streaking toward home plate and,
occasionally, away from it. Thirty batters struck out, even
Henry Aaron missed a line drive, and Jim Fregosi, who played

regularly in the stadium for the California Angels, started to advise his American League colleagues as they went to bat: "Good luck, you guys."

"Bob Gibson threw a couple of pitches," said Carl Yastrzemski, "that I never did see."

"I wonder," speculated a network man, rising to the occasion, "if it wouldn't be better TV if *both* teams wore white uniforms."

In the midst of the confusion stood Fred Haney, the general manager of the Angels, then the most successful expansion team in baseball, a team that had finished in third place in its second season while the Mets, Astros, and Senators were still setting records on the laugh machine. Now in 1967, in the palatial new stadium in the citrus and neon groves of Southern California, hard by Disneyland, with 46,000 persons surrounding Gene Autry and Bob Reynolds and the other owners, it was Haney's turn to conduct his daily broadcast on a local station and *really* give the fans a report. But no — he is reminded of the rule that *no other* broadcast is permitted in the park except the exclusive network job on the All-Star Game. So good old Fred Haney must leave his new ball park in the seventh inning to go to a nearby home that has been wired for sound and there, in a makeshift studio, deliver his report on the great events taking place back in *his* sold-out stadium.

"Are we surrendering too much to TV?" asked Frank Cashin, the lawyer, writer, and advertising man who helped run the Baltimore Orioles. "I don't know. In nineteen sixty-six, we won the World Series, drew a record attendance of one million two hundred thousand, grossed nine hundred thousand dollars, and netted four hundred fifty thousand dollars. But a million dollars of the revenue came from radio and TV. Without it, the team would have *lost* that half-million. What's the alternative? Raise ticket prices? Drop two farm teams? That's surrendering too."

What was happening was natural enough — television, having risked all that money on sports events, could not risk artistic disaster by letting the chips fall where they may during the ball games. To protect their investment, in a business wracked with recrimination, the TV people not only had to cover an event but also had to stage it. Natural enough, but dangerous enough, because the same "natural" impulse had devastated the old quiz shows. It was zeal, it was competition, it was prestige, it was money — it was greed.

It was the same impulse that caused constant interruptions in the late-night talk shows, even during serious conversations with serious guests like Dr. Christiaan Barnard during a lengthy appearance on the Dick Cavett Show. The subject was heart transplants, their opportunities, and their morals, and it was a formidable discussion — riddled with commercials.

Sometimes the interruptions were physical, as they were the afternoon the Philadelphia 76ers played the New York Knicks while ABC's cameras caught it all from courtside. The network had just paid $17,000,000 for three years of televising the league's basketball games, but that didn't provide too much balm when Archie Clark of Philadelphia crashed into a camera in the first quarter and went to the hospital with a severely bruised hip. "They think it's a joke," complained Jack Ramsay, the coach of the 76ers, "but I've lost a player." Nor was Ramsay impressed with the turnabout justice of things later when Nate Bowman of New York collided with the same camera and limped away with a bruised thigh.

Sometimes it was the fans who were stung. When the 1971 Super Bowl game was played in the Orange Bowl, the National Football League imposed a blackout on home TV sets within a seventy-five-mile radius of the sold-out stadium. The howling for TV equaled the howling for tickets. But Pete Rozelle, trying to steer between twin rocks, said a little unhappily:

"We've had four court tests and won them all. The first game in L.A. missed selling out by over thirty thousand, and we don't intend to let pro football become a studio sport. Lifting the Super Bowl blackout could lead to further lawsuits to lift it on all championship games played in cities where weather is a factor."

The emergence of pay-TV in the seventies seemed to supply some relief for the hometown fan; at least, by paying a price, he could sit home and watch the local team play even when free-TV was blacked out. But life was not that simple either, as one viewer in Connecticut protested in a letter to the sports editor of the *New York Times*.

"When the subject of the benefits of pay TV comes up," he wrote, "as it is sure to do during this decade, sports fans should remember that the 1970 World Cup soccer finals were available only for a $12.50 (top-price) ticket via closed-circuit TV. This event was televised free to home sets at its last occurrence in 1966."

Still, about 4,500,000 of the 80,000,000 sets in the United States were owned by cable subscribers who were paying $270,-000,000 a year for their joy and, by the end of the seventies, it was calculated, there would be 27,000,000 customers paying $4,000,000,000. In New York alone, Sterling Manhattan Cable Television signed a five-year contract with Madison Square Garden for the home games of the Knicks and Rangers, plus the National Horse Show, tournament tennis, college basketball, track meets, and the Westminster Kennel Club show. At the other end of the scale, the Department of Labor was reporting that the average family was spending just under twenty-eight dollars a year for all spectator admissions.

The pull of TV was not lost on the athletes either. When the player representatives of the twenty-four major league baseball teams held their winter meeting in 1970 (in Hawaii, which has minor league baseball but major league sunshine) their deliberations included this point, according to the minutes of the meeting:

"Mr. Miller reminded the board that the present television contract with NBC expires at the end of 1971, and that we have been advised that negotiations are already under way between the owners and the networks for a new contract to be effective beginning in 1972."

The real commercial in this, Miller made clear in a letter to the owners, was that "the players and the Players Association will not waive their *property rights.*" He meant that the players were reasserting their claim to a property right in relaying their images by TV, and in selling the images to sponsors. Ergo, a bigger slice of the pie.

"Sports is a bad investment, generally speaking," said Bill MacPhail, observing the costs, claims, and complaints on all sides. "The network needs it for prestige, for image, to satisfy the demands and desires of our affiliated stations. The rights have gotten so costly that we do sports as a public service rather than a profit-maker. We're doing great if we break even."

Carl Lindemann, who once drew a snarl from Dick Young of the *New York Daily News* for saying the San Diego Stadium was "the best ever built for television," put the changing values in these terms for pro football: "We invested $42,000,000 for a five-year period with one thought in mind — to create a competitive league. The merger of the two leagues wasn't contemplated by us at all. There's no doubt that television made the game of pro football, or that our moving into the AFL pact saved the league."

"So many sports organizations have built their entire budgets around television," said Roone Arledge, painting the picture with superlative brush strokes, "that if we ever withdrew the money, the whole structure would collapse."

One man who did not think the whole structure would collapse was James M. Crawford Sr. of Webster, Texas, and his optimism may have been more symbolic than Arledge's pessimism.

Mr. Crawford, clearly riding the crest of the wave, was awarded patent number 3,490,410 by the United States Government because he had invented a sign of the times: clapping mittens.

They were mittens with resilient pockets for the hands, with clappers or blades of wood, plastic, or metal up front that would make a lot more noise than human palms. The idea, the inventor announced, was to enable spectators at sporting events to render loud and coordinated applause for the home team.

And well they might. With or without television, but preferably with, professional sports and leisure-time sports stormed ahead to loud and coordinated applause — and often to loud and coordinated payoffs.

Bobby Moore, captain of England's World Cup soccer team, already was in the $60,000-a-year bracket. Ten players in Italy reported earnings above $60,000, six went over $75,000, and George Best of Manchester United, Robert Perfumo of Argentina, Amadeo Carrizo of Colombia, and the great Eusebio of Portugal cleared $100,000. And, at the pinnacle stood Edson Arantes do Nascimento of Brazil, the one and only Pelé, the onetime shoeshine boy who outscored and outearned them all. After scoring more than 1000 goals in fourteen seasons, he was drawing $144,000 a year from soccer and up to $500,000 from real estate, a ceramics factory, coffee advertising, and a TV series in which he played the part of a detective. Out of consideration for his financial standing, he even was elected a director of Banco Industrial de Campino Grande and, out of consideration for his civic standing, was declared a "national resource" of Brazil.

When Pelé and his teammates won permanent possession of the World Cup, they flew home to share prizes worth $750,000 — in a country with a per-capita income of $215. They split $553,700 in "promised" prize money; they were met by President Emilio Médici with checks for $6600 apiece that had *not* been promised; they received Volkswagens from the mayor of

São Paulo; they split 300,000 shares of stock distributed by Electrobas do Brazil, the country's giant utility, whose president announced that the team had brought the nation together again; they were deluged with television sets, refrigerators, electric stoves, radios, stereos, electric shaving equipment, and other applicances; and they were given two days off when national holidays were declared in their honor.

If the frenzy was more manageable in, say, auto racing, the reward was not substantially less. In a business that did not flourish until after World War II, more than 33,000,000 persons a year were paying their way into tracks to watch the bullets whip by — 400,000 of them alone at Indianapolis every spring when three dozen men steered little cars through the pack for $1,000,000 in purses. There was road racing, oval racing, and drag racing, and not all the customers understood what might happen when a dragster lifted his foot too quickly from the throttle of a 1500-horsepower supercharged engine running on 100 per cent methanol blends. But they understood precisely that while thirty-five professionals made $100,000 a year behind the wheel and a Mario Andretti made a million on all fronts, the dollars were paid for in drama and even death.

They knew that in 1968 the toll took Jim Clark of Scotland, Mike Spence of Britain, and Lodovico Scarfotti of Italy, the son of one of the founders of Fiat, and a month later Jo Schlasser of France. In 1969, John Woolfe of Britain died in Le Mans when his Porsche 917 came out of a turn, hit an embankment, and exploded. A month later, Leon Dernier of Belgium died when his Japanese Mazda R100 hurtled off the road on an S-bend during the Francorchamps twenty-four-hour race in Belgium. Six months later, in February of 1970, Tab Prince of Georgia was killed two days after his thirty-second birthday at Daytona Beach, a year after Don MacTavish of Massachusetts had hit a wall on the same track and not survived. In June, it was Bruce McLaren of New Zealand, spinning out of control in a high-speed run at Goodwood, England, while testing an experimental car at 180 miles an hour — McLaren, who once had said, "We're not making as much money as some people think, but we're having fun."

Three weeks later in the Netherlands, a twenty-eight-year-old heir to a British brewery fortune, Piers Courage, who had lived through a twirling spin the day before and through a crash two months before, died when his car whipped into the woods and exploded. The race was won by Jochen Rindt of Austria, who two months later bounced his Lotus Ford off a guardrail at Monza, Italy, lost a wheel, smashed into the rail again, and died in the wreckage with a broken trachea, crushed thorax, and broken left leg.

But neither rain nor gloom nor snow stayed the racers, whether on wheels or on skis or on beasts. When Monticello Raceway in upstate New York offered $10,000 in prizes for snowmobile drivers over its half-mile trotting track in 1970, a horde of 300 professional racing men were joined by business executives, students, harness drivers, and housewives in what was described as "the fastest-growing winter sport in the United States." That was only half the number who turned out at International Falls, Minnesota, a week later — with prizes posted by snowmobile makers and the Campbell Soup Company. But the field in Monticello at least had the distinction of being started officially by Tex Enright, a Cherokee Indian and former stock-car driver who once had been pronounced dead in Dover, Delaware, after a crash that fractured his skull in three places and cracked several ribs. His mission at Monticello was declared to be safety.

And in case people thought bullfighting was an afternoon's joust conducted by a handful of handsome Spaniard matadors for Ava Gardner's glances and Ernest Hemingway's prose, it had come a long way from the days when Pope Pius V threatened to excommunicate all Catholics involved in, or *viewing*, it and from the days when Isabella I tried to talk Spanish nobles out of entering the ring. Now it was listed as a $25,000,000-a-year business or art or exhibition, if not sport, and the toll in bulls was far heavier than the toll in anything else — 3500 in one year in Spain alone.

Five thousand miles west, a twenty-six-year-old rodeo cowboy named Larry Mahan wrestled bulls in a way that might have impressed Spain's 193 professional big-league matadors. He did it in 60 rodeos a season, rode 250 broncos, manhandled 100 bulls, basked in the title of the world's best rodeo cowboy, and collected $60,000. He paid several hundred dollars out of his own pocket just to reach the scene — someplace like Cheyenne, Wyoming — and even paid seventy-five dollars for an entry fee. But then he and the 500 other professional nomads on the circuit thrilled 15,000,000 customers in 1500 rodeos every year and, along the way, took a few mean rides on 1500-pound Brahma bulls — no stirrups, no saddles, no bridles, just a braided rope and all that prize money.

Even the animals were growing glamorous and going international. An eleven-month-old cocker spaniel puppy was flown 4817 miles from Rio de Janeiro to New York in 1970, competed in the American Spaniel Club specialty, became the first Brazilian-bred dog of his breed to be shown in North America — and still won no ribbon.

But the racing dogs were winning more than ribbons, even east of Eden in places like Jakarta, where the Hong Kong Southwest Development Company spent $3,000,000 to build a "canidrome" at a track seating 12,000 persons who bet anywhere from a few pennies to $100 on 250 imported Australian greyhounds. The racing created jobs for 200 Indonesian boys and girls, mostly high school and college students, who served as kennel kids or who sold gambling tickets. Religious groups opposed the idea, but the city prevailed — and collected $20,000 a month in gambling taxes. But the Oriental mind had a counterpart in

America, where 12,000,000 fans paid their way through turn-stiles at thirty-five dog tracks and bet $652,000,000 in a year — from which the seven approving state treasuries siphoned off $44,000,000 in taxes.

If it moved, people watched it move and bet on it, and governments taxed it. Even horse auctions in mid-Manhattan attracted the improvers of the breed, because they realized it was a short haul down the road to the racing strip. When Madison Square Garden, no less, held its first trotting auction in 1970, about 2500 persons appeared, spent $611,500, and bought ninety-three yearlings. One of them, the noted driver and trainer Stanley Dancer, coughed up $33,000 for the best of the bunch, a chestnut colt named Departure. And, although Dancer already had spent $5,000,000 for other trotters a few months before, he immediately notified all hands that the horse's name would be changed to Nevele Arrival and coughed up fifty dollars more to make it official.

The mania didn't slacken even when no prize money was offered in return. The United States had not lost a challenge for the America's Cup in a century, 1870 to be exact, and yet the overseas challenges kept coming and the cost be damned. Four American twelve-meter yachts vied in 1970 for the glory and the expense of defending the Cup, while boats from France and Australia competed for a whole summer for the glory and expense of capturing it. They finally came to snarls and international incidents over the disqualification one foggy day of the French yacht, *France,* commanded by Baron Marcel Bich, the head of a $2,000,000 syndicate. The baron might have been vexed because the laundry bill for towels alone came to $236 and the bill for sails to $60,000. But that was only money and, when pressed for a reason for all the outlay of energy and cash, he shrugged and said: "For the honor. Because you have never lost the cup. What we like is to participate. The honor is to participate."

For the pleasure-seeking man with a bankroll, as opposed to the honor-seeking syndicate with a bankroll, there was always the Boat Show. You came, you saw, you probably spent. In New York, $5,000,000 worth of equipment was put on view and on sale every year in the Coliseum, and it ranged from surf-boards to houseboats. The seagoing amateur always had stepped up in class after a visit to the show and the inventions it introduced: In 1905, something called a motorboat, which was displayed in a large pool of water to prove it wouldn't sink; in 1911, the hydroplane; in 1920, the outboard motor; in 1929, the airboat; in 1936, the radiotelephone; in 1948, the plastic boat; in 1954, the high-speed outboard; in 1960, the "pleasure submarine"; and in 1965, the high-speed houseboat.

In Paris, meanwhile, an economy ravaged by World War II produced in 1970 a fleet of 1300 luxury craft for 350,000 potential customers. A decade earlier, when the sixties began, there were 100,000 pleasure boats throughout France and now, as the seventies began, there was one million, from kayaks and rubber rafts to a two-seat open submarine for the strong of heart.

Even the outright landlubbers joined the cavalcade of sports, pastimes, fun, and games, with or without television, with or without international acclaim. They even posted prizes worth $21,000 for the United States open pocket billiards championship in Chicago, with twenty-one state and metropolitan winners among the thirty-two men and eight women unshackling the cue sticks. The defenders were Luther Lassiter, drawing a bead on $5000 first-place money for the men, and Dorothy Wise for the ladies. Mrs. Wise was a fifty-five-year-old grandmother and the most she could win was $500. But that was a matter of honor too. The competition included Jean Balukas of Brooklyn, the runner-up in the U. S. Masters, who was eleven years old, and Grandma Wise wasn't about to let her generation down.

* * *

But if it was the best of times, it was the worst of times, as people long had suspected. And, as in all the gold rushes of history, there was a bad guy for every good guy, a deficit for every surplus, a minus for every plus, and a problem for every opportunity. That is, it was a struggle, and the balance sheet of human frailty might not be calculated for a long time.

In Great Britain, where even Rolls-Royce found the path too steep in 1971, the boom in basketball began to pall because money was needed for something besides importing tall men from abroad. It might be all right for Real Madrid to provide Spanish passports and jobs in industry for 6-foot-8-inch Americans, and 400 professionals from the United States already were causing a basketball boom in Europe in the seventies. But the overextended and underpaid English decided it wasn't their cup of tea.

In Montreal, austerity led Mayor Jean Drapeau to plead poverty when the subject got around to reopening "Man and His World," the successor to the Expo 67 World's Fair, built and operated by the city, the Province of Quebec, and the federal government. "Man and His World" drew 12,500,000 visitors in five months, lost $5,000,000, and cast gloom over the city's other baubles — the Montreal Expos baseball team and the 1972 Olympics. The mayor said money was the root of civic evil and hinted he might resign.

In Tokyo, where seven baseball players were suspended in a gambling scandal, the president of the railroad company that owned the Nishitetsu Lions announced he was assuming responsibility and was resigning his executive job. The board of directors accepted, and fans were admitted free to outfield seats in Heiwadai Stadium for the rest of the season to "atone" for the scandal.

In Rome, the government of Italy raised the gambling tax to 17 per cent after it had collected only $4,500,000 on racing bets that totaled $208,000,000. One problem was that bookies were supposed to collect the tax on winning bets, and refused, while other bettors assigned their tickets to their banks, who were not required to reveal the names of "clients." So the government decided to increase its take, for whatever that was worth. The result: 225 gambling shops promptly closed their doors, the jockeys announced they would race horses up the Via Veneto to dramatize their opposition, and the government lowered the tax to 7 per cent.

In Paris, a horse owner sued Yves Saint-Martin, the leading rider in the land, for $6000 because his mount had been disqualified. The horse had been assigned a weight of 116⅗ pounds; Saint-Martin checked in at 119½; he rode, won, then weighed in at 122½, and was set down. "I am probably not going to make the weight," predicted Saint-Martin, a jockey of unquestioned integrity, as he returned to the paddock a winner. "I drank a beer and put a sweater on underneath my silk." The horse, Chateau d'Ys, went out and won $40,000 in his next start. Saint-Martin was not so lucky. He lost the case and had to pay the owner the $6000, which was the amount of the lost purse.

When a disgruntled bettor tried to cash in on the decision, though, he was rebuffed by the court. But a year later, another bettor won $2720 from a jockey whose horse had led into the home stretch, suddenly weakened, and finished fourth.

Back in Italy, where the weekly soccer pool brought the government $32,000,000 in taxes in a year plus $35,000,000 in subsidies for the Olympic Committee, the finance minister began looking into the economics of the top soccer clubs. The minister, Luigi Preti, a Social Democrat and a soccer fan, focused his inquiry on Helenio Herrera, who was earning $240,000 a year as coach of the Roma Club. "I wouldn't say that Mr. Herrera's responsibilities," the finance minister said, "are heavier than those of the foreign and interior ministers — or, for that matter, of the finance minister."

In Florence, the city of beauty and art, the Fiorentina soccer team lost two games in a row and the president, Nello Baglini, fined the team heavily, then ordered the players to cut their long hair, shed their hippie clothes, and stop showing up for practice in luxury sports cars.

One thing seemed certain in the relentless rush for money: the bigger the prize, the bigger the stampede. And the stampede of athletes, agents, lawyers, owners, television executives, sponsors, fans, and bettors was certain to be joined by a stampede of government officials. Politicians might not condone the rush to bigness, and on both legal and moral grounds they might resist it with subpoenas, injunctions, and antitrust suits. That was one thing. But they also needed new sources of revenue, especially during the twin terrors of inflation and recession, so they might as well tax the stampeders. And that was another thing.

In Britain, the government began to permit — and to tax — off-track betting as the sixties started. Betting shops sprouted and, by the time the seventies opened, there were 15,000 in business — 2000 more than the number of drugstores. They ranged from seedy hole-in-the-wall caves to cushy parlors with bright lights, soft couches, closed-circuit TV to display the odds, and loudspeaker broadcasts of the races. Sometimes, a touch of class distinction was added with special sections for people willing to bet ten pounds or more.

"We'll take bets on anything," one of the clerks behind the cage said. "Horses, dogs, the date of the landing on Mars, the winner of the next election. Just name it."

They even took bets by credit card and, in a country where the racetracks were distant and the petrol expensive, that proved decisive. By 1970, off-track bets accounted for 90 per cent of the total, the average attendance at tracks slipped from 7339 a day to 5200, and half of England's sixty-four race courses were losing money.

In Japan, where no off-track betting had been allowed before the war, the fruits of American occupation included gambling in the western manner: cheaper tickets (down to twenty-eight cents), no limit on the number of bets, and an "either order" wrinkle that paid off on the two-one selection as well as on the one-two. The new off-track business was conducted in fifteen centers, eight of them in Tokyo alone, each of them modern buildings six or seven stories tall with ticket windows on every floor.

"On some racing days," a salesgirl reported, "a customer will stick his hand through the narrow window to receive his ticket, and then be unable to extricate his hand because so many people are pushing against him from behind."

Undaunted by such inconvenience — just as horsemen like Stanley Dancer were undaunted by the inconvenience of paying $47,000 a year for horseshoeing a trotting stable — the New York Legislature in 1970 adopted "An Act to amend the pari-mutuel revenue law and the local finance law." Its purpose, the transcript said, was to establish "a public benefit corporation to operate a system of off-track betting in the city of New York."

The "public benefit" aspect of the law was roughly the same as the French government had in mind in 1971, when it increased the tax on pari-mutuel betting to contribute to "the protection of nature." But, regardless of semantics, the Legislature pushed bravely forward and created the New York City Off-Track Betting Corporation, headed by Howard J. Samuels, an industrial executive from upstate who had tried for the Democratic nomination for governor and failed.

Samuels was an intelligent, sincere man who conceded that he didn't know too much about either horses or betting. But he waded into the stream, planned to set up 1000 betting windows in 100 off-track parlors, plus 150 telephone stations to handle 75,000 "accounts," and suggested that the program be expanded to cover all sports since $1,500,000,000 was being bet illegally in New York every year and most of that involved football, baseball, and basketball.

Mayor Lindsay, up to his jowls in red ink, managed a smile when he visted the corporation's offices at 49 Chambers Street and was asked to speculate on the revenue that might come tumbling in.

"If we only break even," he said, "it will be Howard Samuels who did it. If we make a few million, it will be the splendid job of Samuels and Lindsay. If we make millions, it will be John V. Lindsay rescuing New York City from the brink of bankruptcy all by himself."

Nobody else managed to join him in the smile though, because the corporation already had been deluged with 15,000 job applications (for 125 starting jobs), the mutuel clerks at Yonkers Raceway went on strike, the management of Saratoga Raceway sued because the tracks got only 1 per cent of the handle, the New York Racing Association balked at paying $1,000,000 to install off-track electronic equipment at Aqueduct, Liberty Bell Park in Philadelphia threatened suit if Samuels crossed state lines, and the horse breeders griped that the sport was being ruined by greedy government anyway.

The ultimate danger lay somewhere between England, where racing itself bit the dust under off-track betting, and Japan, where the customers were being trampled in the rush to the windows. Even in Las Vegas, the one place in America where betting had long since been deemed patriotic, the moral was clear: A horse track on the outskirts of town had failed because people could get more action by *not* going to the track.

As for the other sports, they already were booming under the bookmakers, who took only a fraction off the top instead of the 17 per cent siphoned off most legal bets by the government. So the average big spender felt much more at home risking $1500 on a football or baseball game, especially since he might tap out on the East Coast action and still turn to the Far West night games to get even — or go broke. At least, nobody else in the stampede would be able to siphon off 17 per cent of zero.

The handwriting was probably on the wall for everybody con-

cerned when Bill Veeck, the original blithe spirit of sports, resigned as president of Suffolk Downs after a billion-dollar conglomerate took over the track in 1971. His wizardry with ideas
had given attendance and betting a shot in the arm, and had
given the state of Massachusetts a shot in the arm with a record
windfall of $8,500,000 in pari-mutuel taxes for ninety days of
racing. But when Veeck tried to gather support for raising the
$14,000,000 to buy the track himself, he got no cheers from the
statehouse, and so the blithe spirit retreated before the business
pincers with the observation: "There are no amateur politicians
in this state."

What he meant was that people in the seventies had acquired
a lesson from the rush of the sixties: It's not necessarily better to
give than to receive. In fact, it may be best simply to *take*. And,
in the Babel of success in professional sports, that wretched message was growing louder.

"There was this golf tournament," said Joe Dey, the golf commissioner, "the Michigan Classic of nineteen sixty-nine — the
first annual Michigan Classic. We called it the instant classic. A
small group of people out to make money, promoters looking
for the gold in the hills. They leased a country club, offered big
prizes, invited big golfers, and then let them tee off before telling them they didn't have the money. The golfers' own Tour
Division paid one hundred thousand dollars to make it up."

"The point of diminishing returns," said Mark McCormack,
not noted for pessimism, "is being reached."

"This is a fast-changing world," observed Vernon Stauffer, the
restaurant man who owns the Cleveland Indians. "It's not just a
baseball crisis now, it's affecting all corporations."

"There's going to be a new four per cent sales tax," said Bob
Short, the owner of the Washington Senators, after raising ticket
prices and gerrymandering his ball park so that it took three
dollars to buy a good seat. "I have to pay ten per cent stadium
rent, fifteen per cent loan interest, and twenty per cent to the
visiting club. Ushers will get raises. I spent one hundred thou-

sand dollars more last season for special police and then there are Ted Williams and Frank Howard to pay."

"I think that outside activities had a lot to do with our losing," said Philip K. Wrigley, the owner of the Chicago Cubs, after his team had folded in the stretch. "I think that all the TV appearances, speaking engagements, the columns the players wrote in the newspapers, the recording sessions, the autograph-signing parties, and other activities took the players' minds off the game."

"They have too many outside interests," said Bud Adams, the owner of the Houston Oilers, explaining why he had switched TV channels to avoid seeing his team lose to Oakland, 56 to 7. "Some of them are only interested in picking up their paychecks."

"It's a logical assumption," said Pete Rozelle, brushing aside complaints that people were confused because nearly half the football teams in his league had shots at the play-off as the season ended, "that during this decade we're going to get to thirty-two teams. In the past decade, we went from twelve to twenty-six."

"I'm pretty sure all our stockholders knew I wasn't going to run the company," Mickey Mantle testified before a Senate hearing on food franchising, "or else they wouldn't have bought the stock."

"I did not intend to make a fast buck," Joe Namath testified before another Senate committee on food franchising. "Furthermore, Mr. Chairman, many of the friends I have made over the years through my football career have acquired a financial interest in this company, and their success is a major concern of mine."

Six months later, Mantle resigned as chairman of his restaurant chain after it had reported a $1,289,777 loss. Four months after that, Namath resigned as chairman of *his* fast-food chain and sold his 145,000 shares of stock after it had reported an eight-month loss of $243,978.

"Eat like the pros," read the magazine ads, touting the nation on "N.F.L. official training-table foods." The ads showed the pros gaining nourishment on "official" foods like sugar, margarine, Peter Pan peanut butter, Ovaltine, Krispy crackers, and Chiquita bananas.

"Hardly anybody has the guts to yell 'Murder!' at what these Pied Pipers are doing," said Vincent J. Bartimo, whose Green Mountain racetrack in Vermont pioneered in Sunday racing but who now was thinking of dropping it. "Our labor unions authorized a strike unless they get triple time for Sundays. Operating costs are going up all the time. And they just keep taking a bigger and bigger tax bite off the top. The states will wind up owning the tracks and then you're going to have the granddaddy of all pork-barrels."

"Football supports everything," conceded Bob Rochs, the assistant business manager for athletics at the University of Texas, whose football team netted $1,000,000 a year. "But with the addition of five hundred thousand dollars worth of AstroTurf and things like that, the profits can be eaten up real quick."

"I definitely think that a winning football team affects the contributions from alumni," reported William Watson, the director of alumni affairs at the University of Florida.

"I was at a wedding," related O. J. Simpson, not entirely convinced that the values were holding up against the tide. "My wife and a few friends and I were the only Negroes there. I overheard a lady at the next table say, 'Look, there's O. J. Simpson and some niggers.' "

"We do have a scalping problem," said Leo J. Palmieri, ticket manager for the New York Jets. "And the biggest problem is that the fines are so small. We heard one scalper tell a cop, 'Hurry up and write out my summons — I've got tickets to sell.' "

"It's a business," said Howard Cosell, the lawyer who became a sports broadcaster. "It's sport to the fans only. Sheer greed dictated the National Basketball Association expansion, nothing else. Sheer greed."

"The viability of major league sports is assured — almost," predicted Michael Burke of the New York Yankees. "My own qualification would be that the people in sports, if they are dim, could blow it.

"Sports franchise owners and players alike could blunt this expanding opportunity if they do not take into account the social function of sports. If either is bent solely on exploiting his own stake, if both haven't learned that greed itself is a form of pollution, then major league sports could be diminished."

"Pro football, which is a cool-weather game," reflected James Reston, "now starts in August. Pro baseball, which is a hot-weather game, now starts in the cold and rain of the capricious spring. Pro basketball, which is an indoor winter sport, now runs from late summer to May. Everybody is out for the Big Buck, and the television contracts are king.

"It is easy to be neutral in the present fight between the sports owners and the sports performers. Both are greedy, and both are caught up in the commercial system, and both may very well be destroyed in the struggle."

Tug McGraw, a twenty-five-year-old $25,000-a-year relief pitcher for the New York Mets and a graduate "jungle fighter" in the Marines, sat in the Shea Stadium bullpen during a baseball game one night and wrote on a piece of lined paper:

"I guess it could be said that I am going through a stage in my life that is nearly impossible for me to understand. It is, I suppose, a period which all the young people (as well as a great many older) in the country (world) are going through.

"It begins with trying to understand myself and wanting to know what I want out of life and also what I expect of life. And before I can even come close to finding these answers, I am struggling to discover exactly how to go about answering them. If by choosing a direction, and finding a reasonable answer, how can I be sure it is the right one?

"Who can I believe in? I believe in God and that is all. How do I know which is the proper way to Him? I want to know the difference between right and wrong. I don't. Sometimes you think you do because you have been brought up a certain way, the way of your parents or school, church or country. But every morning you wake up only to discover that your parents are divorced, your school is not with it, and your church is struggling, and worst of all, your country is falling apart.

"Where have I been, what have I learned, who has taught me, where am I now, and most of all, where am I going? I mean here on earth, in this world.

"To try to understand or figure any of what is going on is nearly impossible. You have to say that compared with any other government that has been tried by modern man, ours, or democracy, seems to be the best or at least offers the most for the people. It seems that we just don't seem to be able to make it work successfully. So it must be the people that are screwed up.

"I really don't know in which direction to head or what to do. Why? Because I'm a people and I'm screwed up. I think the reason I love baseball so much is because when I come into a game in the bottom of the ninth, bases loaded, no one out, and a one-run lead . . . it takes people off my mind."

• • •

Now, here, *you see, it takes all the running you can do, to keep in the same place. If you want to get somewhere else, you must run twice as fast as that.*

— *Through the Looking Glass*

Index

Index